D0497196

Garden Centres & Gardens of Great Britain

Edited by Barbara Vesey
Line Drawings by Sarah Bird

© Travel Publishing Ltd 1999
in conjunction with
The Garden Centre Association

Published by:
Travel Publishing Ltd
7a Apollo House, Calleva Park
Aldermaston, Berks, RG7 8TN

In conjunction with:
The Garden Centre Association
38 Carey Street, Reading, Berkshire, RG1 7JS

ISBN 1-902-00732-8
© Travel Publishing Ltd 1999

Printing by: Ashford Press, Portsmouth
Cover: Lines & Words, Aldermaston
Cover Photographs: Burall Floraprint and the Garden Centre Association
Maps by: © MAPS IN MINUTES ™ (1998)
Line Drawings: Sarah Bird
Editor: Barbara Vesey

All information is included by the publishers in good faith and is believed to be correct at the time of going to press. No responsibility can be accepted for errors.

CONTENTS

INTRODUCTION

The publication of a guide on garden centres and gardens is probably a "first" but reflects the increasing numbers of people interested in gardening, gardens and related products for whom visiting a garden centre is an enjoyable and relaxing experience. The number of garden centres has not only increased in recent years but they have become sophisticated retailers of a more diverse range of gardening and related products. The book aims to provide useful information on those products and services as well as giving directions on how to get to the garden centre. In addition it gives readers details of local gardens to visit thus maintaining the theme of a "gardener's day out".

The guide does not contain every garden centre in Great Britain but all garden centres in the guide are members of the Garden Centre Association whose standards ensure that they are of the highest quality. Indeed this not only applies to products and services but to gardening advice, and the "hints & tips" section of the guide contains just some of the expert guidance which is freely available from GCA garden centres in verbal and written form. We would like to thank the Garden Centre Association staff and its members for their help in producing this guide. We hope you not only enjoy reading it but enjoy visiting the garden centres and gardens it recommends.

Finally we would be happy to receive your comments on the guide and on the garden centres and gardens visited. In addition if you wish to recommend garden centres or gardens which could be included in future editions please do not hesitate to write to us.

Travel Publishing Limited

FOREWORD

Garden Centres & Gardens of Great Britain is, I hope, the first of many editions guiding people with an interest in gardening and related activities to some of the leading garden centres in this country whose standards are assured by their membership of the Garden Centre Association or the "GCA" to use its shortened title. The GCA is probably not universally known by the general public and I think a few words on the history of garden centres and how and why the Association was formed may be helpful in understanding the standards of excellence which the GCA promotes.

How it all started

The Garden Centre Association (GCA) has its origins in the very roots of the garden centre movement which, surprisingly is still less than 40 years old. The term garden centre was not coined until the early 1960's – before that, gardeners bought their plants from nurseries or by mail order.

Garden centres as such began to take off after the idea that plants could be sold in containers all the year round – an American development – was pioneered in the U.K. by a handful of forward–thinking nurserymen. This had the effect not only of spreading demand beyond the traditional planting "bottlenecks" of Spring and, in particular, Autumn (especially for roses), but also of making plants easy to transport and to handle as a retail commodity.

Stewarts, Russells, Wyevale and Notcutts (who coined the title Planters for their first cash and carry retail unit), were among those early "container revolutionaries" who helped to shape the garden centre industry we know today.

By 1968, the movement was sufficiently well developed to need specialist representation so a "Garden Centres Group" was formed within the Horticultural Trades Association (HTA). One of its first decisions was to set up an inspection scheme for members, who were entitled to "Approved Centre" status.

The following year, the group joined the European Alliance which eventually became the International Garden Centre Association (IGC) but it was not until 1979 that it became independent of the HTA and appointed David Nichol as a full-time administrator. In 1986, the group finally adopted the name of The Garden Centre Association and moved into its own freehold premises in Reading.

Today the Garden Centre Association has about 175 members – widely regarded as being among the UK's most progressive garden centres. As the market has grown and the expectations of customers have increased, many have developed to become full-scale "leisure destination centres" offering a rich and rewarding shopping experience based around plants and related products for the home and garden.

What does the GCA do?

The executive Committee recently redefined the Association's mission as

"A resource which improves member's businesses by enabling communication, raising standards and assisting members to promote themselves."

Simply stated, the association believes that sharing information and experiences at all levels, from boardroom to the shop floor, can help members to achieve excellence in horticultural retailing – the ultimate aim of each and every GCA member.

All the garden centres featured in this book are members of the Garden Centre Association. Members must reach a certain standard to join the Association and are then audited every other year to ensure their standards are maintained. The inspections are carried out by an independent consultant who has "hands-on" experience within the garden centre industry. The inspections cover all aspects including plant and product quality, range and display of product, facilities available to the customer and the service which is available from the staff.

What makes a GCA garden centre different?

There are a number of important features which assure the high standards of excellence in GCA garden centres: -

· Minimum of one year plant guarantee

This covers all hardy plants, trees and shrubs and means that providing the plant has been treated correctly, if it fails, the Garden Centre will be obliged to replace it. GCA centres do offer the best quality plants available and therefore you can be assured of success in your own garden.

· Qualified staff to help and advise you

The GCA organises national and regional training for staff members covering all subjects from houseplant care to using a gas barbecue and from planting a hanging basket to selecting the correct secateurs. Most members also have their own in-house training packages and use their local horticultural colleges to ensure you get the right advice from knowledgeable staff.

· Consistently high standards of display and presentation

This is ensured through our annual audits and is also encouraged through the GCA competitions which cover areas such as houseplants, outdoor plant areas and Christmas display competitions.

· Comprehensive range of gardening products

All members must offer a full range of gardening accessories and equipment. This is an integral part of membership and therefore guarantees you a worthwhile visit. GCA garden centres are independently owned and run by people who have a genuine interest in plants and gardens. This enthusiasm exudes throughout their Centres and makes them a vibrant and interesting place to visit.

THE INTERNATIONAL GARDEN CENTRE ASSOCIATION

The International Garden Centre Association continues to go from strength to strength and in recent years new countries have joined including South Africa, Australia and New Zealand as well as Japan. Each year the IGC hosts a Garden Centre Congress in a different country. This lasts for one week and involves a talk by the best garden centres and horticultural businesses in that part of the world. The Congress is attended by around 300 people - all garden centre operators from all over the world. It provides outstanding opportunities for information sharing and enables our members to continue to learn from the best gardening retail ideas from around the world.

Fortunately, Great Britain has the best garden centres in the world, although closely followed by Germany, Holland and the United States, and our aim is to ensure that this pre-eminence continues.

I do hope you like this guide. Please do not hesitate to fill out a reader response form if there is any comment you wish to make about garden centres you have visited or indeed any aspect of the wonderful world of gardening.

Beryl Stafford,
Chairman of the Garden Centre Association

HOW TO USE THE GUIDE

ABOUT THE GUIDE

The Garden Centres featured in this guide are organised by county and then alphabetically. As well as detailed information about each of the garden centres covering their history, specialities, products and services, facilities and expertise there are also maps showing their location together with detailed directions.

Associated with each garden centre are three gardens, chosen not only for their interest and importance, but also because they are located within easy reach of the garden centre.

ABOUT EACH ENTRY

Each entry contains details of the garden centre and three neighbouring gardens to visit and provides the following information:-

· The full name, address, telephone number, fax number, e-mail address or web site where applicable.

· Illustrated background information on the garden centre and the products and services it provides.

· A map of the precise location of the garden centre and directions on how to get there.

· A detailed easy-to-use summary of the products and services offered by the garden centre.

· Brief details, including directions, opening times and cost of entry (where applicable) of three gardens to visit within the vicinity of the garden centre.

FINDING A GARDEN CENTRE

If you are seeking a garden centre in a particular area then

Either:

Turn to the Contents Page and select the appropriate county. Go to the relevant pages of the book and choose the garden centre from the entries contained in that section.

Or:

Turn to the Map Section at the rear of the book and select the appropriate map for the area of your choice. Each garden centre is marked on the map with a box containing the page number for the entry. Turn to the relevant page.

If you know the name of the garden centre

Go to the Alphabetic Index for Garden Centres to the rear of the book and locate the garden centre by page number. Turn to the relevant page.

Finding Garden Centres offering specific Products or Services

Turn to the Table of Products and Servicesat the rear of the book and identify the particular products and/or services from the list provided. The page numbers of the garden centres offering these products and services are given for each category. Turn to the relevant page or pages.

FINDING A GARDEN

If you are seeking a garden in a particular area then

Either:

Turn to the Contents Page and select the appropriate county. Go to the relevant pages of the book and choose the gardens from the entries contained in that section.

Or:

Turn to the Map Section to the rear of the book and select the appropriate map for the area of your choice. Each garden centre is marked on the map with a box containing the page number for the entry. Turn to the relevant page and select the appropriate garden.

Or:

Go to the Alphabetic Index for Gardens to the rear of the book, which is sectioned by county, and locate the garden by page number. Turn to the relevant page.

FINDING PRODUCTS AND SERVICES

If you wish to identify which garden centres offer a specific product or service, or which products and services are offered by a specific garden centre, then go to the index of products and services at the rear of the book and use the cross-referencing tables.

HINTS AND TIPS

This section is not intended to be a comprehensive encyclopaedia of gardening but aims to provide easy-to-follow advice on the essential areas of garden care & maintenance and also guidance on growing a selection of the more difficult plants and shrubs. We hope that the hints & tips contained in the following pages will contribute to many happy hours of gardening and help you create an attractive garden. We are indebted in particular to the following garden centres for their expert contributions:-

Cadbury Garden Centre, Congresbury, Bristol

Cowells Garden Centre, Newcastle-upon-Tyne

Jack's Patch Garden Centre, Teignmouth, Devon

We would also point out that all garden centres in this guide will be only too pleased to provide you with expert advice on the many and varied aspects of the wonderful world of gardening.

These hints and tips are organised into the following broad categories:

PLANTING

Container-grown Shrub, Climber or Perennial

- Dig a hole about twice as wide and twice as deep as the size of the pot your plant is in now.

- Mix some of the soil from the hole 50:50 with some well-rotted garden compost, or a mixture of peat /coir and a little bonemeal.

- Having watered the plant thoroughly and removed the pot, plant to the same depth as it was in the pot, (the exceptions would be clematis, and some roses) and firm soil around it gently. Water again.

- Your newly planted plant will take several months to get its roots out. During this time it is vital that it is not allowed to dry out, particularly during spring, summer and autumn. We recommend a minimum of 2 gallons (about 1 large bucketful) a day per plant during the growing season in the absence of torrential rain. Larger shrubs (particularly evergreens and conifers) may well need more

Ornamental Trees, Fruit Trees and Standard Roses

- Dig a hole about twice the depth and width of the rootball. Fill the hole with a mixture of soil and garden compost (or peat / coir). Bonemeal added at this stage will stimulate root growth, and hence get your tree established more quickly.

- Thoroughly water the hole, and the tree, remove the pot, and plant to the same depth as it was in the container. It is vitally important with grafted trees, that the graft union (the lump near the bottom of the stem) is at least 7cm (3") above soil level, or the tree may die rapidly. Firm in well.

- Insert a supporting stake adjacent to the tree (avoiding spearing any major roots) and check it does not chafe against the branches. Always use the correct tree straps (rose straps for standard roses) with buckles. Never use wire or string, which can cut into the bark of your tree, causing disease or mutilation.

How to Fix your Tree Tie

- Thread the strap around the tree trunk and through the loop, which is then positioned between the stake and tree to prevent rubbing. The buckle should be on the stake. Avoid nailing the strap to the stake, as it will need to be loosened as the tree grows thicker. Use two tree ties - one about 5cm (2") from the top of the stake, and the other about 20cm (8") from the ground. Fit a rabbit guard if vermin or pets are likely to be a problem.

· Exceptionally large specimen trees may require heavy duty stakes. Here are a couple of suggested methods:-

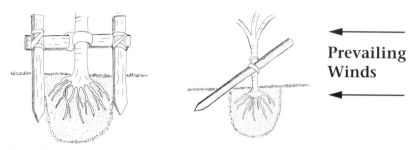

Prevailing
Winds

· Trained trees to be planted against a wall (a superficial fence is less important) are best planted 60cm (2') out from the base of the wall to avoid the wall's rainshadow and to allow the trunk room to swell.

· Multi - stem trees are ornamental trees grown in threes to give three times the amount of bark interest for a similar size head. They will need a stake for each main trunk, angled outwards at 45°.

Watering and Aftercare

· Do not allow the tree to dry out during the season following planting!

· During the growing season when it is in leaf, a recently planted tree will need a minimum of 10 gallons of water a day (about 5 large bucketfuls) in the absence of very heavy and prolonged rain. Very thirsty varieties (such as poplars and willows) and large specimen trees may need more. Check daily!

· Feed in spring and early summer with Vitax Q4 or a seaweed based fertilizer

· Keep base free of competing weeds and turf. In a lawn, cut a circle approximately 90cm (3') in radius around the tree to allow access to water and feed.

· Loosen the buckle on the tree straps as the tree grows and the trunk thickens.

GROWING & POTTING ON

INITIAL CARE OF SEEDLINGS

· Always ensure that the compost your seedlings are in is moist but not too wet

· When you get them home, keep the pots in a light frost-free place. If this is a window sill , turn the pots once a day to prevent the seedlings bending towards the light.

· On cold nights, move away from the window pane.

TRANSPLANTING SEEDLINGS

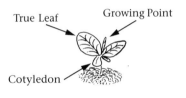

True Leaf   Growing Point

Cotyledon

· When your seedlings have two true leaves and are growing well, it is time to pot them on into a slightly stronger compost.

· Fill a transplanting tray with a good compost. (Premier multi-purpose or Levingtons, but beware of cheap, poor quality brands). Do not firm or water the compost at this stage.

· Tease the young seedlings apart after knocking them out in the compost. The longer you leave them the more difficult this will be as the roots will become intermingled. When you handle the young plants always pick them up by the leaves and never by the stem or roots.

· Dibble a hole in the centre of each of the pack units and with the Dibber ease the roots of the seedlings into the hole. Gently push the compost back around the plants but do not firm too much.

Dibber

· When the trays are filled and planted, lightly water in the seedlings and then place them in the propagator or back on the window sill or greenhouse bench.

· To begin with, only water when the surface of the compost has dried out. As the plants grow bigger and stronger more water can safely be given. Feed once a week with *Miracle Gro*, *Phostrogen* or any good plant food, increasing to twice a week as the plants get bigger.

Initial Care of Baby Plants

· Always make sure that your baby plant's compost is moist but never over-wet.

· When you get them home, keep them in a light, frost-free place. If this is a window sill, turn the plants daily to prevent them from becoming lopsided. On very cold nights it is a good idea to take the plants away from the window.

Potting On Baby Plants

· For best results the baby plants need to be potted into fresh compost, in a bigger pot or tray, before being planted in their final position.

· Fill the container or pot with a suitable compost, such as Premier Multipurpose, Levingtons or a peat free compost. *Do not firm or water at this point.*

· Make a hole in the compost and transplant the baby plant into it. *Do not remove the mesh pot containing your baby plant.* The pots are specially designed to let the new roots grow right through the holes in the pot. If you try to remove the pot you will inevitably damage the roots and slow down your plant's growth. *Do not firm the compost.*

· Water plants in well but make sure that they are not left standing in water. No further water should be given until the roots have reached the edge of their new pot or unless the surface has dried out.

· Once the plants have been established and are growing away, feed and water regularly with a good plant food such as *Miracle Gro, Magi Grow, Phostrogen* etc.

· When you are ready to plant your plants in their final position, be sure to water them well first. Use a good quality container compost. Cheap alternatives usually give disappointing results. Feed and water regularly for best results.

COMPOSTING

It Pays to Compost

Garden compost is a domestically created version of what naturally forms on woodland floors in the wild - a soft crumbly, sweet smelling humus made from broken down leaves and vegetable matter which has been digested by natural organisms over a period of time. It is probably the single most useful material a gardener could wish for - and it's free!

What Compost can do for your Garden

· Compost is the ultimate soil conditioner - it bulks up sandy soils and lightens heavy clay.

· It helps the soil retain nutrients so they remain available to your plants.

· It feeds the billions of microscopic flora and fauna in the soil which manufacture plant nutrients and make your soil naturally fertile and living.

· It balances soil acidity - making acid soils sweeter and limey soils more acid.

· Encourages and feeds beneficial earthworms.

· It helps retain moisture in times of drought.

· It makes soil easier to dig and plant.

· Warms up heavy clay soils early in the season.

· Extends the range of plants you can grow.

· Makes an excellent nutrient-rich, moisture-retentive mulch for putting around the base of trees and shrubs.

· Puts to use tons of kitchen and garden waste which would otherwise clog up landfill sites or be burnt, causing more atmospheric pollution.

· Encourages good, sturdy, disease-resistant plants.

· Can be sieved and used as the basis for home-made potting compost, or to fill in dips in lawns.

· It makes an excellent planting mix to put in the holes when planting trees and shrubs.

How to Compost

To make your own constant supply of compost, you will need some form of compost heap or container. If this is divided into at least two parts, you can fill up one whilst using the other. Normally it will take some months to accumulate enough vegetable and fruit waste to fill the average sized bin. In the meantime the other will be rotting down nicely. Composting is incredibly easy as long as certain principles are borne in mind:

·   Only compost soft, uncooked vegetable matter. Avoid meat, dairy and cooked material (these may smell and attract animals) and woody material (which will not rot down quickly enough).

·   A compost heap (or bin, box or bag) needs a certain amount of air. This is for the beneficial bacteria which will break down your compost. Without adequate ventilation other forms of anaerobic bacteria will proliferate instead and these can make your compost slimy and smelly.

·   You can compost heavy wet substances like grass mowings (minus weed-killer residue!), but only add this type of material in small layers mixed with more easily composted vegetable waste. Grass mowings should not make up more than about 25% of the total volume.

·   If your heap gets too wet and heavy it will benefit from "turning" - that is forking over to let air in. A "tumbling" type compost bin will do this automatically as you rotate it.

·   A compost heap needs a certain amount of moisture to work. Cooler, shadier corners of the garden are better sites for compost heaps than hot, sunny ones. Hose your heap down if it gets very dry in summer (lots of woodlice in it are usually an indication it's too dry).

·   The microscopic organisms which break down and digest your vegetable waste need nitrogen to do so. Normally this is taken temporarily from the surrounding material. However, if you add extra nitrogen for the organisms to use as a "digestive aid", the composting process will be speeded up enormously. Suitable "compost activators" include "Garotta", the organic "Biotec" range and dried blood.

·   The heat generated by a large compost heap (approx. 1.8m x I. 8m x 90cm (6'x6'x3')) will be enough to kill weed seeds in it, particularly if the heap is turned so that all material spends some time in the warm centre. For smaller scale bins, it may be wise to avoid composting seeding weeds.

·   Never attempt to compost the roots of perennial weeds such as bindweed, ground elder or couch grass as they will take over your heap!

CHOOSE THE RIGHT COMPOST HEAP FOR YOUR GARDEN

The Compost Bag

No garden is too small to compost and the compost bag proves it. Several can be tucked into the odd shady corner and can be shaken or tipped to turn the contents over. Makes small quantities at a time.

The Plastic Compost Bin

Ready-made bins in various designs, often with a handy access hatch near the base so you can remove finished compost whilst continuing to add new material to the top. Makes small or medium quantities according to the size of the bin. The compost bin sits directly onto the ground, which should be well dug over first. Fill with alternating layers of garden soil (or old compost from a previous heap) and 30cm (12") deep layers of mixed vegetable matter, plus compost activator (if you're using one).

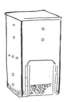

The Compost Heap

Normally contained within some form of restraining wooden framework. Make your own of any size you like, or buy ready-made slatted wooden boxes. Set directly on well dug earth as for the plastic bins.

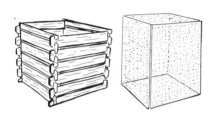

The Tumbling Compost Bin

A plastic bin designed to rotate, thus regularly mixing and turning all your composting material inside. Makes small / medium quantities.

The Worm Bin

A fun way of making compost more quickly, the worm bin is a favourite with children. A starter colony of special striped "brandling" worms, (these are also sometimes called "Tiger Worms" or "Red Worms"), are kept in a damp, ventilated bin. The softest raw vegetable and fruit waste from the kitchen is added to the top. The worms will quickly make this into mature compost, which builds up below. Because the worms only live in the top few centimetres, the box should never be forked over or disturbed and the vegetable matter put on the top only. You can get brandling worms from a neighbour's established compost heap or from a fishing shop. You only need a few to start as they will soon breed.

WATERING

With the run of increasingly dry seasons, using water efficiently has become more important then ever before.

PLANTING AND AFTER CARE

Container-grown plants can be planted any time of the year as long as the ground isn't frozen or waterlogged. However, all plants require continuous watering for some months after planting until their roots have grown out and they can fend for themselves. Planting in Autumn when natural rainfall is plentiful and Winter is coming on, means there are unlikely to be serious demands on your watering before Spring. When planting in dry weather, ensure the plants rootball is soaked just before planting (dip in a bucket of water if dry). Many people totally underestimate how much daily water a newly planted shrub or tree needs - at least 2 gallons for shrubs and 10 gallons minimum during the growing season for trees in dry weather.

WATERING IN THE GARDEN - LABOUR SAVING TIPS TO SAVE TIME AND MONEY

·   Grow the right plant in the right place - if you have a dry, sunny border then plant drought-tolerant varieties of plant, or you will be forever watering! Note that "drought tolerant" plants only become so after their roots have grown out and the plant has become established.

·   Ensure your soil is capable of holding moisture until the plants can drink it. Regular additions of organic matter such as garden compost, leaf mould peat or coir will give it moisture-holding bulk.

·   Water regularly - particularly new plants. If the interval between waterings is too long, the underground peaty rootball will dry out in its centre. Subsequent superficial waterings will then soak down the sides, leaving the centre dry and the plant dying, although being apparently still 'watered'. To rewet, saturate the whole area with a running hose.

·   Use mulches around your plants to prevent water from evaporating before the plant can drink it. Good 'mulch' materials include garden compost, rotted leaves, composted bark, carpet squares, slate, cardboard, broken terracotta or grass mowings. Note that roses dislike wood products. Uncomposted, shredded conifer material is best used only for mulching other conifers because of harmful resins leaching out.

· Water only in the cooler parts of the day in Summer so that water is not lost through evaporation before the plant can use it all - early morning or evening is best.

· If you haven't mulched, prevent a hard baked, impervious layer forming on the surface which prevents subsequent wanderings soaking in. Break up the smooth surface layer gently with a fork before applying more water.

· Water only what really needs watering! Many established plants don't need repeated watering during the routine dry Summer weather and are usually fine in all but extreme drought periods.

Get your water to where it's needed - around plant roots. Here are some tips:-

- Build a low earth embankment around the base of your plant so the water cannot run away from the area where it is needed - this is particularly important on slopes.

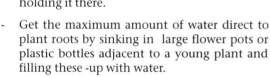

- On a very sandy soil, you can line a cone shaped hole around the rootball of a newly planted plant with newspaper or rag. This has the effect of channelling the water to the root area and holding it there.

- Get the maximum amount of water direct to plant roots by sinking in large flower pots or plastic bottles adjacent to a young plant and filling these -up with water.

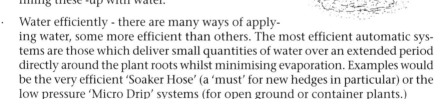

· Water efficiently - there are many ways of applying water, some more efficient than others. The most efficient automatic systems are those which deliver small quantities of water over an extended period directly around the plant roots whilst minimising evaporation. Examples would be the very efficient 'Soaker Hose' (a 'must' for new hedges in particular) or the low pressure 'Micro Drip' systems (for open ground or container plants.)

PATIO TUBS AND HANGING BASKETS

Growing plants in containers is more labour intensive than growing them in the open ground and will involve much more watering. The following tips will help but are still no substitute for watering itself:-

· Use the largest size container you can, the bigger the volume of soil, the more water it will hold and the less it will heat up and evaporate water.

· Increase the water-holding capacity of the compost by mixing in special moisture retentive granules such as 'Swell Gel'.

· Put plants with similar watering needs all together in the same tubs to save watering varieties which don't need it.

- Use non-porous pots (e.g. glazed or plastic ones). If you do use terracotta or reconstituted stone, line the inside sides with plastic or paint the inside with a silicon compound to stop water being drawn out through the sides like a wick.

- Both sun and wind desiccate! If you place tubs and baskets in shadier, sheltered positions you can save hours of excess watering over the summer.

LAWNS

Although it generally recovers fairly rapidly from drought damage, grass is a shallow rooted, high maintenance, garden feature. Here are some tips:-

- Consider reducing the size of your lawn. Far lower maintenance alternatives include other lawn forming plants more suitable for dry conditions (e.g. Acaena, Thyme or Chamomile), low massed plants with stepping stones or alpines set amongst gravel, bark, pebbles or slate.

- Don't mow your lawn too short in summer, the longer the grass, the deeper its roots and the more it shades itself.

- During hot spells, leave the mowings lying on the surface as a partial mulch, removing them later when the rain returns.

- Always use an Autumn lawn feed - this will strengthen and deepen the roots of your grass to resist drought damage the following summer.

- Annual Autumn top dressing will help moisture retention the following season.

- Small lawns can can be divided up into imaginary squares each one being watered on a different day on a rota basis in times of water shortage.

- Some varieties of lawn grass are slightly more tolerant of dry conditions than others.

- Any tree or shrub planted in a lawn will take the lawn's water, whilst the grass will take the plant's water. It is always better to plant shrubs and trees away from grassed areas.

VEGETABLES

As with ornamental plants, some vegetables are better under dry conditions than others (see lists below). You can save time and money by concentrating on these.

- If you grow varieties needing more water, plant them as close to your water source as possible.

- Grow vegetables with the same watering needs in groups.

- Some vegetables can be grown through mulches of plastic, cardboard, newspaper or carpet to keep in moisture.

- All vegetables will need plentiful watering at sowing and transplanting times. After that, water only when necessary. Over watering makes slug-prone, lush growth.

Crops which need little or no watering once established:-

Parsnips, Shallots, Turnips, Swede, Beetroot, Carrot, Broccoli, Onions, Asparagus, Scorzonera, Leaf Beet, Jerusalum Artichoke.

Crops which need water at certain key stages:-

Peas and Broad Beans - as they begin to flower, as the flowers fade and as the pods swell.

Potatoes - from flowering onwards.

Sweetcorn - when tassels start to appear on the cobs onwards.

Courgettes - when the fruit form and swell.

Kohlrabi - as the bulbous stems begin to develop.

French beans - before sowing. Otherwise water as required only if plants show stress.

Crops which require constant watering throughout:-

Runner Beans, Celery, Cucumbers, Lettuces, Cabbage, Spinach, Cauliflower, Radishes, Chinese Leaf Crops, Leeks, Marrow, Tomatoes, Pumpkin, Squash.

PRUNING

Although there are many sophisticated pruning techniques that gardeners have developed over the years, the basics are quite simple.

WHY DO WE PRUNE?

To keep a plant from getting bigger

·   The best example is of course a hedge, which needs regular pruning to keep the plants roughly the same size over a long period. For most types this involves regularly cutting off the most recent growth .

To keep a plant healthy and active

·   Remove any diseased or dead wood with a clean cut and treat with a wound preparation.

·   Remove weak "twiggy" growth to encourage new strong shoots.

·   Prune most plants after flowering, to avoid cutting off flower buds and to encourage new flower buds for next year.

·   Tender shrubs, like hardy fuchsias, should be left unpruned until winter is safely over. The old wood helps to protect the lower buds, and stops them from sprouting too soon. In March, when the danger of harsh frosts has largely passed, this old wood can be cut away and strong new shoots will come from the base.

·   Spring flowering plants like some Clematis, can be tidied with light trimming in the autumn and if necessary pruned harder after flowering in early summer, to encourage strong new growth which will flower next year.

·   Summer flowering plants can be cut back hard in Spring to encourage vigorous new shoots that will flower well.

·   Fruit bushes like blackcurrants need the oldest unproductive wood removing to make room for new vigorous growth. Usually a third is pruned away each year so the bush is completely renewed every 3 years.

To make a plant grow into a shape other than its natural form.

·   Espalier and cordon fruit trees, topiary, bonsai , standard fuchsias, pollarded trees and wall-trained shrubs are all examples of cutting away unwanted shoots and training the new growth into a desired form.

CONTAINER GARDENING

Almost any plant can be grown in a container, provided:-

· The container is big enough.

· The soil is suitable for the type of plant you are planning to grow

· The container is in a suitable position for the plant to be happy

SIZE OF CONTAINER

Choose a container which allows room for the plant to grow. A rough "rule of thumb" is that there is as much root in the soil as leaves above. Also, volumes increase (and decrease) very rapidly with changes of pot diameter - a 15" tub has nearly twice the volume of a 12" tub. A medium conifer, for example (which naturally grows to 8ft in ten years) would be unhappy in a 14" shrub-tub, but thrive for many years in a 24" half-barrel.

SUGGESTION

If you wish to grow a large plant in a small container think about treating it as a "temporary resident". Plan to release it to a "retirement" position in the open garden after 3 or 4 years, where it should (with a little initial care) be happy for many more years.

THE RIGHT SOIL

Different plants need different types of soil in which to succeed. *Don't Panic !!!* (It's not as confusing as it sounds). Plants that naturally live in moist, peaty situations, e.g. moorland or woodland, would not be suitable in a gritty, well-drained potting soil. Likewise, plants that thrive in dry sunny positions would not really enjoy a fibrous, peaty moisture-holding compost.

Most plants in containers will be happy in a mixture containing lots of peat, with some soil and grit. A good quality multipurpose compost made especially for pots, tubs, hanging baskets and window boxes is recommended for container growing. There are (predictably) a couple of exceptions to this guideline:-

· Lime-hating (ericaceous) plants, e.g. Rhododendron, Heathers, Azalea, Camellia, Pieris and Magnolia. These need a *lime-free* compost.

· Rockery type plants. These are happiest in a free-draining mixture, so to two bucketfuls of "standard" compost, add 1/2 bucket of coarse gritty sand.

CHECKLIST FOR CONTAINER GROWING

· Choose the right plant for the position.

· Remember that the food contained in the compost you buy will only last for roughly 6-8 weeks. After that you will need to replenish it. During the growing season (April-September) feed once a week with a liquid plant feed such as *Phostrogen, Miracle Gro or Maxicrop*.

· Once a year (Springtime is best) carefully scrape away the topmost inch of compost from your pot and replace with fresh. At the same time, sprinkle a small handful of a general fertiliser such as Fish, Blood & Bone, Bonemeal or Vitax around the plants (take care not to leave any fertiliser on the leaves of the plants)

· Remember to water regularly! Plants in containers will dry out faster than those growing in the open ground. Check your containers regularly (every day in Summer) and, if they are dry, give them a *Good Soak*. A plant growing healthily in a container will lose up to a gallon of water on a hot, sunny day. Remember, tubs and containers will also need checking in Winter.

· Allow for drainage, especially in Winter. It is a good idea to raise your container up off the ground on small stones or blocks of wood. As well as allowing free drainage, this will stop a build-up of woodlice and debris. A pot that can drain freely in Winter will not suffer frost damage which is usually caused by a mass of water-logged soil expanding, causing the pot to crack.

RECIPES FOR TUBS AND HANGING BASKETS

It is possible to produce tubs and hanging baskets for all times of the year. In order to create your own recipe from the information below follow these simple instructions:-

· Select the season you require. If your site is shady, use only the plants marked with a 🌥 .

· Plants are grouped into types according to their size and shape:-

  A plants are large feature plants.

  B plants are medium fillers.

  C plants are trailing or prostrate plants.

Create your own combinations by referring to the illustrated planting plans.

· The plants shown are based in a 42cm (14") tub or basket. For a smaller or larger container, adjust the number of plants accordingly.

· Where only a tub or hanging basket is pictured, you can easily adapt the plan for the other, by adding (or leaving off) plants on the underside of the basket.

· Where a listed plant is marked 🌷 this indicates bulb, meaning it may be possible to purchase it in a pot towards flowering time. To be sure however, it is recommended planting as a dried bulb 2-3 months before flowering time. Planting your basket well in advance also gives plants time to fill in.

· For the best results, a quality Compost is a must! Special lightweight hanging basket compost is available otherwise use a good multipurpose compost. If you want to include any plants marked ![] fill the whole tub or basket with Ericaceous (Rhododendron) compost.

· Remember to keep your tub or basket watered constantly throughout the Summer - this may mean more than once a day for some baskets. If you have a row of tubs or baskets, try "Growdrip" a drip watering line which will effectively water a series of baskets at the turn of a tap.

· The Spring & Summer arrangements should be fed fortnightly with a liquid fertilizer such as liquid seaweed, "Flowerite", "Miracle Gro" or "Phostrogen". Others can have slow release "Osmacote" plugs inserted in the soil at the time of planting.

SPRING (MARCH – MAY)

A huge range of fresh flowering bulbs enlivens a colourful Spring arrangement. Plant as dry bulbs the previous autumn or as potted groups in February

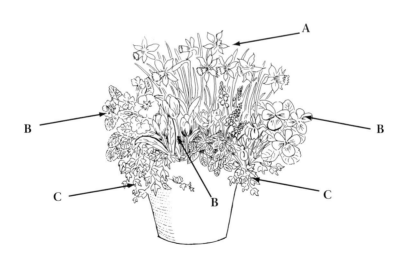

A Plants

Cineraria, dwarf Conifer, Hebe, medium Narcissi, Wallflowers.

    Euonymus (*Microphyllus* ,*Emerald'n Gold* , *Emerald Gaiety*).

    Erica Darleyensis vars.

    dwarf Japanese Azaleas.

B Plants

Polyanthus, Primrose, Leucanthemum Hosmariense (Rhodanthemum), Bellis Daisy, dwarf Narcissi, Ranunculus.

Primula spp.,Primula "*Wanda*", Violets.

Anemone Blanda, Anemone De Caen, Chionodoxa, Crocus, Grape Hyacinths, Hyacinth, dwarf Iris, Puschkinia, Scilla, dwarf Tulips.

Bluebell,Snow Drops.

C Plants

Ajuga, Variegated Ivy, Lamium, Vinca Minor.

Summer (May-September) - For Very Hot & Sunny Conditions

Extremely hot sites can be challenging for many bedding plants; these are our recommendations:

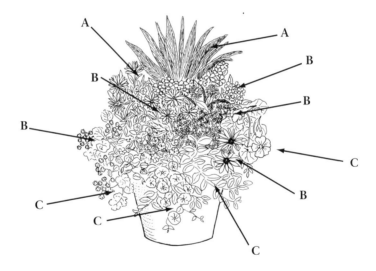

A Plants

African Marigolds, Argyranthemum (Marguerites), Cineraria "*Silver dust*", Cordyline, Cosmos, Geranium, Helianthus, Pelargonium, Pyrethrum (Silver Feather), Salpiglossis, Salvias.

B Plants

Calendula, Convolvulus (bushy), Eschscholzia, dwarf French Marigolds, Gazania, Helichrysum (bushy), Helichrysum (paper flower), Mesembryanthemums, Osteospermum, Phlox, Portulaca, Tagetes.

C Plants

Cobaea, Trailing Convolvulus, Felicia, Trailing Geraniums, Helichrysum (trailing), Nasturtium, Sweet Pea.

SUMMER (MAY-SEPTEMBER) - FOR SUNNY CONDITIONS

All the plants listed in the "very hot' section can be used in addition to those below which prefer it a little cooler.

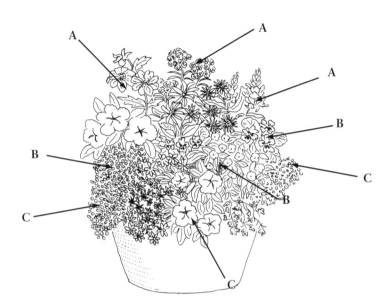

A Plants

Antirrhinum, Asters, Celosia, Cuphea, Dahlia, Kochia, Lantana, Larkspur, Lavatera, Lilies, Matricaria, Nicotiana, Penstemon, Rudbeckia, Stocks,Sweet William, Zinnias.

B Plants

Ageratum, Alyssum, Aptenia, Asteriscus, Calceolaria, dwarf Carnation, Chrysanthemum, Coreopsis, Dianthus, Godetia, Heliotrope, Limnanthes, Lobelia (upright), Nemesia Schizanthus, Pansies, Petunia.

C Plants

Trailing Antirrinhum, Bacopa Brachycombe, Eccremocarpus, Trailing Lobelia, Lotus, Lysimachia, Nepeta, Trailing Petunias, Seaveola, Thunbergia, Tropaeolum, Trailing Verbena.

Summer (May-September) - For Half Sun, Half Shade

Some bedding plants will stop flowering when shade increases. Those listed here will take up to half a day in the shade. You can also use all the plants from the "shade" list below.

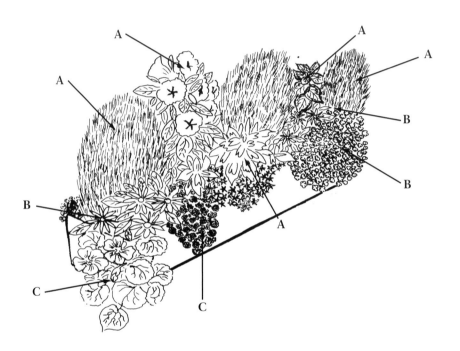

A Plants

Coleus, Kochia, Larkspur, Lavatera (annual), Nicotiana, Rudbeckia, Stocks.

B Plants

Ageratum, fibrous Begonias, Calceolaria, Calendula, Echium, Isotoma, Lobelia, Mimulus, Myosotis, Nemesia, Poppy, Primula, Reseda.

C Plants

Bidens "Aurea", Nasturtium, Polygonum *"Pink Bubbles"*, Rhodochiton.

SUMMER (MAY-SEPTEMBER) - FOR SHADE

(constant dappled light or only 2-3 hours of sun per day)

Predominant shade is not a bedding plant's favourite location, but a few will tolerate it. You will get a much wider range of colour if you mix these bedding plants with shade tolerant shrubs or perennial plants.

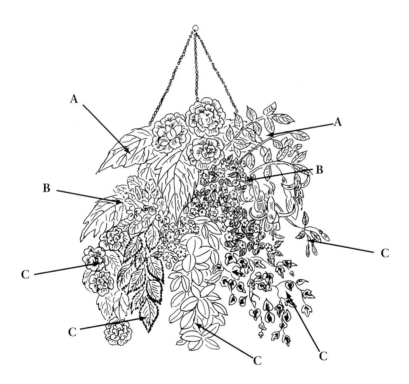

A Plants

Tuberous Begonias, Bush Fuchsias.

B Plants

Impatiens, Vinca (Madagascar Periwinkle), Violas.

C Plants

Ajuga, Trailing Begonias, Trailing Fuchsias, Trailing Ivies, Vinca Major/Minor, Lamium.

Autumn (September-October)

Replace your exhausted summer bedding plants with some bright new seasonal colour.

A Plants

Cineraria, dwarf Conifer, Cosmos (annual), Dahlias, Euonymus, ornamental Grass, dwarf Hebe, Patio / miniature Roses, Sages (coloured leaf), Salvia (bedding), Schizostylis (perennial).

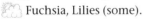 Fuchsia, Lilies (some).

Nerine.

B Plants

Diascia, Winter Pansy, Thymes (coloured leaf forms).

Cyclamen, Impatiens, Violas.

Colchicum, Sternbergia.

C Plants

 Ajuga, variegated Ivy, Lamium.

Gentians

WINTER (NOVEMBER - JANUARY)

Don't leave your old summer baskets rusting and empty! Winter needs brightening up!

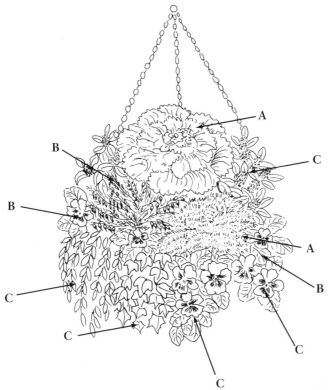

A Plants

Ornamental Kale/Cabbage, Cineraria *"Silver Dust"*, Hebe (eg Pinguifolia Pagei).

Bergenia Cordifolia (varieties of), dwarf Conifers, (eg Thuja *"Rheingold"*, Juniperus *"Blue Star"*), Euonymus *"Emerald n' Gold"* , *"Emerald Gaiety"*, Sarcoccoca , Skimmia *"Rubella"*.

Penettya Mucronata.

B Plants

Prostrate Conifers (eg Juniperus *"Blue Carpet"*), Winter Pansies.

Eranthis (Winter Aconite)

Heathers- Erica or Calluna.

Gaultheria Procumbens.

C Plants

Ajuga, Ivies, Vinca.

WINTER (JANUARY – MARCH)

As early winter feature plants fade, so the new heralds of spring take over.

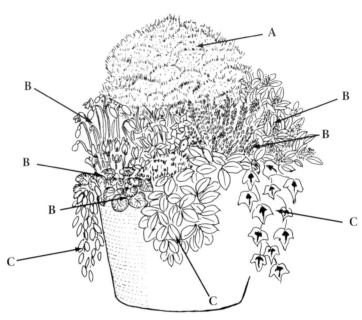

A Plants

Cineraria *"Silver Dust"*, Dwarf Conifers (eg Ellwoodii, Juniperus Comm. *"Compressa"*, Thuja *"Rheingold"*, Thuja Smaraagd, Cham. Pis. *"Boulevard"*) Sarcoccoca, Skimmia *"Rubella"*.

B Plants

Winter Pansies,

 Calluna (foliage), Erica Carnea or Erica Darleyensis.

Bergenia Cordifolia.

 Anemone Blanda, Anemone de Caen, Chionodoxa, Crocus, dwarf Daffodils, dwarf Iris, Scilla, dwarf Tulip.

 Cyclamen coum, Snowdrops.

 Gaultheria Procumens.

C Plants

 Ajuga, Ivies, Vinca.

SMALL GARDENS

A small garden doesn't have to look cramped and claustrophobic. Here are some tips from the world of professional garden designers:

- Cover up fences and walls with climbing plants to avoid a cramped "garden-in-a-box" look. The boundaries are camouflaged and become less obvious.

- Create vistas if you can. While using trees to block overlooking neighbours, you can also encourage a sense of distance by 'framing' any attractive views you do have and leading the eye towards them using paths running in that direction or with an eye catching feature giving a focal point.

- Make sure everything is in scale – keep flowers, pools, paths, patios, pergolas, statues and benches small and dainty and they will make your whole garden look bigger. Most pots and some ornaments come in different sizes to suit different settings. If your features are too large and out of scale, the whole garden will look smaller.

- Use flower/leaf colours carefully. Bright colours, particularly reds, oranges and yellows should be used very sparingly near the house, or not at all. Pastel shades have a lighter, airy feel to them. You can add to the impression of distance by planting flower colours towards the 'blue' end of the rainbow furthest away, and those at the 'red' end of the rainbow nearer the house, or the position from where the garden is normally viewed.

- Eliminate straight lines. Straight lines create a sense of constriction.

- Curves create a sense of space. This applies to paths, lawn edges, walls, terraces or ponds. If it can't be built in a sweeping curve, at least cover it up with plants The most spacious shape for a small lawn is one which imitates a pool of water.

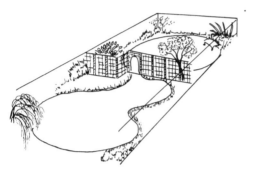

- Don't subdivide a small garden unnecessarily with terraces, raised beds or walls or it will look even more "bitty". If you have to build retaining walls, make them curved and disguise them with covering plants. The exception would be a very long narrow garden, where partially blocking the view can make it look wider

- Use tricks of false perspective to create impressions of depth or width. For example the ellipse shape persuades the eye that it is really, looking at a circle, side on, which therefore looks 'deeper' than it really is. The rear posts on this pergola are actually slightly shorter and closer together than the front ones. The side beams are closer together at

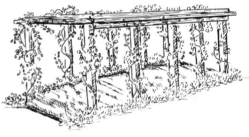

the back than at the front of the pergola. The top beams are closer together towards the back than they are at the front.

- The rear posts look further away. They are actually slightly smaller. The front poles of the rustic fence are taller than the rear ones, and the horizontals slope downwards towards the arch. Use a large mirror as a feature on a solid wall to create a reflected view to create the impression of a further garden.

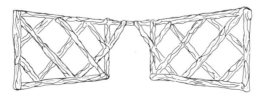

WILDLIFE GARDENING

WHY CREATE A WILDLIFE GARDEN?

· *Selfish reason* - Observing wild birds, butterflies and animals in your garden will give you enormous pleasure.

· *Unselfish reason* - With intensive farming and development putting ever-increasing pressure on the countryside, wildlife is increasingly coming to depend on gardens for survival.

DOES MY GARDEN HAVE TO BE LEFT TO GROW WILD?

No! You only need to make small changes to dramatically improve the wildlife value of your garden.

SOME SUGGESTIONS FOR WILDLIFE GARDENS

· Create odd corners of thick vegetation. Overlapping layers of trees, shrubs and flowers provide good cover. Maybe let the weeds grow behind an ornamental shrub where they don't show anyway. Or plant a thick, low-growing shrub in behind.

· Don't keep all of your garden too neat and tidy! Leave seed heads on plants for birds to eat. Leave fallen fruit for insects and birds to feed on. If possible, leave an area of grass to grow long and go to seed.

· Spread grass clippings and leaves around under your shrubs. As well as providing moisture retention to help the plant grow, these will soon become colonised by insects and worms - valuable food supply for birds and small mammals such as hedgehogs. Similarly, an old log left on the ground makes a good place for beetles and other insects to breed.

· Grow some of the older garden flowers, and even wild flowers. These have more nectar than many modern, larger hybrids.

· Avoid using sprays more than necessary and if possible, select natural products such as *Pyrethrum*. As your garden becomes richer in wildlife, with more varied habitats, natural predators such as blue tits, ladybirds and hoverflies, will control many of the pests.

· Hedges, banks and walls can offer valuable sites for wildlife. Don't tidy them too rigorously, and especially don't start trimming your hedge during the nesting season (April-June).

· Create a small pond or wet area if you can. This will enrich your wildlife enormously. Birds and mammals will come to drink. New plants will start to flourish, and aquatic animals such as water beetles, dragonflies, toads & newts will soon arrive.

HOW MUCH EXTRA WORK IS INVOLVED?

As you can see, wildlife gardening, probably means less, rather than more, work. In fact you've now, got the perfect excuse for things being a little bit untldy!

PLANTS FOR PROVIDING FOOD AND SHELTER FOR BIRDS, BEES & BUTTERFLIES

· Berberis - A very versatile shrub. There is a wide variety for the rock garden as well as for the shrub border, for hedging, covering banks or screening and for growing on its own as a showy specimen piece. There are also both dwarf and giant varieties available. Any reasonable garden soil will do, in sun or partial shade.

· Buddleia - A favourite shrub, as a walk down any street in late summer will show. The popular varieties are tough and easy to grow. All have pretty flower clusters. Any reasonable garden soil will do, provided it is well drained.

· Chaenomeles - This garden favourite is better known as Japonica, Japonese Quince or Cydonia. The reason for its popularity is obvious – it thrives in all soil types, in sun or shade, and its Spring flowers are followed by golden fruits in the Autumn. Grow it in the border, against the wall or hedge.

· Cotoneasters – Come in all shapes and sizes, ranging from prostrate ground covers to 20ft trees. The general feature of all varieties is the abundance of showy berries and rich foliage colours in Autumn. All Cotoneatsters are hardy and tolerant of poor conditions.

· Daphne – The ever popular Daphne mezereum is a common sight in February or March, when its stiff upright stems are clothed with purpish-red flowers. Prefers humus rich soil, in sun or partial shade.

· Hebe – These evergreen shrubs come in all shapes and sizes. Most Hebes are neat compact bushes with shiny oval leaves and spikes of colourful flowers. Hebe is easy to grow even in smoky or salt-laden air, and many types flower all Summer and Autumn long.

- Mahonica – This popular evergreen shrub has pretty foliage with holly-like leaflets, fragrant yellow flowers early in the year and a crop of blue-black berries later in the season. Thrives in shady situations and is often planted under trees.

- Pyracantha (Firethorn) – Clusters of small white flowers appear early in June, but this shrub is grown primarily for its massed display of berries in the Autumn. Any reasonable garden soil will do, including chalk. Thrives in sun and partial shade.

- Skimmia – This shrub is neat and compact, with red berries glistening above oval leaves which persist all Winter. Acid soil is essential. It succeeds best in partial shade.

- Syringa (Lilac)– One of the mainstays of the British shrub border. The flowering season is short, but the fragrance and size of blooms more than compensate for it. All reasonable garden soils are suitable, but chalky ones are best. Choose a sunny site.

- Viburnum – A large genus of garden shrubs with varieties to produce colour all year round and to suit almost every purpose – ground cover, screening, specimen plants and bushes for the shrub border. Viburnams are divided into three basic groups: the Winter flowering group, the Spring flowering group and especially the Autumn berry/leaf colour group.

There are also a wide range of other plants and trees which can be used:-

Shrubs

 Ilex (Holly), Rhus.

 Amelanchier, Aucuba, Sambucus, Stransvaesia.

 Fuschia, Potentilla, Spirea, Ceanothus, Cytisius (Broom), Prunus Laurocerasus (Laurel), Ribes (Flowering Currant), Weigela, Buxus (Box), Cistus, Escallonia, Lavender, Tamarix.

Herbacious Perennials

 Achillea, Aster, Erigeron, Helenium, Sedum, Solidago.

Small Trees

 Betula (Silver Birch), Malus (Crab Apples), Sorbus (Mountain Ash, etc.).

Conifers

 Large conifers provide excellent shelter and nesting sites.

ORGANIC GARDENING

Most people know that organic gardeners do not use chemical sprays or fertilizers. However, organic gardening does not mean doing nothing! Plants will always need some form of feeding and protecting from pests and diseases. Organic gardening is a holistic growing technique which encourages a naturally fertile soil and strong healthy plants. This then reduces the need to fertilize and spray them.

ORGANIC GARDENING HAS MANY ADVANTAGES, SUCH AS:

· Organic gardens are vibrant with life - organic methods encourage beneficial wildlife.

· Food crops have an undeniably better flavour, are more nutritious, and contain no chemical residues.

· Plants become sturdy, strong-growing and naturally resistant to pests and diseases.

· Organic methods cause the minimum of environmental impact.

· The structure and natural fertility of your soil are enhanced.

· Organic methods encourage re-use of materials, so there is less waste.

· Organic fertilizers are far less likely to cause root burn or toxic build up in the soil than chemicals and are generally more easily absorbed.

· You can have your own resident "Task Force" of natural predators living on site ready to attack any pests. If you provide them with all year round refuges such as log piles and compost heaps. Dead foliage and flower heads left overwinter on perennials will shelter ladybirds.

SOIL

Managing the soil is the very foundation of organic gardening. The idea is to feed the soil more than to feed the plants, and the key ingredient is garden compost from the compost heap. This is added regularly to all parts of the garden (dug in or applied as a mulch) to create a soil which is easy to work, well-drained yet moisture retentive when needed, and rich in the microscopic fungi and creatures which manufacture plant nutrients. The reason why chemical fertilizers are never used here is because they kill this soil life. The result is a soil which is living, fertile, retains nutrients well and produces vigorous and naturally disease-resistant plants. To keep a constant supply of compost available, organic gardeners keep at least two compost heaps or bins on the go at any one time, filling up one whilst using the other. Compost can be made from all soft, raw fruit and vegetable kitchen waste, plus any suitable garden waste.

Fertilizers

A balanced, compost rich soil (coupled with good crop rotation in the case of vegetables) will give excellent overall results. However, to give an extra boost, for example to specifically encourage flowers, fruit or leaf production, a number of fertilizers which contain only natural substances are available (see list below)

Certain nutrient-rich leaves can also be dug in to rot down and release their goodness into the soil. Comfrey leaves are very high in potassium for flowers and fruit. "Green Manures" are varieties of quick-growing seed which are dug in to release their nutrients when they are several inches high.

When growing plants in tubs or containers it will be difficult to avoid using some form of extra feed, because the soil management principle cannot be used effectively in an enclosed artificial environment. For bedding plants, herbs and strawberries Maxicrop's liquid seaweed extract is good. Other liquid feeds can be made by fermenting the leaves of Comfrey or rotted farmyard manure (eg "Lady Muck") in a non-metallic container of water.

The following products are normally considered acceptable by organic growers:

· Peat or Coir - a soil conditioner or basis for home-mixed potting compost.

· Ground limestone - organic form of garden lime. Good for calcium to raise soil ph and to lighten heavy clay soils.

· Bonemeal - encourages root growth. Good when planting.

· Fish and bone - for fruit, flowers and roots.

· Dried blood - for leafy growth and to speed up compost heaps.

· Calcified seaweed/seaweed meal - excellent broad spectrum granular fertilizer with trace elements and growth stimulant effect.

· Maxicrop liquid seaweed extract - quicker acting form of above.

· "Rooster" - pelleted chicken manure.

· "Lady Muck" - bags of farmyard manure.

Weed Control

Prevent weeds taking over by hand weeding, hoeing, burning or mulching. Mulches either prevent weeds coming up or suffocate them once they are there. Many substances can be used depending on how ornamental you want it to look - chipped bark, gravel pebbles, slate, broken clay tiles,.leaf-mould, grass mowings, cardboard, black plastic or tarpaulin are examples. The 'Weed Wand' will burn off weeds using heat.

For areas which are just about to be planted with shrubs or ground cover plants, you can lay landscape fabric first and plant through this. Landscape fabric allows rainfall through whilst suppressing weeds. An ornamental mulch on top will conceal it. If desired, salt applied to paths and driveways will inhibit weed growth there, but may "creep" after rainfall.

PESTS AND DISEASES

Working with, not against, nature and prevention are the two basic principles. Like humans, plants have a certain natural immunity to attack by disease and pests. This immunity will be highest when the plant is vigorous and happy with its situation. If it is under stress in any way, the plant's immunity falls, and it may succumb to attack. For optimum disease resistance, consider the following:

- Plant the right plant in the right place. There are plants suitable for all sorts of situations and one which is suited to your situation will do best.

- Choose disease resistant varieties. Roses and fruit trees for instance, can vary enormously in their resistance to disease under the same conditions.

- Use only balanced, organic fertilizers. High nitrogen chemical fertilisers can stimulate a lot of soft, disease-prone, green growth.

- Rotate your planting of vegetable crops to avoid planting the same type of plant in the same place year after year. Some problems like onion rust, maize smut or tomato virus can occur for just this reason.

- Ensure that your plants do not go short of water or food during the growing season as this stresses them.

- Use "companion planting" techniques to avoid problems eg marigolds planted alongside tomatoes deter whitefly, while chives grown next to apple trees are said to prevent mildew and lavender next to roses to prevent blackspot.

- Encourage natural predators to your garden to do the work for you; planting poached egg plants (Limnanthes) in your border will attract hoverflies which will eat aphids. If you can set up a fish-free pool with surrounding ground cover planting and a ramp for access in and out, you can encourage frogs and toads which will eat copious amounts of slugs for you. The Zeneca range of "Natures Friends" includes live predators which will eat slugs, vine weevil larvae, whitefly, caterpillars and red spider mite.

- Practice good husbandry (weeds can harbour diseases and pests and compete with your plants).

- Try and avoid monoculture (planting large areas of the same plant together) as they are easily targeted by pests.

There are many non-chemical pest and disease controls available - examples would be soap based insecticides and fungicides, traps for codling moths on apples, grease bands for winter moths on apple trees, collars for cabbages, traps for whitefly, liquid copper fungicide and many more.

CREATING A LAWN

Before Starting consider the following points

What type of lawn do you want? Seed mixes are available for shady lawns, hard wearing play lawns or lush 'bowling green' type lawns. Turf is more limited, but there is some choice here too.

· Do you want a formal, straight edged lawn or a more gentle curving shape? (on a very crumbly, sandy soil, plastic lawn edging will be necessary).

· Make sure there is access to the lawn, but run paths alongside it, never straight on to it, or worn bald patches will result.

· To avoid fiddly trimming, leave a narrow gap where a lawn adjoins a path, wall, fence, patio or driveway.

· If you must grow a tree in your lawn be sure to leave a wide area around the base of the trunk free from grass. As well as making mowing easier and preventing mower damage to the trunk, trees prevent grass growing and grass prevents trees growing well.

· No grass grows well in dense shade, but if your lawn is to be lightly or partly shaded, use a special shade-tolerant grass seed mix. A densely shaded area would be better planted with shade-tolerant ground cover plants or made into a border.

· Slopes steeper than 30° are difficult and dangerous to mow and should either be terraced or planted with ornamental plants.

· To avoid mowing problems and compaction in a confined area make grass paths at least 3 feet (90cms) wide.

Site Preparation

Preparation of the site is extremely important and it pays to do it properly as mistakes made at this stage cannot be put right easily later. Choose a day when the soil is neither frozen nor very wet at least three weeks in advance of your sowing time. (Note that grass seed can only be sown in early Autumn or in Spring).

Step by Step Preparation

· Clear away all large stones, tree stumps and debris.

· Treat the area with 'Roundup' or 'Tumble Weed' to kill perennial weeds. Do this whilst the weeds are in active growth and allow at least three weeks for it to completely take effect. Remove the dead weeds.

- If necessary, level out any uneven areas. If there is only a thin layer of top-soil, remove this first, level the sub-soil layer, then replace the top-soil.

- If your soil is heavy, improve drainage. There are various ways of doing this - if it is not too bad, add lots of organic matter (garden compost, peat, coir) or add "Claybreaker" to the top-soil.

- If the ground is very poorly drained and the site is flat, remove the topsoil, create a layer of grit and rubble about 10" (20cms) deep below the topsoil layer.

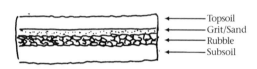

- If the area is sloping and very poorly drained, a soakaway in the lowest corner of the lawn will draw the water away from the area.

- Improve the soil by digging the area over well and incorporating organic matter such as sieved garden compost, coir or peat.

- Firm the area down by stepping on it, heels down, with overlapping steps then rake it over with a rake to a fine, crumbly tilth. You can ensure it is level at this stage by dragging a ladder sideways across it with a rope.

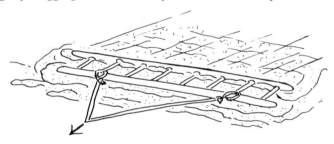

Lawns from Seed

Sowing Grass Seed

- The best time to sow is early autumn (around early-mid September). Spring is also acceptable, although extra watering may be necessary to get the grass established in dry weather.

- Choose the right seed mix for the desired lawn type and a day when the soil is damp under the surface but not sticky on top. Full sowing instructions can be found on your grass seed packet, but aim for about 1 1/2 oz (42.1 gms) per square yard.

- You can either sow by hand spreader such as an adjustable lawn spreader or a hand held mechanical spreader for even distribution.

- Rake the loose surface to create slight ridges to discourage heavy rain washing the seed into 'pockets'.

- If broadcasting the seed by hand, weigh the seed needed to cover small measured areas of the site in advance and distribute the seed both from side to side and up and down as you go to prevent any linear effects.

- Afterwards, rake the area over lightly to partially cover the seed.

Aftercare

- Even if the seed contains a bird repellent, birds will have to be kept off the seeded area, so use criss-cross black thread stretched between the stakes, or pea and bean netting.

- Use a fine sprinkler to water so the area does not dry out before the grass is fully established. Normally germination will take a fortnight or so and the grass will be ready to cut (with sharp blades and the mower set high) when it is 2-3in (5-7cms) high.

LAWNS FROM TURF

Preparation of the site is as described earlier. Always allow an extra 5% or so for wastage when calculating quantities of turf, and do not store turf rolled up for more than two days after delivery. Turf can be laid any time when conditions are suitable but will require regular watering in dry weather.

Laying Turf

- Mark out the edges of your proposed lawn with sand (for curved edges) or string stretched between stakes (for straight lines).

- Make the first row along one side of the area, pushing each turf firmly up against its neighbour and gently tamping down with a spade or home-made tamp and using a spirit level to check they are all level. Add or remove soil as necessary.

- Having established this first row, line up subsequent rows to it. Note that the turves should be staggered to form a brick-like pattern and that you will need to stand on a plank to work on the row in front. When you get to the edges make sure only large pieces are used (use up smaller bits somewhere in the middle or they may crumble away).

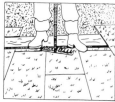

- Brush fine loose soil, sand and peat or coir into any cracks between the pieces to help them knit together.

- Trim the edges with an edging iron, using the plank you are standing on as a guide for straight lines or a hosepipe laid on the ground for curves.

Aftercare

- Do not allow the turf to dry out until fully established or shrinkage may result. You can start mowing (with the mower blades sharp and set high) when the turf has obviously begun to grow.

- If small bumps or hollows appear, add some sieved sand and peat mix in the Spring to level them out. If the site has been properly prepared, major undulations should not be a problem.

DIFFICULT PLANTS AND SHRUBS

BONSAI

To raise Bonsai, basically all you need to know are the common techniques. You simply need to remember that a Bonsai requires the four essentials :- water, light, air and food. As long as these principles are followed a tree should live to a ripe old age. There is no mystique to Bonsai, it really is quite easy, a logical extension of ordinary gardening practice.

LIGHT

Light is absolutely essential for the well being of trees. All Bonsai require as much natural light as possible. Variegated trees and some other varieties need greater levels of light than others. A site close to a bright window is ideal. However, protect from direct sunlight in mid-summer as this can be harmful.

WATER

Bonsai are little trees so they take in a lot of water. As they are kept in shallow containers they dry out quickly. Check each day by touching the surface of the soil. Water until water emerges from the holes in the base of the pot. Avoid washing away loose soil - when possible try to use rain water. If tap water has to be used, allow it to stand for 2 or 3 days before use. Reduce watering in winter. Never water during the middle of the day when the sun is on the tree. Droplets on the leaves cause scorch marks as they catch the sun.

HUMIDITY

Indoor Bonsai from the tropics love humid conditions. It is important to mist spray the foliage daily. However, keep the spray off the flowers as this will cause them to fade. Humidity may also be improved by standing your Bonsai on a tray of damp gravel. Water on the gravel will gradually evaporate and create a humid atmosphere.

AIR

Keep away from draughts but ensure a regular change of air. Air is of course the source of carbon dioxide which is needed by plants to produce food. Like leaves, roots need to breath; if soil air is excluded, which happens when the soil is water-logged, the roots will suffocate.

Feeding

Bonsai are not miniaturised through starvation. In order to get the trunks to thicken up and the tops to develop Bonsai need to be fed. A consistent feeding pattern will produce a strong healthy Bonsai. Feed once a fortnight in Spring and Autumn, applying liquid or solid fertilizers. Avoid fertilizers that are high in nitrogen as this produces lush, sappy growth. Always use fertilizers at their weakest strength. Food which is too strong will cause damage to the roots. Flowering trees will also benefit from a yearly feed with sequestrene. Never feed trees which are dry- always water them first.

A Simple Guide to Fertilizers

- Nitrogen (N) - the food needed to produce leaves & shoots

- Phosphate (P_2O_5) - the food used to develop a good root structure.

- Potash (K_2O) - the flower and fruit making feed.

An easy way to remember is NPK = Leaves - Roots - Flowers & Fruits

Camellias

Camellias have the unfair reputation for being difficult and delicate. In fact they are less difficult and fussy than Rhododendrons.

Positions

Cold winds and frosts can damage the flower buds, so they should be grown in the shelter of other shrubs, or close to a wall. A good idea is to try and place your camellia where the early morning sun will not scorch the flowers if they happen to be covered in frost.

Soil

Camellias dislike lime or chalky soils, but are more tolerant of this than Rhododendrons. Work plenty of Irish Peat and/or Forest Bark in and around the planting holes. Spread some Forest Bark in a layer around the plant as well.

Pruning

No regular pruning is required. If there is any straggly growth, or it is desired to train the plant, then April/May is the best time to cut.

Feeding

The buds for next year are starting to form as early as June. So if your plant seems shy to make buds, then this is the time to scatter a handful of potash. Or you could water on a liquid that is high in potash, such as a tomato food. If the leaves are looking yellowish, it can be a shortage of either iron or nitrogen. It is recommended that "Maxicrop with Iron" is applied which is a liquid feed and will solve both problems.

GROWING IN TUBS

Most camellia varieties will grow happily in tubs, though not as vigorously as in the ground. Constant watering and occasional liquid feeding will be required. The following Camellia varieties are particularly recommend for tubs - St. Ewe, E.G.Waterhouse, Elsie Jury, Anticipation and Inspiration

PESTS AND DISEASES

Camellias are not much troubled by diseases, and the only pests are usually aphids on the young shoots and buds. These can be easily killed with any general insecticide. If the buds start to drop off, this is usually stress caused by dry soil conditions or cold damage.

CLEMATIS

Clematis, the most popular group of climbers, are easy and adaptable to most conditions. A little care, however, will be greatly rewarded.

USES

Clematis provide quick colourful cover of walls and arches, or for rambling through other trees and large shrubs. For a more permanent cover, the Montana species are best, as the mat of woody branches lasts through the winter.

POSITION

Clematis prefer full or part sun. Some varieties, notably the Montana group, will grow quite happily in a light position on a north wall. The striped varieties, such as Nelly Moser and Bee's Jubilee, tend to fade quickly in full sun. All clematis require a cool, moist root-run, and if the sun falls fully on the soil around the plant, it is strongly suggested that small shrubs or bedding plants are planted around the base.

PRUNING

There are three basic divisions for pruning purposes:-

1. The species varieties (ie.without Hybrida in the name). These need no regular pruning, but can be trimmed after May flowering if they are becoming untidy.

2. The early flowering hybrids such as Bee's Jubilee, Nelly Moser, President, Lasurstern. Remove straggly and crowded shoots in February, and then after flowering, cut back last year's growth to two strong buds on each branch.

3. The later flowering hybrids. Cut back last year's growth to two strong buds on each branch, in February.

OTHER TIPS

·   Clematis need something to cling on to. A few wires will do, but plastic or wooden trellis looks best when the leaves fall in winter.

·   Mildew can be a problem in certain seasons. The plant is unlikely to be killed, but a spray of "Benlate" will clear the attack.

·   Watch out for slugs eating the young shoots as they start in the Spring, Scatter some pellets around each plant at that time.

·   An unexplained disorder known as Clematis Wilt appears occasionally, when a healthy shoot wilts and withers away for no apparent reason. Cut out the affected shoot and do not worry! A new shoot normally grows up from the base.

RHODODENDRONS

Any of this large and varied group of plants can be enjoyed in most gardens, providing a few basic needs are appreciated

POSITION

Although Rhododendrons appreciate partial shade and shelter, most of the varieties will be perfectly happy when fully exposed to wind and sun once they are established.

SOIL

This is very important. A reasonably fertile, peaty soil is best. Rhododendrons will not tolerate lime. If your soil is limey or chalky, then the plants can be established by digging a large hole and filling it with a mixture of coarse peat, soil and coarse grit. The plant can then be planted in this mixture. An annual dressing of rotted leaves, farmyard manure or ICI Forest Mulch will also help considerably.

WATERING

Rhododendrons make only thin, fibrous roots that are vulnerable to drying out. Ensure that your plants are kept well watered until they are established. A covering of ICI Forest Bark, rotted leaves or similar, each spring will help to keep the soil moist, especially in sunny positions.

FEEDING

Rhododendrons are particularly fond of a good nitrogen feed just after flowering. A couple of handfuls of "fish, blood & bone" or bonemeal is best given in May or June. A slow release fertiliser called Osmocote in pellets can also be used.

Sequestrene is a good general tonic, especially for plants growing in chalky soil. It will help to clear any yellowing leaves that appear.

PRUNING

No regular pruning is necessary and should be avoided. Any spindly or damaged shoots can be cut out in Spring. If you wish to help growth in the early years, then it can be beneficial to remove the spent flower heads by carefully breaking them out with finger and thumb. Do not use secateurs!

WISTERIA

Successful outbreaks of "Mass Wisteria" can be achieved with correct pruning. There are two easy steps to remember:

1. In August/September seek the new long green whippy growths that the plant has made during the year. Cut these back by half.

2. In the January following, find the shoots that you have cut back already, and cut these back to three buds.

Apart from pruning, Wisterias are generally trouble-free. They are tolerant of shade. However. more flowers will be produced on a sunny site.

GARDEN CENTRES & GARDENS

This section is organised, for England, by county and within each county the Garden Centres are listed alphabetically. Entries for Scotland and Wales follow.

WILLINGTON GARDEN CENTRE
SANDY ROAD, WILLINGTON, NR BEDFORD MK44 3QP
TEL: 01234 838777 FAX: 01234 838135

Founded in 1898 by the grandfather of the present owners, **Willington Garden Centre** began life as a cut-flower nursery supplying towns in the north of England and Scotland. It became a garden centre in 1972, and over the last few years has seen considerable investment in the garden plant area, plant house, landscaped grounds and water feature nestling beside the outstanding Garden Room Restaurant. The horticulturally trained staff can offer friendly, knowledgeable advice and information on all aspects of gardening and water gardening. All the centre's trees, shrubs and hardy garden plants are covered by a two-year guarantee. To complement the fine selection of bedding and garden plants, the Centre has a great choice of stone and terracotta pots, landscape materials, rustic features, garden ornaments and water features. The beautifully landscaped grounds provide a wonderful source of inspiration. Alternatively, if you are looking for professional assistance a garden design service is available.

The Plant House offers a host of brightly coloured flowering houseplants for the home, conservatory or office. All foliage houseplants are sold with a one-year guarantee. There is a good selection of cacti and succulents and a Bonsai display. For the perfect gift choose from unusual ceramics, glassware, silk or dried flower arrangements, stationery and books. The card shop is well-stocked with an imaginative range of cards and wrap for all occasions.

Specialising in garden and conservatory furniture, the Garden Centre can offer a delivery service to anywhere in the country. No visit to Willington would be complete without a meal or snack in the Garden Room Restaurant. The patio areas provide an ideal setting to relax and enjoy the very special atmosphere. This Centre is well worth a visit as are its sister centres - Frosts at Woburn Sands and Millets Farm Garden Centre, near Abingdon. *Open: opening hours are revised seasonally; please ring for details.*

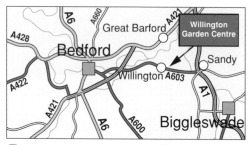

Directions:

From the A1 take the A603 towards Bedford. Willington Garden Centre lies about 3 miles on the right-hand side in the village of Willington.

Aquatics	Dried & Artificial Flowers	Houseplants
Barbecues	Fencing	Information Desk
Books & Stationery	Fruit Trees	Large Car Park
Christmas & Seasonal Displays	Garden Construction	Paving
Clothing	Garden Design	Plant Guarantee
Conservatories	Garden Furniture	Plants
Credit Cards Accepted	Garden Machinery	Restaurant/Coffee Shop
Cut Flowers	Garden Products	Seeds & Bulbs
Disabled	Giftware	Trees
Display Gardens		

LOCAL GARDENS

The Swiss Garden, Old Warden, Biggleswade 01767 627666

Nine-acre garden said to have been created in the early 19th century for the Swiss mistress of the third Lord Ongley. Leased by Bedfordshire County Council in 1979 after long years of neglect, it has since been restored. Dotted with footbridges, interlinked ponds, ironwork bridges and tiny 'Swiss' cottages. Romantic design with daffodils, rambling roses, rhododendrons, azaleas, spring-flowering shrubs. Cedar of Lebanon, largest Arolla pines in England, 150-year-old pieris, variegated sweet chestnut. Grotto and fernery. Further 10-acre native woodland with picnic area by the lake. *Open: Jan-Feb and Oct Sun 11-3; Mar-Sept Mon-Sat 1-6, Sun and Bank Holiday Mon 10-6 (last admission 5.15). Guided tours. Entrance: £3.00 (concs £2.00).*

Embankment Gardens, The Embankment, Bedford 01234 267422

Bedford Borough Council garden, dating back to 1890. Running along the banks of the River Ouse, it affords wonderful views of Mill Meadows and an iron bridge designed by John J Webster. Avenue of plane and lime trees, formal layout designed by John Lund, urns, statuary, symmetrical beds, miniature yuccas and pampas grasses. *Open: all year, daily. Entrance: free.*

The Lodge, Sandy 01767 680551

Royal Society for the Protection of Birds reserve, with seven acres of formal gardens, good lawns, terraced fish pond. Wellingtonias, large weeping birch, colchicums, acers, sweet chestnuts. Large wisteria, mature conifers, camellias. Two small walled gardens with Garrya elliptica and clematis. All plantings are reared according to organic principles. Wildlife garden cultivated in association with the Henry Doubleday Research Association. 7m E of Bedford off the A1/B1042. *Open: all year, daily dawn-dusk. Entrance: £2 (OAPs £1, children 50p, RSPB members free).*

SQUIRE'S GARDEN CENTRE, WINDSOR
MAIDENHEAD ROAD, WINDSOR, BERKSHIRE SL4 5UB
TEL: 01753 865076 FAX: 01753 831097

Founded in 1935, the Squire's group is a family business which comprises seven garden centres, a rose nursery and herbaceous and bedding plant nurseries. The company seeks to maintain high standards combining quality plants and gardening products with the best service to gardeners and a tradition of working with the local community. The **Squire's Garden Centre at Windsor** is located not far from Windsor Race Course, near the attractive village of Bray in this historic locality with its Castle, Royal Park and Savill Gardens.

This Centre offers a wide variety of trees, shrubs, bedding plants, herbaceous plants, houseplants, garden supplies, gifts and garden furniture. It was the only Garden Centre in Berkshire to receive the Garden Centre Association Award of Excellence for 1997/8. It offers excellent gardening advice to complement its extensive range of garden products.

Spa Conservatory Village on site offers a huge selection of conservatories, sheds and greenhouses together with a handsome variety of cane conservatory furniture.

The Kitchen Garden Coffee Shop serves hot and cold snacks and lunches. Special Customer Evenings are held each year offering a mixture of talks and demonstrations as well as the opportunity to wander around the Centre, browse and chat over a glass of wine. *Opening Times: Monday to Saturday 9.00 am - 6.00 pm; Sunday 10.30 am - 4.30 pm; Spring late-night opening Friday and Saturday to 7 pm. until end of June.*

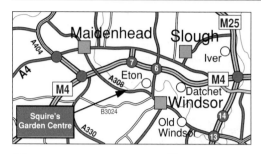

Directions:

From Junction 6 of the M4 take the Windsor road and at the first slip road turn right on the A308 towards Maidenhead. After about 1 mile Squire's Garden Centre lies at the roundabout junction with Maidenhead Lane on the right.

(Barbecues icon) Barbecues	(Fruit Trees icon) Fruit Trees	(P) Large Car Park
(Books icon) Books & Stationery	(Garden Furniture icon) Garden Furniture	(Plant Guarantee icon) Plant Guarantee
(Christmas icon) Christmas & Seasonal Displays	(Garden Products icon) Garden Products	(Plants icon) Plants
(Conservatories icon) Conservatories	(Giftware icon) Giftware	(Restaurant icon) Restaurant/Coffee Shop
(Credit Cards icon) Credit Cards Accepted	(Greenhouses icon) Greenhouses & Sheds	(Seeds icon) Seeds & Bulbs
(Dried Flowers icon) Dried & Artificial Flowers	(Houseplants icon) Houseplants	(Trees icon) Trees
(Fencing icon) Fencing	(Information icon) Information Desk	

LOCAL GARDENS

Frogmore Gardens, Windsor 01753 868286 (Estates Manager)

At Windsor Castle, 30 acres of landscaped gardens. Fine and unusual trees, flowering shrubs, flowers and lawns. Large lake. Royal Mausoleum, built for themselves by Prince Albert and Queen Victoria, who broke with royal tradition in favour of the serenity of this spot. On B3021 between Datchet and Old Windsor. *Open: telephone for details. Coaches by appointment only. Entrance: house, gardens and mausoleum £4.70 (OAPs £3.70, children £2.70 - children under 8 not admitted).*

Savill Garden, within Windsor Great Park, Wick Lane, Englefield Green 01753 847518

35-acre woodland garden. Masses of hydrangeas, camellias, magnolias, rhododendrons, hostas and ferns. Formal area with herbaceous borders and modern roses, alpines and an interesting dry garden. Large (36.5 by 18-metre) temperate house with mimosas, weeping Kashmir cypress, eucryphias, tree ferns and delicate shrubs. 5m S of Windsor off the A30. *Open: Mar-Oct daily 10-6; Nov-Feb daily (except 25th-26th Dec)10-4. Entrance: £3.80 (OAPs £3.30, children under 16 free; groups of 20 or more £3.30 per person). Guided tours available for groups - book direct.*

The Valley Gardens (Windsor Great Park), Wick Road, Englefield Green 01753 847518

The royal gardener Sir Eric Savill began this garden, one of the best examples of the 'natural' English gardening style, following his development of the Savill Garden. On the north side of Virginia Water, and divided by several shallow valleys. Fine collection of trees (including maples and flowering cherries) and shrubs, deciduous and evergreen azaleas, heather garden, large collection of hollies. 5m S of Windsor off the A30. *Open: daily all year, 8-7 or dusk. Entrance: car and occupants £3 (coins only accepted); £4.00 in Apr, May & Oct.*

BOOKER GARDEN CENTRE
CLAY LANE, BOOKER, NR MARLOW, BUCKINGHAMSHIRE SL7 3DH
TEL: 01494 532532 FAX: 01494 520894 EMAIL: bookergc@csi.com

Originally established in 1972, **Booker Garden Centre** was completely rebuilt in 1988. The garden centre is set into the side of a hill overlooking rolling countryside and is evocative of country living, with the original brick and flint building. This was once two farm-workers cottages and now houses a delightful tea-room. A true down to earth, traditional garden centre, it stocks a wide range of garden products and provides services and facilities to meet all your gardening needs. The site is multi-level both indoor and out and ramped pathways lead to various areas dedicated to the many aspects of gardening. Each level offers a different experience.

The main plant area is sited at ground level and *Connoisseurs Corner* is one highlight of any visit here. Not just for the everyday gardener but for the plant collector and for people who want instant gardens, the plants available are ready for planting out - and hey presto, you create a beautiful and healthy garden. The range of specimen plants on offer changes all the time, and the centre can supply almost any plant, shrub or tree you need. Just ask, and the helpful, qualified staff will track it down for you.

The garden centre stocks a huge range of top quality garden furniture all the year round and there is a large, light and airy, well-stocked pet area. Everything you need for the perfect water garden can be found in the *Waterlife Studio* - statuary, ponds, pumps, pebbles, and much more. For watering the garden, the centre offers a wide range of solutions including micro-irrigation and "pop-up" watering systems. Jacuzzis and spas are also on display and the centre offers a comprehensive selection of first-class gardening tools. *Open: Monday to Saturday 9-6, Sunday 10.30-4.30.*

Directions:

From junction 4 of the M40 take the A4010 towards Aylesbury. At the third roundabout turn left and, after crossing a roundabout and the M40 motorway, Booker Garden Centre will be found on the right.

Aquatics	Floristry	Information Desk
Barbecues	Fruit Trees	Large Car Park
Books & Stationery	Garden Construction	Paving
Christmas & Seasonal Displays	Garden Design	Pet Products and/or Pets
Conservatories	Garden Furniture	Plant Guarantee
Credit Cards Accepted	Garden Machinery	Plants
Disabled	Garden Products	Restaurant/Coffee Shop
Display Gardens	Giftware	Seeds & Bulbs
Dried & Artificial Flowers	Greenhouses & Sheds	Trees
Fencing	Houseplants	

LOCAL GARDENS

West Wycombe Park, West Wycombe 01628 488675

National Trust. Landscape garden with many 18th-century temples and follies, much of it the work of the second Sir Francis Dashwood, influenced by his travels to Russia and Asia Minor. Temple of Venus, Temple of Music (by Nicholas Revett) and Temple of the Winds. Wonderful vistas. Lake in the shape of a swan, with attractive flint and wooden bridges and a cascade. 2m W of High Wycome off the A40. *Open: April-Aug Sun-Thurs (April/May Sun-Weds) and Bank Holiday Mon 2-6 (last admission 5.15); house open July-Aug Sun-Thurs 2-6 (last admission 5.15). Entrance: £2.60; house and grounds £4.50.*

Stoner Park, Stonor 01491 638587

Grounds and parkland of Tudor building with 12th-century origins. Flower and vegetable garden. Lawns leading up to a terrace with stone urns, pools and planting along the steps. Orchard with lavender hedges, espaliered fruit trees, cypresses. 5m N of Henley-on-Thames on the B480. *Open: please telephone for details. Entrance: £4.50 (children under 14 free).*

Greys Court, Rotherfield Greys 01491 628529

National Trust. 8 acres amongst which are the ruined buildings and walls of the original fortified manor. Wisteria, white, rose and cherry gardens, kitchen garden, lawns. Ice-house, Archbishop's maze. Donkey wheel and tower. The Jacobean house with 18th-century alterations stands on the site of the original 13th-century manor fortified by Lord Grey in the 1300s. 3m W of Henley-on-Thames off the B481. *Open: late April-Sept Mon-Weds and Fri-Sat 2-6 (last admission 5.30). House open April-Sept Mon, Weds, Fri 2-6. Entrance: £3.20 (children £1.60); house and garden £4.50 (children £2.25).*

FROSTS GARDEN CENTRE
NEWPORT ROAD, WOBURN SANDS, MILTON KEYNES MK17 8UE
TEL: 01908 583511 FAX: 01908 585238 WEBSITE: www.frostsgroup.com

Established in 1946, **Frosts at Woburn Sands,** is a family business, which began as a cut-flower and tomato nursery; by 1962 it was one of the first garden centres in the UK. Voted Garden Centre of the Year in 1997/98, the whole centre has an ambience of quality and style. Set amongst landscaped grounds with extensive water features there is ample free parking in shaded areas. The Garden Room Restaurant serves home-cooked meals and snacks, delicious salads and its own-recipe Salmon Fishcakes. Frosts' reputation is founded on the quality of the plants on sale and its knowledgeable, long-serving staff. The large garden plant area is well stocked with trees, shrubs, hardy garden plants, herbs and seasonal bedding. All trees and hardy garden plants are covered by Frosts' two-year guarantee. There is a good selection of containers, garden ornaments, landscape materials and specialist staff on hand to give tips and advice. Beside the garden centre shop is the magnificent Palm House, which contains large, specimen tropical plants, many of which are obtained to fulfil contracts for interior planting schemes all over the country. The garden centre shop itself includes a large Flower Shop, with both local and Interflora delivery services. Displays of houseplants are a joy to behold - with orchids, azaleas and bougianvilleas nestling alongside luscious green foliage plants. The Aquatic department specialises in coldwater and tropical fish, aquaria, pumps and self-contained water features. All livestock is covered by a seven-day guarantee.

The extensive Gift department provides inspiration for all those seeking unusual presents for family and friends. Garden and conservatory furniture is very well displayed, care advice and guarantees are thoughtfully explained in helpful factsheets, and the garden centre can arrange delivery. Frosts at Woburn Sands won a Silver Medal at Chelsea Flower Show and there is no doubt that anyone visiting this centre will come away filled with ideas and enthusiasm. In common with its sister centres Willington Garden Centre, near Bedford and Millets Farm Garden Centre, near Abington - the emphasis is on quality and service. Also on site: Fresh fruit and vegetable shop; Chocolate Shop; Pet Supplies; Garage Door Centre; Conservatories. *Open: opening hours are revised seasonally, please ring for details.*

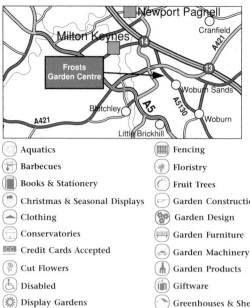

Directions:

From Junction 14 of the M1 follow the A5130 towards Woburn Sands. Frosts Garden Centre is on the right just before the railway crossing.

Aquatics	Fencing	Houseplants
Barbecues	Floristry	Information Desk
Books & Stationery	Fruit Trees	Large Car Park
Christmas & Seasonal Displays	Garden Construction	Paving
Clothing	Garden Design	Pet Products and/or Pets
Conservatories	Garden Furniture	Plant Guarantee
Credit Cards Accepted	Garden Machinery	Plants
Cut Flowers	Garden Products	Restaurant/Coffee Shop
Disabled	Giftware	Seeds & Bulbs
Display Gardens	Greenhouses & Sheds	Trees
Dried & Artificial Flowers		

LOCAL GARDENS

Toddington Manor, Toddington 01525 873924/872576

These beautiful gardens have been restored by the present owners and now comprise a Pleached Lime Walk with herbaceous and hosta borders. Large walled garden with delphinium and peony borders. Extensive herb garden. Many shrub and climbing roses plus a yellow and white rose garden.many trees including wellingtonias, beech, lime and yews and a new wild flower meadow. Large woods with 2 lakes and 3 ponds in gardens. Also rare breeds of sheep, pigs and goats. Vintage tractor collection. Cricket matches at weekends. Gift shop and tearoom. 1m NW of Toddington. *Open: 10 days each month from May; ring for full details. Entrance: £3.75 (OAPs £3, children £2, family £10, special rate for groups).*

Woburn Abbey, Woburn 01525 290666

Humphrey Repton-designed park and garden. Large hornbeam maze, 18th-century temple created by Chambers. Sweeping lawns, herbaceous borders, rose garden designed by Anita Pereire. Ponds with rare water lilies, springtime narcissi and daffodils - more than 100 varieties. Orchids, fritillaries, tulip trees, viburnums. Camellia house. Deer park Teas. 1½m from Woburn Village, on A4012. *Open: Jan-20th Mar and Oct Sat-Sun 10.30-3.45; 21st Mar-26th Sept daily 10-4.30. Entrance: £5 per car (includes all passengers); Abbey and park £7.50 (OAPs £6.50, children £3, under-12s free).*

Ascott, Wing, Leighton Buzzard 01296 688242

National Trust 30-acre Victorian garden with 20th-century over-plantings by Arabella Lennox-Boyd. Terraced lawns with mature ornamental and specimen trees. Bulbs, mirror-image herbaceous borders. Formal gardens, Dutch garden. Magnolias. Lily pond and wild garden. Box and yew topiary. ½m E of Wing, 2m SW of Leighton Buzzard off A418. *Open: April and 27th Aug-Sept Tues-Sun 2-6; May-25th Aug Weds and last Sun of month 2-6 (last admission 5). Entrance: £4 (children £2, under-5s free; house and garden £5.50/£2.50).*

BRAMPTON GARDEN CENTRE

BUCKDEN ROAD, BRAMPTON, HUNTINGDON, CAMBRIDGESHIRE PE18 8NF

TEL: 01480 453048 FAX: 01480 414994

Brampton Garden Centre is a spacious and well-stocked garden centre boasting large open and undercover display areas. The Centre is nicely paved throughout with plenty of room to browse at your leisure. The Centre offers an A-Z of shrubs, including evergreen varieties, climbing and wall plants, flowering and foliage plants and much more, with an accent on the Centre's wide range of conifers. Dwarf, spreading and medium varieties are all on offer here, backed up by specialist advice from the helpful and knowledgeable staff. Roses and clematis are also much in evidence at this fine garden centre, where the range of plants are tastefully laid out with attractive trellis-backed stands for easy access.

Water features for the garden are one important highlight at this Centre as well, offering both novice and experienced gardeners a wealth of ideas for adding striking and unusual water features to your garden, no matter how small. One such idea is using converted barrels fitted with water pumps to make a talking point and attractive feature for your garden. The Centre stocks pots from around the world, and unusual stone troughs and other stone products.

The landscaped themed gardens can help you plan, choose plants and maintain the perfect garden, to suit every taste, lifestyle and pocket. For the complete garden, there's a range of Australian-style gas barbecues, diverse range of garden furniture, parasols and garden loungers, summer houses and decking, lighting displays for both interior and exterior use, and candles and aromatics.

The Centre's licensed cafe serves morning coffee, light lunches and snacks, cakes, pastries, ice-creams and cream teas in attractive and relaxing surroundings.

Directions:

From the A1 follow the red signs to RAF Brampton. Brampton Garden Centre is located opposite the main entrance.

Aquatics	Dried & Artificial Flowers	Information Desk
Barbecues	Fencing	Large Car Park
Books & Stationery	Fireworks	Paving
Childrens Play Area	Fruit Trees	Plant Guarantee
Christmas & Seasonal Displays	Garden Design	Plants
Clothing	Garden Furniture	Restaurant/Coffee Shop
Credit Cards Accepted	Garden Products	Seeds & Bulbs
Disabled	Giftware	Trees
Display Gardens	Houseplants	

LOCAL GARDENS

Cambridge University Botanic Garden, Cambridge 01223 336265

40-acre garden with diverse plant collections grown for three purposes: education, research and pleasure. Of international renown, this garden has a winter garden, woodland garden, lake and stream garden, sandstone and limestone rock gardens, stunning landscape of mature trees and wildflower meadows. Alpine House. Beds with over 80 different families of flowering plants, tropical and other glasshouses. *Open: summer daily 10-6, winter daily (except 25th-26th Dec) 10-4. Entrance: Nov-Feb Mon-Fri free; Mar-Oct admission charge.*

Thorpe Hall, Longthorpe, Peterborough 01733 330060

L-shaped garden composed of a series of borders and parterres. Bold herbaceous border, oval pond, architectural Victorian parterre with ornamental grasses and other perennials, clipped box, yew, laurel and bay. Spreading cedars, ancient yews. Three grand and gracious Grade II-listed Georgian pavilions, linked by a long vista. Western edge of Peterborough between A47 and A605. *Open: daily all year (except 25th-26th Dec and 1st Jan) 10-5; Entrance: by donation.*

The Manor, Hemingford Grey 01480 463134

Lovely garden designed and planted by Lucy Boston (author of the Green Knowe Books, set in this storybook locale), who lived in the 12th-century manor house. Enclosed by river, moat and wilderness. 4 acres with topiary in the shape of chess pieces; large herbaceous borders with scented plants. Over 200 old roses. Ancient yews, superb copper beech. 4m E of Huntingdon off the A14. *Open: Garden open daily 10-6. House open by prior arrangement. Entrance: £1 (children 50p). No parking at house.*

BARTON GRANGE GARDEN CENTRE
CHESTER ROAD, WOODFORD, CHESHIRE SK7 1QS
TEL: 0161 439 0745 FAX: 0161 439 0840

Established in 1963, **Barton Grange Garden Centres**, comprising this Centre, one in Preston and another in Bolton, has an enviable reputation as a leader in the field of gardening and outdoor leisure. Having developed its own wholesale plant-growing division, Barton Grange can offer a high quality range of trees, shrubs, seasonal bedding plants and houseplants. To complement this range of plants, the Centre can supply you with everything from tools and fertilisers to garden furniture, water features and a range of pets and pet care products. Covering 13½ acres, this esteemed Centre offers a large area of display gardens including two large ponds with wildfowl, landscaped by a team of expert designers.

Set in the Cheshire countryside on the edge of the Peak District, this Centre has knowledgeable and conscientious staff including nine highly qualified horticulturists and two trained florists. The Centre also boasts a complete and professional landscape gardening service - from back garden rockeries and patios to major parkland schemes, the Centre is well equipped to provide a comprehensive service to suit your individual tastes, requirements and budget.

The household goods department and gift shop are also well worth a visit, providing a good day out for all the family. The Farmhouse Restaurant serves a selection of breakfasts, snacks, light meals, cakes, teas and coffees in a relaxed and pleasant surroundings. Seasonal events and promotional days are held throughout the year, consisting of children's weekends, workshops demonstrating the techniques behind various planting schemes and creating the perfect hanging basket, an October fireworks festival and special Christmas events. August Bank Holiday sees the Centre's annual Dutch bulb festival. *Open: January to November Monday to Saturday 9-5.30 (Thursdays until 8 p.m. April to November), Sun 10.30-4.30; December Monday to Friday 9-8, Saturday 9-5.30, Sunday 10.30-4.30.*

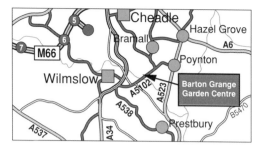

Directions:
From junction 6 of the M66 take the A538 towards Wilmslow. At the A34 turn left towards Manchester and Barton Grange Garden Centre lies on the left.

Aquatics	Fencing	Houseplants
Barbecues	Fireworks	Information Desk
Books & Stationery	Floristry	Large Car Park
Christmas & Seasonal Displays	Fruit Trees	Pet Products and/or Pets
Conservatories	Garden Construction	5 Year Plant Guarantee
Credit Cards Accepted	Garden Design	Plants
Disabled	Garden Furniture	Restaurant/Coffee Shop
Display Gardens	Garden Products	Seeds & Bulbs
Dried & Artificial Flowers	Giftware	Trees

LOCAL GARDENS

Capesthorne Hall and Gardens, Macclesfield 01625 861221

A distinctive and varied garden: daffodil lawn, rhododendrons, azaleas, herbaceous border, lake and arboretum. Memorial garden with Georgian chapel. Park is a shining example of English 18th- and 19th-century landscaping; woodland walks, man-made lakes, mature trees. Teas, light lunches, suppers by arrangement. Free car park. 5m W of Macclesfield off the A34. *Open: April-Oct Weds, Sun and Bank Holidays noon-6; house open 1.30-3.30. Entrance: gardens and chapel £3 (OAPs £2.50, children 5-18 £1.50); Gardens, House and Chapel £5.50 (OAPs £5 children 5-18 £2.50).*

Willow Cottages, Prestbury 01625 828697

Small cottage garden intensively planted for a variety of colours, shapes, scents and textures. Providing year-round interest, this gem covers less than one-tenth of an acre. Just behind the Admiral Rodney Public House in Prestbury, 2m NE of Macclesfield off the A538. *Open: May-July 2.30-5 (maximum of 10 visitors at any one time); ring for further details. Entrance: £2 (children £1).*

Gawsworth Hall, Macclesfield 01260 223456

Impressive manor house with two lakes to the north end of the house, lawns, large yew tree. To the west there's a formal garden with modern roses, annuals and a wealth of stone ornaments, circular pool and fountain, sunken lawn with shrub borders and perennials. To the south more lawns, a high yew hedge, herbaceous borders. To the west, mature trees. Small conservatory housing classical statues. Mid-June to mid-August there are open-air theatre performances in the garden. 3m SE of Macclesfield off the A536. *Open: garden early April-early Oct daily 2-5; Hall open. Entrance: hall, park and garden £4.20 (children under 16 £2.10, groups of 20 or more £3.00 per person).*

BENTS GARDEN CENTRE

WARRINGTON ROAD, LEIGH END, GLAZEBURY, NR LEIGH, CHESHIRE WA3 5NT
TEL: 01942 262006 FAX: 01942 261960

Bents Garden Centre is a cornucopia of indoor and outdoor plants, containers, bulbs and a most impressive collection of trees, shrubs, conifers, perennials, bi-annuals, annuals, roses and rockery plants. Here you will find just what you want to suit your garden, your tastes and your pocket. Among the specialities of this comprehensive garden centre are old-fashioned roses - which the centre has grown for over 50 years - over 300 varieties of cottage garden herbaceous plants, and over 100 varieties of conifers. In addition it has one of the largest selections of bedding plants, and has received many awards for its outside plant area.

The Centre, which is now one of the largest in the North West, has a long history of growing - on the Centre's 60 acre Nursery - and is committed to offering quality plants with the highest standard of customer advice. A family run Centre since the early 50's Bents offers one of the best shopping environments in the area, whilst maintaining an enthusiastic and friendly level of service.

Gone are the days when Garden Centres only sold plants, seeds and gardening equipment - these days so much more can be found. At Bents a huge selection of gifts, home furnishings, books, fresh and silk flowers can be found alongside traditional products such as indoor and outdoor plants, containers and bulbs. The florist shop also produces beautiful decorative sprays of fresh flowers - as the Centre's logo reads - *Bents is Much More than Just a Garden Centre.*

Further attractions will include landscape display gardens around the 3 acre lake and a new downstairs restaurant. *Open: Monday to Friday 9-5.30 (late nights March to December until 8 p.m); Saturday 9-5.30, Sunday 9-5.*

Directions:

From junction 11 of the M62 take the road to Warrington. At the A574 junction turn right and Bents Garden Centre can be found on the right at the junction with the A580, just after the village of Glazebury.

Aquatics	Fencing	Golf Shop
Barbecues	Farm Shop	Houseplants
Books & Stationery	Fireworks	Information Desk
Childrens Play Area	Fishing	Large Car Park
Christmas & Seasonal Displays	Floristry	Paving
Clothing	Fruit Trees	Pet Products and/or Pets
Conservatories	Garden Construction	Plant Guarantee
Credit Cards Accepted	Garden Design	Plants
Cut Flowers	Garden Furniture	Restaurant/Coffee Shop
Disabled	Garden Products	Seeds & Bulbs
Display Gardens	Giftware	Trees
Dried & Artificial Flowers		

LOCAL GARDENS

Tatton Park, Knutsford 01565 654822

Among the many outstanding features of these 50-acre grounds are the orangery by Lewis Wyatt, fernery by Paxton, Greek Monument, African hut, and Italian, rose and Japanese gardens. Swamp cypresses, tree ferns, hybrid azaleas and rhododendrons, tall redwoods, bamboos and alpines. 10m SE of Warrington off the A6/M56. *Open: April-Oct Tues-Sun and Bank Holiday Mon 10.30-6; Nov-Mar Tues-Sun (except 25th Dec) 11-4. House open April-Oct as gardens, but noon-4. Entrance: gardens £3; Discovery saver ticket - any two of house, old hall, farm, park and gardens £4.50 (children £2.50, family £12.50).*

Arley Hall and Gardens, Arley, Great Budworth 01565 777353

12-acre garden with twin herbaceous borders, walled gardens, azaleas, rhododendrons. Hybrid and species shrub roses. Avenue of 14 quercus Ilex trees clipped to the shape of giant cylinders, yew hedges; rock garden, woodland garden. Specialist plant nursery. 5m W of Knutsford off the A50. *Open: April-Sept Tues-Sun and Bank Holiday Mon 11-5 - advisable to ring for confirmation. Hall open Tues and Sun. Entrance: £4 (concessions £3.40); hall and gardens £6.50 (concessions £5.40).*

Dunham Massey, Altrincham 0161 941 1025

National Trust. Over 20 acres on an ancient site. Elizabethan mount planted with false acacias, moat lake, 18th-century orangery. Fine mature trees and lawns; extensive range of herbaceous perennials and shrubs suited to the acid conditions. Waterside plantings; hosta garden and moss garden. Also a further 350 acres of deer park, laid out from before the 18th century. 3m SW of Altrincham off the A56. *Open: daily April-Oct, 11-5.30. House open Sat-Weds April-Oct noon-5 (last admission 4.30). Entrance: £3; car park £3; house and garden £5.*

BROOKSIDE GARDEN CENTRE

MACCLESFIELD ROAD, POYNTON, CHESHIRE SK12 1BY
TEL: 01625 872919 & 875088 FAX: 01625 859119

Founded in 1962, **Brookside Garden Centre** specialises in an exceptionally wide range of specimen perennials, bedding plants, flowering shrubs and fruit trees, set off by landscaped set pieces to help visitors decide. Other wide-ranging selections include quality garden stoneware, garden sheds, rustic furniture and conservatories - the whole service backed up by a knowledgeable and helpful sales staff. Indoors, Brookside's large giftshop offers a tempting selection of indoor and tender plants together with displays of pottery, giftware and garden accessories.

The jewel in Brookside's crown, however, is the true-to-scale working miniature railway. Famed for its meticulous attention to detail and the quality and variety of its rolling stock, it features six small engines which take visitors on a half-mile tour through the beautifully landscaped gardens. This 7¼-inch gauge steam railway line travels along a circuit laid out round the lovely Norbury Brook. Along the way, numerous period enamel advertising signs recapture the feel of the golden age of steam. The four-platform station is an authentic recreation of a GWR station; there are two turntables, semaphore signals and a full-size (non-operational) Aughton Road signal box (rumoured to  have its own resident ghost). The interior of the station waiting room houses a railway museum. The line's flagship engine is a scale LMS 4-6-0 6100 Royal Scot.

Other attractions include the Advisory Aquatics Centre, with fish and lilies, souvenir shop, children's play area, and Romany's Restaurant, serving delicious teas and snacks. There is also a lovely picnic area. Throughout the site there are footpaths; special attention has been paid wherever possible to the requirements of people with disabilities. On the A523, 1-2m from the M62/3. *Open: summer Mon-Fri 9-6; late nights Thurs/Fri -7.30; Sat/Sun 9-5. Winter Mon-Sat 9-5; Sun 10-5. Entrance: free; nominal charge for train rides.*

Directions:

Take the A6 south from Stockport and at the A523 junction in Hazel Grove turn right. Brookside Garden Centre is on the left midway between Hazel Grove and Poynton.

Aquatics	Farm Shop	Houseplants
Barbecues	Fencing	Information Desk
Books & Stationery	Fireworks	Large Car Park
Childrens Play Area	Fishing	Paving
Christmas & Seasonal Displays	Floristry	Pet Products and/or Pets
Clothing	Fruit Trees	Pick Your Own
Conservatories	Garden Design	Plant Guarantee
Credit Cards Accepted	Garden Furniture	Plants
Cut Flowers	Garden Machinery	Restaurant/Coffee Shop
Disabled	Garden Products	Seeds & Bulbs
Display Gardens	Giftware	Trees
Dried & Artificial Flowers	Greenhouses & Sheds	

LOCAL GARDENS

Hare Hill Gardens, Over Alderley, Macclesfield 01625 828981

National Trust 10-acre garden with walled garden planted with clematis and vines. Surrounding large woodland garden with a fine display rhododendrons and azaleas. Also a good collection of hollies and other specimen trees and shrubs. Borders planted with agapanthus and geraniums. 5m NW of Macclesfield, N of B5087 between Alderley Edge and Prestbury. *Open: April-Oct Wed/Thurs/Sat/Sun/Bank Holidays 10-5.30; special opening for rhododendrons mid- to late May, daily 10-5.30. Entrance: £2.50, children £1.25.*

Dunge Hidden Valley Gardens, Windgather Rocks, Kettleshulme 01663 733787

In a small valley and set in 5 acres, at 1,000 ft the highest garden in Cheshire. A wide range of rare and unusual plants, apines, herbaceous plants and shrubs, numerous walks. Great variety of rhododendrons and azaleas, also acers, magnolias. Perennials include rodgersias, euphorbias, meconopsis, corydalis. Seats positioned at the best viewpoints back down the valley. Surrounding 118 acres of farmland converted to wildlife conservation areas. Signed from B5470 Macclesfield-Whaley Bridge Rd. *Open: 1st April-31st August Tues-Sun 10.30-6. Entrance: May/June £2 (£2.50 weekends); April/July/Aug £1.50 (£2 weekends); children 50p.*

Lyme Park, Disley, Stockport 01663 762023/766492

National Trust 17-acre garden of Palladian-style Lyme Hall. Foremost NT garden for high-Victorian-style bedding. Many rare and old-fashioned plants. Two 150-year-old camellias; Dutch garden, Gertrude Jekyll-style herbaceous border, wooded ravine garden with stream, rhododendrons, azaleas, ferns, shade-loving plants. 300-year-old lime avenue, rose garden. Teas. 6m SE of Stockport just W of Disley on A6. *Open: 26th March-Oct, Fri-Tues 11-5; Wed/Thurs 1-5; Nov-20th Dec Sat/Sun noon-3. Guided tours by arrangement. Entrance: garden £2 (park: pedestrians free, car £3.50 includes occupants).*

BURLEYDAM GARDEN CENTRE
CHESTER ROAD, LITTLE SUTTON, SOUTH WIRRAL L66 1QW
TEL: 0151 339 3195 FAX: 0151 339 1549

Burleydam Garden Centre has been owned since 1989 by Sally and Adrian Cornelissen and offers exceptional service from knowledgeable staff. With a huge selection of plants and garden accessories, this comprehensive garden centre always has expert help on hand to assist you with choosing the best plants. The Centre supplies an excellent quality of nursery stock coming from a long tradition in horticulture and always holds a fine selection of specimen stock and unusual plants such as tree ferns and palms. The impressive entrance resembles a stylised house adorned with sunflowers and dozens of baskets of dried flowers, creating a profusion of colour and a warming welcome to all customers.

One of this garden centre's specialities is its huge range and display of garden furniture. Pride of place goes to the specialist stock of rough-hewn Thai furniture not seen anywhere else. Created from reclaimed Thai boats, this attractive and eye-catching range of furniture will beautify any garden.

This wonderful garden centre also stocks a marvellous range of bamboos together with dedicated areas for bonsai plants and cacti. The layout of the centre is made up of a series of rooms to create the idea of being in various gardens, so you can judge for yourself the different styles, treatments and ideas that you could put to work in your own garden. One area of the centre is devoted to a very impressive display of dried and silk flowers. Another features the Portmeiron range of pottery, ceramics and crockery, together with hand-thrown painted terracotta ware. There is also an area selling a variety of delicious preserves, special treats and sweets, and a large and comfortable cafe serving a selection of hot and cold meals, snacks, cakes and beverages. *Open: Monday-Saturday 9-5.30 (until 5p.m. January to February); Sunday 10.30-4.30.*

Directions:

From junction 5 of the M53 take the A41 south towards Chester. Burleydam Garden Centre lies on the right just before the village of Little Sutton.

Aquatics	Fencing	ⓘ Information Desk
Barbecues	Fireworks	℗ Large Car Park
Books & Stationery	Floristry	Pet Products and/or Pets
Christmas & Seasonal Displays	Fruit Trees	Plant Guarantee
Clothing	Garden Design	} Plants
Credit Cards Accepted	Garden Furniture	Restaurant/Coffee Shop
Disabled	Garden Products	Seeds & Bulbs
Display Gardens	Giftware	Trees
Dried & Artificial Flowers	Houseplants	

LOCAL GARDENS

Ness Botanic Gardens, Neston Road, Ness 0151 353 0123

Begun in 1898 using seeds from plants collected by noted plant hunter George Forrest, 60-acre gardens with a great many interesting features. Lombardy poplars, Scots pines and holm oaks shield specialist areas of salix, sorbus, primulas, betulas and rhododendrons from the northwest winds blowing off the Irish Sea. Also heathers; rose and herbaceous gardens. Maps, guides and information on interesting trails available. 10m NW of Chester off the A540. *Open: daily Mar-Oct 9.30-dusk; Nov-Feb (except 25th Dec) 9.30-4. Entrance: telephone for details.*

Birkenhead Park, Birkenhead 0151 647 2366; Ranger 0151 652 5197

World's first park to be built at public expense, designed by Joseph Paxton and opened in 1847. The design of New York's Central Park was heavily influenced by Birkenhead Park. Split into two by a road, the eastern side has a lake, Swiss-style bridge and two islands, banks planted with shrubs and trees. Western side has another lake planted round with rhododendrons and weeping willows. 1m from Birkenhead centre, S of the A553. *Open: daily all year during daylight hours. Entrance: free.*

Thornton Manor, Thornton Hough, The Wirral 0151 336 4828

Gardens created for Lord Leverhulme. Garden designed for promenading and walking with large lawns, broad stone paths and excellent views. Includes lake, mixed beds of shrubs, perennials and annuals. Walled garden covered in climbers. 3 m south of Birkenhead on minor road linking A5137 to B5136 at Thornton Hough. *Open: limited opening in Spring and Summer . Telephone for details. Entrance: £2, OAP's £1, Children 50p*

GORDALE GARDEN CENTRE
CHESTER HIGH ROAD, BURTON, SOUTH WIRRAL, CHESHIRE L64 8TF
TEL: 0151 336 2116 FAX: 0151 336 8152

Still owned and personally managed by the Nicholson family, who founded Gordale back in 1948, **Gordale Garden Centre** occupies 10 acres of both covered and open areas, providing plenty to do whatever the weather. A particularly attractive feature of this excellent garden centre is its park like setting, complete with pond, peacocks and other ornamental fowl, which provides interest and inspiration for the young and old. The professional, knowledgeable and friendly staff are always on hand to offer specialist advice and information.

Gordale offers a large selection of trees, shrubs, bedding plants and landscape items. The indoor area has a wonderful array of houseplants, including many unusual varieties not generally available. Complimenting this are ceramics, candles, silk, dried and fresh flowers, patio furniture, barbecues, lighting, giftware and Christmas goods - everything you need to enhance your garden and home.

The light and airy coffee shop seats 180 people and serves light refreshments, home-made cakes and Gordale's renowned ice cream. It is an excellent place to sit and relax and enjoy the surroundings. *Open: January to February, Monday to Saturday 9-5, Sunday 10.30-4.30; March to December, Monday to Wednesday and Friday 9-6, Thursday 9-8, Sunday 11.00-5.00.*

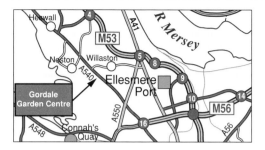

Directions:

Gordale Garden Centre lies about 5 miles northwest of Chester on the A540.

Barbecues	Fencing	Houseplants
Books & Stationery	Fireworks	Information Desk
Christmas & Seasonal Displays	Floristry	Large Car Park
Credit Cards Accepted	Fruit Trees	Plant Guarantee
Cut Flowers	Garden Furniture	Plants
Disabled	Garden Machinery	Restaurant/Coffee Shop
Display Gardens	Garden Products	Seeds & Bulbs
Dried & Artificial Flowers	Giftware	Trees

LOCAL GARDENS

Zoological Gardens, Upton-by-Chester 01244 380280

The UK's largest zoological gardens covering 110 acres of glorious award winning gardens, has won the prestigious 'Britain in Bloom' award for the best large tourist attraction in the region 7 times. Spectacular spring and summer bedding plant displays, many plants grown in the zoo's own nurseries. Features include a butterfly garden, floral clock and South American garden. Currently constructing Roman garden in time for the Millennium. The 20 gardeners are also responsible for appropriate planting in the animal habitats including Tropical Realm, with its exotic plants and trees. *Open: daily 10:00, various closing times according to season. Closed Christmas Day. Phone for admission prices.*

Ness Botanic Gardens, Neston Road, Ness 0151 353 0123

Begun in 1898 using seeds from plants collected by noted plant hunter George Forrest, 60-acre gardens with a great many interesting features. Lombardy poplars, Scots pines and holm oaks shield specialist areas of salix, sorbus, primulas, betulas and rhododendrons from the northwest winds blowing off the Irish Sea. Also heathers, rose and herbaceous gardens. Maps, guides and information on interesting trails available. 10m NW of Chester off the A540. *Open: daily Mar-Oct 9.30-dusk; Nov-Feb (except 25th Dec) 9.30-4. Entrance: telephone for details.*

Grosvenor Park, Chester

The main ornamental park in Chester, covering 16 acres. It is ideally situated adjacent to the historic walled city and borders the river Dee with its famous 'Groves' and pleasure crafts. Typically Victorian in layout with avenues of trees, shrubs and ornamental bedding. The latter, planted twice yearly, provide a spectacular and colouful display in spring and summer. Mature trees planted in the 1870's mix with new plantings, particularly attractive being the two California Redwoods. *Open: daily dawn to dusk. Admission free.*

GROSVENOR GARDEN CENTRE
WREXHAM ROAD, BELGRAVE, CHESTER CH4 9EB
TEL: 01244 682856 FAX: 01244 679036

From humble beginnings in 1975, **Grosvenor Garden Centre** has continued to improve and expand; recent redevelopment is being complemented by further planned development to be completed by the year 2000. Covering 14 acres, this attractive and well laid out Garden Centre is bursting with ideas for home and garden. The welcoming, expert staff are always on hand to help you with choosing the right plant for every garden. Lovely scents and colours meet visitors as they examine the Centre's range of top-quality outdoor plants, trees and shrubs, including conifers, fruit trees, alpines and heathers, herbs, hedging and borders, bedding plants, bulbs and seeds, and a wide selection of indoor plants. All hardy plants in containers come with a two-year guarantee.

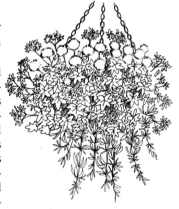

The Centre's range of ornaments, statues and fountains, bamboo fencing and trellises is second to none. With one of the largest collections of pots, containers, tubs, troughs and wall baskets in terracotta, wood and stoneware, as well as a variety of attractive hanging baskets, this complete resource for the garden also offers aquatic plants, tropical and freshwater fish. Major seasonal displays include furniture, bulbs and christmas decorations. In addition there are displays of camping equipment and trailer tents.

The Bookshop has something to interest all the family, from a comprehensive selection of gardening books to books for children, while the Floristry department boasts a huge variety of silk, dried and fresh flowers. Other amenities include the Candle Shop, gift shop, and the Orangery Cafe which serves cakes, hot and cold snacks and light meals. The Centre hosts four open evenings annually, with guest gardeners meeting the public and speaking on a range of subjects. The Centre also organises coach parties to famous gardens throughout the UK and the rest of Europe. *Open: April-Oct Mon-Sat 9-6, Sun 10-4; Nov-Mar Mon-Sat 9-5; Sun 10-4.*

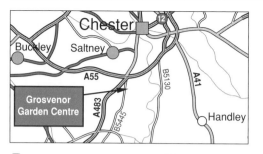

Directions:

From the A55 Chester Ring Road take the A483 towards Wrexham. At the first roundabout turn left on the B5445 and Grosvenor Garden Centre is on the left.

Aquatics	Display Gardens	Giftware
Barbecues	Dried & Artificial Flowers	Greenhouses & Sheds
Books & Stationery	Fencing	Houseplants
Camping Equipment	Floristry	Information Desk
Childrens Play Area	Fruit Trees	Large Car Park
Christmas & Seasonal Displays	Garden Construction	Plant Guarantee
Clothing	Garden Design	Plants
Conservatories	Garden Furniture	Restaurant/Coffee Shop
Credit Cards Accepted	Garden Machinery	Seeds & Bulbs
Cut Flowers	Garden Products	Trees
Disabled		

LOCAL GARDENS

Bodrhyddan, Rhuddlan 01745 590414

French-style box-edged parterre garden, designed by William Andrews Nesfield, whose son, William Eden Nesfield, designed the 1875 alterations to the house. Formal garden, water garden, clipped yew hedges. Woodland walk with mature trees, four ponds and new plantings, leading to St Mary's Well, revered since pagan times. Well pavilion designed in 1612 by Inigo Jones. Picnic area. 4m from Rhyll and Prestatyn off the A5151. *Open: June-Sept Tues and Thurs 2-5.30; ring for further details. House open. Entrance: house and garden £3 (children under 16 £1.50).*

Erddig, Wrexham 01978 355314

National Trust-owned example of early 18th-century formal design. Old roses, woodland garden and spring bulbs. Large walled garden, varieties of fruit trees. Canal garden, fish pool. Lake, National Collection of Hederas. 2m S of Wrexham off A525. *Open: 20th Mar-Oct Sat-Weds 11-6 (5 p.m. after 30th Sept). Tours for groups by prior arrangement. House open noon-5 (4 p.m. after 30th Sept). Entrance: £4 (£2 children/family ticket £10/prebooked groups of 15 or more £3.20 per person); house and garden £6 (£3/£15/£5).*

Ness Botanic Gardens, Neston Road, Ness 0151 353 0123

Begun in 1898 using seeds from plants collected by noted plant hunter George Forrest, 60-acre gardens with a great many interesting features. Lombardy poplars, Scots pines and holm oaks shield specialist areas of salix, sorbus, primulas, betulas and rhododendrons from the northwest winds blowing off the Irish Sea. Also heathers; rose and herbaceous gardens. Maps, guides and information on interesting trails available. 10m NW of Chester off the A540. *Open: daily Mar-Oct 9.30-dusk; Nov-Feb (except 25th Dec) 9.30-4. Entrance: telephone for details.*

HIGH LEGH GARDEN CENTRE
HIGH LEGH, KNUTSFORD, CHESHIRE WA16 0QW
TEL: 01925 756991 FAX: 01925 757417 EMAIL: jclhome@globalnet.co.uk

High Legh Garden Centre is one of the country's premier centres. With plenty on offer, this garden centre of excellence makes a great day out for all the family, whether they are expert gardeners or enthusiastic beginners. The nursery, with its numerous outdoor beds and covered areas, contains a wide variety of trees, plants and shrubs. As a member of the Hillier Premier Plant Scheme, the centre enjoys access to more unusual outdoor plants. All are grown with great care and attention, and the friendly, knowledgeable staff are on hand to advise and assist all customers.

In the Planthouse there's a vast selection of familiar and more unusual house plants and planted arrangements - perfect for your home or conservatory. Cacti are a speciality here, with every conceivable type available to grace your home, office or conservatory.

Having the right tools for the job can, as any gardener will tell you, make any gardening chore much more of a pleasure. This centre offers leading brands of garden tools, watering equipment and an extensive range of chemicals and fertilisers. Each season the centre has the latest designs in garden furniture made from the finest wood and resin. The gift department is brimming with unusual and attractive gifts, ornaments and cards, complemented by the book department with titles to suit all ages. For the children there's a range of garden toys, games and accessories, and a safe and enjoyable outdoor play area.

The Greenhouse Cafe serves a delicious variety of home-cooked meals, cakes and snacks. Also on site are several franchises which include designer knitwear and leisurewear, patios and driveways, conservatories and leisure buildings, an aquatic centre and a specialist turf supplier. *Open: Monday to Saturday 9-6 (5 in winter), Sun 10.30-4.30.*

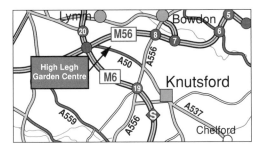

Directions:

From Junction 19 of the M6 take the A556 towards Manchester. At the A50 junction turn left and High Legh Garden Centre can be found on the left in the village of High Legh.

Aquatics	Dried & Artificial Flowers	Information Desk
Barbecues	Fencing	Large Car Park
Books & Stationery	Fireworks	Paving
Childrens Play Area	Floristry	Pet Products and/or Pets
Christmas & Seasonal Displays	Fruit Trees	Plant Guarantee
Clothing	Garden Furniture	Plants
Conservatories	Garden Products	Restaurant/Coffee Shop
Credit Cards Accepted	Giftware	Seeds & Bulbs
Disabled	Greenhouses & Sheds	Trees
Display Gardens	Houseplants	

LOCAL GARDENS

Tatton Park, Knutsford 01565 654822

Among the many outstanding features of these 50-acre grounds are the orangery by Lewis Wyatt, fernery by Paxton, Greek Monument, African hut, and Italian, rose and Japanese gardens. Swamp cypresses, tree ferns, hybrid azaleas and rhododendrons, tall redwoods, bamboos and alpines. 10m SE of Warrington off the A6/M56. *Open: April-Oct Tues-Sun and Bank Holiday Mon 10.30-6; Nov-Mar Tues-Sun (except 25th Dec) 11-4. House open April-Oct as gardens, but noon-4. Entrance: gardens £3; Discovery saver ticket - any two of house, old hall, farm, park and gardens £4.50 (children £2.50, family £12.50).*

Peover Hall, Knutsford 01565 632358 (guide); 01565 830395 (estate office)

15 acres with five walled gardens, lily pond and herb, white, rose and pink gardens. Land-scaped park dating from the 18th century with lake, 19th-century dell, rhododendron walks, blue and white border, purple border, Church walk, pleached lime avenue, fine topiary. 3m S of Knutsford on the A50. *Open: May-Sept Mon and Thurs 2.30-5; hall open May-Sept Mon (except Bank Holiday Mon) 2.30-4.30. Entrance: £2 (children £1); hall, stables and garden £3 (children £2).*

Arley Hall and Gardens, Arley, Great Budworth 01565 777353

12-acre garden with twin herbaceous borders, walled gardens, azaleas, rhododendrons. Hybrid and species shrub roses. Avenue of 14 quercus Ilex trees clipped to the shape of giant cylinders; yew hedges; rock garden, woodland garden. Specialist plant nursery. 5m W of Knutsford off the A50. *Open: April-Sept Tues-Sun and Bank Holiday Mon 11-5 - advisable to ring for confirmation. Hall open, but times vary. Entrance: £3.60 (concessions £3); hall and gardens £6.10 (concessions £5.20).*

PETER BARRATT'S GARDEN CENTRE
YARN ROAD, STOCKTON-ON-TEES TS18 3SQ
TEL: 01642 613433 FAX: 01642 618185

Peter Barratt's Garden Centre in Stockton, like its sister centre in Newcastle, is a large and comprehensive garden centre offering everything you need to create the perfect garden. The indoor and outdoor areas are pleasant and welcoming, and all products are well-displayed and easily accessible. Outdoor plants are the speciality of this distinguished garden centre. The Plantarea offers a wide range of lovely plants, including bulbs, bedding and perennial plants, fruit and ornamental trees, shrubs, conifers, climbers, alpines and heathers.

To complement this excellent range of plants, the centre stocks a comprehensive choice of gardening sundries and accessories, including containers in all sizes, stoneware and ceramics. In addition, you will find a wide selection of floristry sundries, silk flowers, composts, fertilisers and gardening tools. For those extras that enhance any garden, there is also a range of fencing, paving, barbecues, garden furniture, greenhouses and sheds.

The Aquatic department offers a selection of pool kits, together with fountains, fonts, cascades and statues that spout water in every way. There is also a variety of pumps, ponds, fish, tanks, aquariums and sundries - everything to create and maintain beautiful water features for the garden. The trained staff are always available to advise on choosing plants for particular situations.

Another attraction of this centre is the range of clothing available, including Stormafit and Acorn fleeces and a selection of sweaters and outdoor wear. The small and well-stocked giftshop has ornaments, pictures and frames, wind chimes, candles and more. The restaurant/coffee shop serves a tempting range of hot and cold meals, snacks and beverages. Special events and gardening demonstrations are held throughout the year, and there is also a dedicated safe play area for children. *Open: Monday to Saturday 9-5 (peak season 9-7), Sunday 10.30-4.30.*

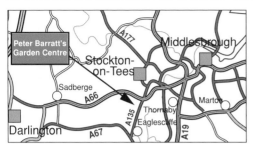

Directions:

From Middlesbrough take the A66 towards Darlington and at the A135 junction turn left.Peter Barratt's Garden Centre is on the right.

Aquatics	Dried & Artificial Flowers	Information Desk
Barbecues	Fencing	Large Car Park
Books & Stationery	Fireworks	Paving
Childrens Play Area	Floristry	Pet Products and/or Pets
Christmas & Seasonal Displays	Fruit Trees	Plant Guarantee
Clothing	Garden Furniture	Plants
Conservatories	Garden Products	Restaurant/Coffee Shop
Credit Cards Accepted	Giftware	Seeds & Bulbs
Disabled	Greenhouses & Sheds	Trees
Display Gardens	Houseplants	

LOCAL GARDENS

Mount Grace Priory, Saddle Bridge 01609 883494

English Heritage. Each of the monk's cells in this ruined Priory had its own garden; now some of these have been replanted. Medicinal and other herbs, each year following a different theme. Also one-acre terraced garden with rock plants, shrubberies, narrow borders and Japanese garden with small pond, azaleas, rhododendrons and colourful maples. 7m NE of Northallerton on the A19. *Open: daily April-Oct 10-6 (dusk in Oct); Nov-Mar Weds-Sun 10-1 and 2-4 (last admission 3.30). Entrance: £2.70 (concessions £2, children £1.40).*

Millgate House, Richmond 01748 823571

A small, characterful and award-winning walled town garden overlooking the River Swale in Richmond, North Yorkshire. Foliage plants including hostas and ferns; old roses, unusual selection of clematis and hostas. 'Maigold' roses hang picturesquely from the Regency balcony of the house. Small trees and shrubs. Lower garden has more than 28 varieties of roses and a specialist collection of hostas. Offers a wealth of ideas for small gardens. *Open: daily mid-Mar to mid-Oct 10-late evening; at other times by appointment. Entrance: £2.*

Ormesby Hall, Ormesby 01642 324188

National Trust. Recent development has transformed the gardens of this great Hall. The main rose beds have been replanted with standards, shrub and bush roses. Holly Walk, new glasshouse. Garden tours on the last Thursday of the month, led by the head gardener. Garden and sales shop. 3m SE of Middlesbrough off the A171. *Open: April-end Oct Tues-Thurs, Sun and Bank Holiday Mon 2-5.30. Entrance: £2.10 (children £1); house, garden, railway and exhibitions £3.50 (children £1.70).*

TRELAWNEY GARDEN LEISURE
SLADESBRIDGE, WADEBRIDGE, CORNWALL PL27 6JA
TEL: 01208 812966 FAX: 01208 814798 EMAIL: trelawney.garden@virgin.net

Trelawney Garden Centre is styled and themed to a traditional railway station, reflecting the days when part of The London and South Western Railway ran through the site from the 1800's to the 1960's. Nestled in the beautiful Camel Valley the centres Planteria and garden area is set by a picturesque lily laden lake, ideal for a leisurely stroll, and is filled with quality locally grown plants, shrubs and trees. The raised beds always hold a fantastic display of seasonal colour and creative planting ideas.

An enormous water wheel dominates the garden as visitors cross the rustic bridge to the children's play area, an imaginative and extensive playground with safe and sturdy equipment, including a likeness of a steam locomotive alongside a miniature station and platform with slides, climbing frames and working signals.

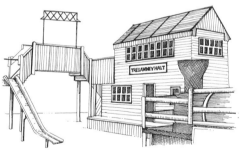

The on-site Carriages Restaurant and Coffee Stop provides delicious early bird breakfasts, freshly baked cakes, morning coffee, full daily carvery, children's menu, snacks and Cornish cream tea's, all home-cooked. From February to December it hosts regular special themed evening menus- booking a must. Trelawney offers three shopping platforms of top quality products for the garden and home and boasts a good range of garden care products, watering equipment, lawn preparations, seeds, tools and accessories, as well as an outstanding selection of spring and summer bulbs.

The superb selection of house plants are imported directly from Holland. The gift area is a treasure trove of books, ceramics, china, ornaments, locally produced goods, jams, preserves, sweets and chocolates, and an excellent variety of fresh, dried and silk flowers which can be transformed into stunning floral displays by their expert florists. At Christmas time Platform 3 transforms from a paradise of top quality garden furniture and barbecues to a Winter Wonderland of stunning festive displays of decorations, lights and Christmas trees. *Open: daily 9.00 - 5.30; Sundays 10.30 - 4.30.*

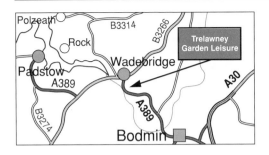

Directions

Take the A389 from Wadebridge towards Bodmin. Trelawney Garden Leisure is 1 mile on the left.

⊞ Barbecues	▥ Fencing	ⓘ Information Desk
▓ Books & Stationery	✿ Floristry	℗ Large Car Park
⍑ Childrens Play Area	ℂ Fruit Trees	▦ Paving
☀ Christmas & Seasonal Displays	▤ Garden Furniture	☗ Pet Products and/or Pets
⏚ Clothing	⚙ Garden Machinery	☗ Plant Guarantee
▨ Credit Cards Accepted	⚘ Garden Products	} Plants
✿ Cut Flowers	▥ Giftware	⑂ Restaurant/Coffee Shop
♿ Disabled	⬠ Greenhouses & Sheds	☀ Seeds & Bulbs
⚘ Dried & Artificial Flowers	⬚ Houseplants	⚘ Trees
⚘ Farm Shop		

LOCAL GARDENS

Lanhydrock, Bodmin 01208 73320

National Trust-owned 30-acre garden forming a horseshoe-shape around the finest house in Cornwall. Famed for early magnolias. Formal Victorian parterres, wooded Higher Garden on the hillside. Begun in 1857, it features rhododendrons, camellias, Irish yews, roses, annuals and herbaceous borders. Woodland walks take in flowering shrubs, rare trees and hydrangeas. 2m SE of Bodmin off A38 and A30, or B3268. *Open: daily Mar-Oct 11-5.30 (Oct 5 pm); daily Nov-Feb during daylight. Entrance: garden and grounds £3.20 (children £1.60), free Nov-Feb; house, garden and grounds £6.40 (children £3.20, family and group tickets available).*

Long Cross Victorian Gardens, Trelights, Port Isaac 01208 880243

A mazelike effect is produced by the hedges protecting this reconstruction of a late-Victorian garden from the ravages of the sea air. This 3-acre garden has been designed specifically to thrive in the salt-laden atmosphere of Cornwall's north coast. Wonderful views of Port Isaac and Port Quin Bays. There are many sections incorporating an ornamental pond, children's play area and pets' corner. 7m N of Wadebridge on B3314. *Open: daily all year. Entrance: £1.40 (children under 14 25p).*

The Japanese Garden and Bonsai Nursery, St Mawgan, Newquay 01637 860116

This 1-acre garden is a reconstruction of an authentic Japanese garden with water features, bamboo grove, and stroll and zen gardens. Featured plants include Japanese Maples, rhododendrons, azaleas, and ornamental grasses. The bonsai nursery is adjacent to the garden. 6m NE of Newquay off the A3059 and B3278. *Open: daily except Christmas Day - New Years Day inclusive, 10-6 (last admission 5pm). Entrance: £2.50 (children £1); bonsai nursery free.*

WEBBS GARDEN CENTRE

BURNESIDE ROAD, KENDAL, CUMBRIA LA9 4RT

TEL: 01539 720068 FAX: 01539 727328 EMAIL:office@webbs-garden-centre.co.uk

Originally established in 1810 by a nurseryman called James Meldrum, **Webbs Garden Centre** was purchased by Clarence Webb in the mid-1800s. It was this same Clarence Webb who introduced the internationally acclaimed Webb's Wonderful Lettuce. The renown of the Webb family continued as, in 1922, James Webb developed a growing area for what would become his prize-winning varieties of dahlias and chrysanthemums. Geoffrey Webb moved the Centre to its present 3-acre site, where his daughter and her husband continue to uphold the company's tradition of service and quality.

A speciality of this centre is its variety of penstemons, with a vast array of over 60 different varieties grown here at the centre, and a huge collection of all forms of herbs and geraniums. If not grown here in the Centre's own nursery, produce is bought in from elsewhere in Britain wherever possible, as with their top-quality houseplants, mainly British grown. In addition this Centre offers a range of outdoor plants, including an exciting array of conifers, rhododendrons, bedding plants, shrubs, and fruit and deciduous trees.

Moving with the seasons, Webbs offers bulbs for autumn colour, fireworks displays in October, and a superb Christmas display.The range of seeds, fertilisers and other garden supplies is second to none. A recent extension to the Centre houses a choice selection of wooden and resin garden furniture, top-of-the-range barbecue equipment and more.

The Aquatic Centre has a full complement of cold-water, tropical and marine fish and accessories. The Coffee Shop serves home-made snacks, soups and meals, seven days a week. Demonstrations on hanging baskets, flower arranging and other gardening techniques are held regularly. *Open: winter Monday to Saturday 9-5, Sunday 10.30-4.30; summer Monday to Saturday 9-6, Sunday 10.30-4.30.*

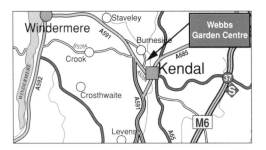

Directions:

From Junction 36 of the M6 take the A591 past Kendal and turn right towards Kendal North. Turn left into Burneside Road and Webbs Garden Centre is on the right..

Aquatics	Fencing	Greenhouses & Sheds
Barbecues	Fireworks	Houseplants
Books & Stationery	Floristry	Information Desk
Christmas & Seasonal Displays	Fruit Trees	Large Car Park
Clothing	Garden Construction	Paving
Credit Cards Accepted	Garden Design	Plant Guarantee
Cut Flowers	Garden Furniture	Plants
Disabled	Garden Machinery	Restaurant/Coffee Shop
Display Gardens	Garden Products	Seeds & Bulbs
Dried & Artificial Flowers	Giftware	Trees

LOCAL GARDENS

Levens Hall, Kendal 01539 560321

10 acres including the first ha-ha in England, laid out in 1694 by Guillaume Beaumont, gardener to James II. Many of the original trees. Primroses, clipped yews, box hedges. Topiary garden, formal bedding, impressive beech circle, herbaceous borders. Fountain Garden with lime avenues; picturesque herb garden. Levens Hall is an Elizabethan mansion boasting excellent panelling and plasterwork. 5m S of Kendal off the A6. *Open: April-mid-Oct Sun-Thurs 10-5. House open. Entrance: £3.90 (children £2.10); house and garden £5.30 (children £2.80; group rates available).*

Sizergh Castle, Kendal 01539 560070

National Trust garden with year-round interest. The Limestone Rock Garden is the largest owned by the NT. Collection of dwarf conifers, primulas, Japanese maples, hardy ferns, gentians, bulbs and perennials. Specimen roses, shrubs and ground cover, lilies. Wildflower areas, 'Dutch' garden, orchard; water garden. 3½m S of Kendal off the A591. *Open: late Mar-Oct Sun-Thurs 12.30-5.30 (last admission 5; castle open 1.30-5.30). Entrance: £2.20; castle and garden £4.50 (group rates available).*

Holme Cragg, Blea Cragg Bridge, Witherslack, Grange-over-Sands 01539 552366

Plantsman's garden making excellent use of the site's natural features. Rocky outcrops are covered in sempervirums, saxifrages, sedums, alpines. Candelabra primulas, rhododendrons, irises, azaleas. Grassy bank clothed in double and single Welsh poppies ranging in colour from yellow to a deep orange. Himalyan meconopsis, natural wildflower area, shrub roses; handsome acers providing good colour. 14m SW of Kendal off the A590. *Open: daily, all year (telephone for details). Entrance: by donation to the Cumbria Wildlife Trust.*

CHATSWORTH GARDEN CENTRE
CALTON LEES, BEELEY, MATLOCK, DERBYSHIRE DE4 2NX
TEL: 01629 734004 FAX: 01629 734005

Chatsworth Garden Centre is situated only one mile from Chatsworth House, in what was once a three-acre walled garden within this famed and gracious estate. This centre has been popular and highly regarded since it opened in 1983, and in a relatively short time has earned a reputation as one of the finest garden centres in the area.

The large garden shop stocks quality herbaceous plants, heathers and alpines, hardy shrubs, fruit trees, rhododendrons, seasonal bedding plants and herbs from nurseries throughout the UK and Europe. With both an indoor houseplants area and extensive outdoor display beds for trees and shrubs, this centre is truly a one-stop shop for all your gardening needs. Everything imaginable for the garden can be found here - from gazebos and other outdoor structures to top-of-the-range gardening tools. The centre also has a superb collection of garden and conservatory furniture, barbecues and accessories, as well as a range of attractive water features, stoneware, garden ornaments and statues to enhance every garden.

The knowledgeable and qualified staff are always on hand to offer courteous and informative advice on all aspects of gardening. Speciality giftware available includes ceramics, silk flowers, cards, books, unusual gifts, ornaments and much more. The dedicated clothing department is another attractive feature of this comprehensive centre.

There are facilities for people with disabilities. When it's time for a break, the 120-seater Coffee Shop offers a range of delicious hot and cold snacks, lunches and cream teas. When a visit to Chatsworth House has whetted your appetite for creating the perfect garden of your own, this is the place to come to make your plans and vision a reality. *Open: daily, Oct to Feb 10-5; Mar to Sep 10-6.*

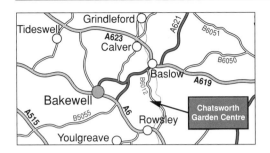

Directions:

From Matlock take the A6 north towards Bakewell. At Rowsley turn right on the B6012 towards Baslow and Chatsworth Garden Centre can be found after 3 miles on the left.

🍖 Barbecues	🌳 Fruit Trees	Ⓟ Large Car Park	
📖 Books & Stationery	🪑 Garden Furniture	🌱 Plant Guarantee	
☀ Christmas & Seasonal Displays	🏭 Garden Products	} Plants	
👕 Clothing	🏠 Giftware	🍴 Restaurant/Coffee Shop	
CC Credit Cards Accepted	🌿 Houseplants	● Seeds & Bulbs	
♿ Disabled	ⓘ Information Desk	🌴 Trees	
🌹 Dried & Artificial Flowers			

LOCAL GARDENS

Chatsworth, Bakewell 01246 582204

100-acre garden which has developed over four centuries, and reflects the changing garden fashions of history. Canal pond, cascade, Emperor Fountain with 84-metre water jet. 18th-century Capability Brown landscaping with fine vista from Salisbury Lawn to the horizon. 20th-century orange borders and white and blue borders, display greenhouse, terrace, conservatory garden and rose garden. Wildflowers, sedges, grasses, moss. Arboretum, pinetum. Large rockery by Paxton. 4m E of Bakewell off the A619/A6. *Open: daily mid-Mar-Oct 11-5. House open. Entrance: £3.75 (OAPs/students £3, children £1.75); house and garden £6.50 (OAPs/ students £5.25, children £3).*

Haddon Hall, Bakewell 01629 812855

16th-century terraced gardens reconstructed this century, on a limestone bluff near the River Wye. Extensive collection of rambling and climbing roses, clematis and delphiniums. Considered one of the most romantic gardens in England, with the fine medieval castle as backdrop. House is not accessible for wheelchairs. 2m SE of Bakewell off the A6. *Open: daily Apr 1-Sep 30 10.30-5.00. (Closed on Sun 18 July); Oct 1 -Oct 31, Mon-Thurs 10.30-4.30; House open. Entrance: hall and gardens £5.50 (OAPs £4.75, children 5-16 £3); no garden-only tickets available.*

Lea Gardens, Lea 01629 534380

4-acre woodland setting with unusual rhododendrons and dwarf conifers, and rare collection of kalmias, azaleas and alpines. The excellent rock gardens also contain heathers, spring bulbs and acers. The rhododendron garden was begun in 1935, and now boasts 550 varieties of rhododendrons and azaleas. There's an excellent booklet available that outlines routes for visitors. Plants for sale. 5m SE of Matlock off the A6. *Open: daily late Mar to early July 10-7; at other times of year by appointment. Entrance: £3 (children 50p).*

FERNDALE NURSERY AND GARDEN CENTRE
DYCHE LANE, COAL ASTON, DRONFIELD, DERBYSHIRE S18 3BJ
TEL: 01246 412763 FAX: 01246 290323

Established in 1982, **Ferndale Nursery and Garden Centre** seeks to provide everything the gardening public need and deserve: helpful, friendly and knowledgeable service and the finest range of high-quality plants. Customers soon find their gardening problems solved, with the result that they return again and again for the kind of advice and service they can find here.

The centres covered, heated area stocks a range of flowering and foliage plants. This area leads to another covered area, which in turn leads to the open outdoor area. Throughout the centre trees, shrubs, groundcover, herbs, bulbs and hundreds of plant species can be found to grace every home, conservatory, office or garden. The specialisation here is flower arrangements; with a truly amazing range of innovative and traditional arrangements to suit every taste and pocket.

The centre also has a good selection of garden implements, and for those finishing touches, there's a variety of garden pots, terracotta and Roman-style urns and plant holders. The attractive giftshop stocks a range of candles and holders, ceramics and ornaments, cards, books and more. The welcoming coffee shop seats over 60 people and serves delicious hot and cold snacks, meals and beverages.

With the byline 'making your world more beautiful', the people at Ferndale are adept at helping you to make your garden glorious. They have found a green thumb on everyone they've worked with, and they can help you find yours. Anyone, no matter how inexperienced, can benefit from their experience and ability. They offer plants and gardening products of the highest quality with a performance guarantee, and they'll give you sound, honest advice. *Open: January to February Monday to Friday 9-5, Sunday 11-5; March to December Monday to Friday 9-6, Sunday 11-5.*

Directions:

From the A61 just north of Dronfield take the B6056 towards Coal Aston. Turn right onto the B6057 and Ferndale Nursery and Garden Centre is on the right.

Aquatics	Dried & Artificial Flowers	Houseplants
Barbecues	Fencing	Information Desk
Books & Stationery	Floristry	Large Car Park
Christmas & Seasonal Displays	Fruit Trees	Plant Guarantee
Conservatories	Garden Design	Plants
Credit Cards Accepted	Garden Furniture	Restaurant/Coffee Shop
Cut Flowers	Garden Products	Seeds & Bulbs
Disabled	Giftware	Trees
Display Gardens		

LOCAL GARDENS

Hardwick Hall, Doe Lea 01246 850430

Late summer- and autumn-flowering herbaceous borders ranging from hot, vibrant colours to soft, delicate ones. Superb herb garden. Mature yew hedges. Orchard. Wildflowers. Famous Elizabethan mansion house. Stainsby Mill, water powered corn mill which has been on site since 13th century. Junction 29 on the M1 then follow the A6175. *Open: daily April-Oct noon-5.30. Country park open daily all year dawn-dusk. House open April-Oct Weds-Thurs, Sat-Sun and Bank Holiday Mon 12.30-5 or dusk (last admission 4.30). Entrance: £3 (children £1.50); house and garden £6 (children £3). Mill £1.60 (children 80p, family £4)*

The Herb Garden, Hall View Cottage, Hardstoft, Pilsley 01246 854268

Luxuriant herb garden in a bucolic setting. Well established parterre. There are three speciality gardens: a lavender garden, a physic garden, and a pot-pourri garden. Great range of herbs on sale, including some unusual and rare species. 6m SE of Chesterfield on the B6039. *Open: daily mid Mar-mid Sept 10-5 (except Tuesdays). Entrance: £1 (children free).*

Sheffield Botanic Gardens, Sheffield 0114 267 1115

Owned by Sheffield Town Trust and managed by Sheffield City Council. Opened in 1836 and being restored with Heritage Lottery funding. Proposals include conversion off Curators House into cafe/restaurant, restoration of the 'Paxton' pavilions and re-instatement of linking green-houses. 19 sheltered areas close to the city centre. 1/2 m from A625. *Open: All year daily except 25, 26 Dec and 1 Jan. Entrance Free.*

GRANGECRAFT GARDEN CENTRE
HOSPITAL LANE, MICKLEOVER, DERBY DE3 5DR
TEL: 01332 514350 FAX: 01332 516136

Established on a greenfield site in 1987, **Grangecraft Garden Centre** is known locally as 'The Gardener's Garden Centre'. It is considered a leading garden centre in the Derby area. The centre aims to provide a large selection of quality plants, sold at competitive prices and backed up with expert advice from its qualified staff.

The extensive sales area is set amid landscaped terraced gardens, a very pleasant environment in which to shop at leisure. From alpines, bedding plants, bonsai plants and climbers to roses, shrubs and trees, this centre boasts an A-Z of plants for all situations. There are easy-to-grow varieties for the new gardener, to the 'Connoisseur Collection' for more unusual and challenging plants. If you still can't find what you want, the centre's Customer Order service will try to source items especially for you. The houseplant area gets fresh deliveries every week, and offers an excellent range of flowering, foliage and conservatory plants. Here you will also find a wide selection of plastic and ceramic pots and covers.

The centre specialises in pergolas, gazebos and other outdoor features to add the finishing touches to any garden. Add to this the centre's comprehensive selection of gardening accessories, sheds, conservatories and glasshouses, water features and seasonal furniture and you have a complete range of everything you need to create and maintain a beautiful garden.

Covering approximately 8 acres, the garden centre features many other facilities, including a large giftware department, Pets and Aquatics department, and floristry department. When you're ready for a breather, the licensed cafe serves a selection of hot and cold beverages, cakes, meals and snacks. You can sit on the lovely veranda overlooking the Koi pond, or sample the fragrant delights of the 'Purley Trellis Rosary' (a 15-foot reproduction Victorian Rosary). *Open: Monday to Saturday 9-5.30, Sunday 10.30-4.30.*

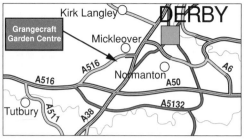

Directions:

From Derby travelling south on the A38 towards Burton take the A516 to Uttoxeter. Take the first left turning and follow the road round to the right into Hospital Lane. Grangecraft Garden Centre is on the right past the new Mickleover Country Park Estate.

Aquatics	Fencing	Information Desk
Barbecues	Fireworks	Large Car Park
Books & Stationery	Fruit Trees	Paving
Childrens Play Area	Garden Design	Pet Products and/or Pets
Christmas & Seasonal Displays	Garden Furniture	Plant Guarantee
Conservatories	Garden Products	Plants
Credit Cards Accepted	Giftware	Restaurant/Coffee Shop
Disabled	Greenhouses & Sheds	Seeds & Bulbs
Display Gardens	Houseplants	Trees
Dried & Artificial Flowers		

LOCAL GARDENS

Melbourne Hall Gardens, Melbourne 01332 862502

A living record of a late 17th-/early 18th-century design in the style of Le Notre, laid out by London and Wise. Terraces run down to a lake; grotto with an inscription ascribed to Byron's mistress Caroline Lamb. Lovely lead statuary including Van Nost's lead urn of The Four Seasons; fountains. The Birdcage iron arbour dates from 1706, and is visible from the house along a long walk hedged with yews. 8m S of Derby off the B587. *Open: April-Sept Weds, Sat-Sun and Bank Holiday Mon 2-6. House open: please telephone for details. Entrance: £3 (OAPs £2, children £2).*

Elvaston Castle Country Park, Borrowash Road, Elvaston 01332 571342

Grade II listed gardens designed in the early 19th century by William Barron. Old English, parterre, Alhambra, Italianate and azalea gardens. Tree-line avenues, herbaceous borders, rose gardens, extensive topiary, large ornamental lake. Moorish temple and boat house; cedars of Lebanon. Barron was able to transplant even 13-metre high mature trees using his unique transplanting machines - one of which is housed at the Royal Botanic Gardens, Kew. 6m SE of Derby on the B5010. *Open: daily all year, dawn-dusk. Estate Museum open April-end Oct. Entrance: free; Estate Museum £1.50 (children 60p).*

Derby Arboretum, Aboretum Square, Derby 01332 716644

This was the first specifically-designed urban park in Britain. John Claudius Loudon was commissioned to oversee its creation; his original plan involved the planting of 1,000 trees. the free leaflet available is very helpful, listing 40 varieties of trees to be found here. The park features trees from all points of the globe. *Open: daily all year. Entrance: free.*

ENDSLEIGH GARDEN CENTRE
IVYBRIDGE, DEVON PL21 9JL
TEL: 01752 898989 FAX: 01752 898990

Endsleigh Garden Centre opened in 1972 on the site of a former chrysanthemum nursery. It has grown steadily since that time under the leadership of MD Robin Taylor, whose father was head gardener at stately Endsleigh House. One of the largest centres of its kind in the South West, its friendly, highly trained staff can offer advice on all gardening needs.

Priding itself on being much more than a garden centre, Endsleigh plays an active role in the local community. Its Garden Room hosts numerous activities throughout the year, open to the public, including garden club meetings, craft fairs, and guest speakers on subjects such as plant pests, bulbs, water gardens and much more. The Centre offers practical demonstrations, entertainment and a plant clinic. These and other community-spirited endeavours have earned the Centre the Investor in People award, to accompany its award as a Garden Centre of Excellence.

The Centre's enormous range of gardening tools and products includes supplies for watering, feeding, weed control and any number of seasonal jobs. The Aquatics base is the place to stop for whatever you need to create a thriving water garden. For the home aquarium, they stock a huge range of tropical fish. Among the wonderful range of trees, shrubs and flowering and foliage plants for sale, the Centre specialises in sub-tropical plants including a fine range of palms. Hardy plants are guaranteed for two years, and the Centre offers a free replanting service for hanging baskets. There's also an extensive selection of quality dried and silk flowers, floristry materials, books and gifts in the large shop area. *Open: Mon-Sat, 9-5 (summer 9-6), Sun 10.30-4.30; closed Easter Sunday.*

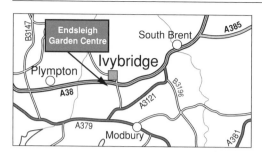

Directions:

Endsleigh Garden Centre lies on the A38 about 9 miles east of Plymouth and 30 miles west of Exeter and just to the west of the B3213 Ivybridge Junction.

Aquatics	Farm Shop	Houseplants
Barbecues	Fencing	Information Desk
Books & Stationery	Fruit Trees	Large Car Park
Childrens Play Area	Garden Construction	Paving
Christmas & Seasonal Displays	Garden Design	Pet Products and/or Pets
Clothing	Garden Furniture	Plant Guarantee
Conservatories	Garden Machinery	Plants
Credit Cards Accepted	Garden Products	Restaurant/Coffee Shop
Disabled	Giftware	Seeds & Bulbs
Dried & Artificial Flowers	Greenhouses & Sheds	Trees

LOCAL GARDENS

Endsleigh House and Gardens, Milton Abbot 01822 870428

Designed by architect Jeffry Wyatt and landscape gardener Humphry Repton for the 6th Duke of Bedford beginning in 1811, Endsleigh, once used by the Duke as a fishing and hunting lodge, is now a country house hotel. The gardens are gradually being restored in an attempt to recapture Repton's 19th-century vision. Woodland; rare tree species in the arboretum; fine views of the upper Tamar. 4m NW of Tavistock on the B3362. *Open: April-Sept Sat-Sun and Bank Holiday Mon noon-4, and by appointment Tues and Fri noon-4. Entrance: by donation (suggested minimum £1.50).*

Lukesland, Ivybridge 01752 893390

Covering 15 acres in the beautiful setting of a small valley around Addicombe Brook, this boasts flowering shrubs, rare trees, wildflowers, lakes, many waterfalls and pools. Large and unusual selection of small- and large-leaved rhododendrons, and one of the largest magnolia cambellii in the UK. Parts of it accessible to wheelchair-users. 1½m N of Ivybridge on Harford Rd. *Open: Apr 18 - Jun 13 Sun, Wed & Bank Holidays 2-6; can take coaches by appointment. Entrance: £2.80 (children free).*

Flete (Country Houses Association), Ermington 01752 830308

15 acres of gardens that overlook majestic valley and River Erme. Landscaped by Russell Page in the 1920s, the gardens include an Italian garden and a water garden, the latter constructed in part by T E Lawrence (Lawrence of Arabia). Fine shrubs and trees. Unusual cobbled terrace spreads from the west face of original Tudor manse. 2m W of Modbury on A379 Plymouth-Kingsbridge Rd. *Open: [need dates/times]. Entrance: £2 (children £1).*

OTTER NURSERIES GARDEN CENTRE
GOSFORD ROAD, OTTERY ST MARY, DEVON EX11 1LZ
TEL: 01404 815815 FAX: 01404 815816

Otter Nurseries was established in 1964. From beginning as a wholesale nursery producing trees, bedding plants and shrubs, it has grown into a thriving garden centre. Otter Nurseries is now unusual in that they produce 70% of all the hardy outdoor plants they sell on site. The Nurseries command over 100 acres of production, where open ground and container plants are grown. With one of the largest stocks of plants in the country, today Otter Nurseries is one of the largest garden centres in the South West of England, retailing virtually all their own plants.

With over an acre under cover, the superb, new, extensive greenhouse is brimming with houseplants, bedding plants, old favourites and more unusual plants for the beginner and experienced gardener alike. Nursery-fresh shrubs, trees, roses, heathers and many other hardy garden plants are sold here, all guaranteed to grow in your garden. The trained staff will be delighted to answer your questions and offer advice.

The centre also boasts a large selection of garden accessories and machinery, and is famous throughout the South West for its huge display and range of garden furniture, especially wooden furniture and three-piece cane suites, for outdoor use and the conservatory, most of which are in stock for immediate collection or delivery. There is a large fencing and paving section, an attractive Koi carp pool, and a vast range of stoneware, giftware, clothing, conservatories, greenhouses and sheds. The information desk is the source for all questions and the centre's superb restaurant, which seats over 240 people, serves a selection of delicious home-cooked food - morning coffee, lunches, afternoon teas and all-day snacks, much of it home-made on the premises. Other features of this distinguished centre include its excellent facilities for people with disabilities and car parking for over 400 cars. *Open: Monday to Saturday 8.30-5.30, Sunday 10.30-4.30.*

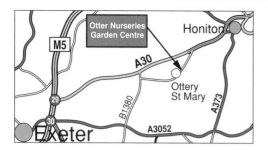

Directions:

From the A30 towards Honiton, take the right turn at the brick monument half a mile after the Fairmile Inn. The road leads directly to the Garden Centre and Nursery.

Aquatics	Fencing	(i) Information Desk
Barbecues	Fruit Trees	(P) Large Car Park
Books & Stationery	Garden Design	Paving
Christmas & Seasonal Displays	Garden Furniture	Plant Guarantee
Clothing	Garden Machinery	) Plants
Conservatories	Garden Products	Restaurant/Coffee Shop
Credit Cards Accepted	Giftware	Seeds & Bulbs
Disabled	Greenhouses & Sheds	Trees
Display Gardens	Houseplants	

LOCAL GARDENS

Burrow Farm Gardens, Dalwood 01404 831285

Secluded garden of 6 acres, created from pasture land. The informal design features many unusual herbaceous plants and shrubs. Ponds, large bog garden. Pergola walk with shrub roses. Woodland with colourful range of azaleas and rhododendrons. Mature trees, candelabra primulas, native wildflowers. The terraced courtyard has later-flowering herbaceous plants. Superb views. Plants for sale in nursery, tearoom, cream teas. 4m W of Axminster off the A35. *Open: daily April-Sept, 10-7. Entrance: £2.50 (children 50p).*

Killerton, Broadclyst 01392 881345

Wonderful, extensive hillside gardens, enclosed by parkland, woods and farmland. Naturalised bulbs down to large open lawns. Rare shrubs and trees including beech avenue, the first plantings of Wellingtonias in England, oaks, Lawson cypresses, maples. Marvellous walks, herbaceous borders. Early 19th-century summerhouse; rock garden, Bear's Hut, icehouse. Fine chapel in its own 3-acre grounds, including the largest tulip tree in England. 7m NE of Exeter off the B3181. *Open: daily all year 10.30-dusk. House and costume museum open Weds-Mon mid-Mar-Oct 11-5.30 (last admission 5). Entrance: £3.50; reduced rate Nov-Feb; house and garden £5.00.*

Knightshayes Gardens, Bolham, Tiverton 01884 253264

Landscaped 'Garden in the Wood' with views over the Exe valley. Collections of unusual plants including birches, acers, camellias, magnolias, rhododendrons, azaleas, roses, alpines, spring bulbs and herbaceous borders, cornus, hydrangeas and many rare and tender plants. 16m N of Exeter off the A396. *Open: daily April-Oct 11-5 (last admission 5; 4 in Oct); Sun Nov-Dec, 2-4 for pre-booked groups only. House open Sat-Thurs (Sat-Weds in Oct), same times as gardens. Entrance: £3.50 (children £1.70); house and garden £5.10 (children £2.50).*

OTTER NURSERIES GARDEN CENTRE
CHITTLEBURN HILL, BRIXTON, PLYMOUTH, DEVON PL8 2BH
TEL: 01752 405422 FAX: 01752 484181

Otter Nurseries produce their own plants and have 100 acres of growing area, which means that virtually any requirements for plants can be delivered to Plymouth daily. This branch site is within easy reach of the main centre in Ottery St Mary, where 70% of the retail plants are grown. There is a wide selection of trees, shrubs, conifers, herbaceous plants, climbers and herbaceous perennials, rockery and alpine plants, topiary and feature plants. In addition, this comprehensive nursery boasts an extensive range of houseplants and conservatory plants, together with accessories such as bowls, baskets, hanging arrangements and more.

This comprehensive garden centre has dedicated departments focusing on paving, fencing, patios, gifts, seasonal displays and garden furniture, which offers a vast choice, most of which are in stock, for immediate collection or delivery. Having the right tools is a necessary ingredient in successful gardening, and so this centre offers a comprehensive range of gardening tools, implements and accessories, to help you create and maintain a garden in tip-top condition.

All staff are knowledgeable and are on hand not only to help you find exactly what you want, but also to give you expert advice and answer any questions. In addition to its superb range of plants, the centre also has an extensive selection of garden ornaments, conservatories and garden sheds, barbecues and gazebos. There is a superb restaurant, seating 80 people, serving delicious home-cooked food, morning coffee, lunches and afternoon teas. Free Car Parking. *Open: Monday to Saturday 9-5.30, Sunday 10.30-4.30.*

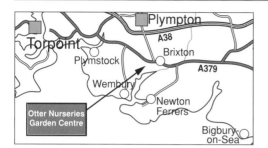

Directions:

Conveniently situated just south of the Plymouth to Kingsbridge road, 4 miles out of Plymouth and 1/4 mile from Brixton, set in the beautiful rolling Devon countryside within 1 mile of the coast.

Aquatics	Fencing	Information Desk
Barbecues	Fruit Trees	Large Car Park
Books & Stationery	Garden Design	Paving
Christmas & Seasonal Displays	Garden Furniture	Plant Guarantee
Clothing	Garden Machinery	Plants
Conservatories	Garden Products	Restaurant/Coffee Shop
Credit Cards Accepted	Giftware	Seeds & Bulbs
Disabled	Greenhouses & Sheds	Trees
Display Gardens	Houseplants	

LOCAL GARDENS

Saltram House, Plympton 01752 336546

National Trust. Fine specimen trees, rhododendrons, azaleas and spring-flowering plants. 18th-century belvedere, orangery and octagonal garden house. Long lime avenue, beech grove, Melancholy Walk with magnolias, Japanese maples, camellias. The house itself is a Grade II listed mansion with superb plasterwork and decorations - including two rooms designed by Robert Adam. 3m E of Plymouth off the A379. *Open: Sat-Sun 6th-21st Mar, 11-4; Sun-Thurs 27th Mar-Oct 10.30-5.30 (last admission 5). House open Sun-Thurs 27th Mar-Oct noon-5.30. Entrance: £2.60; house and garden £5.60.*

Buckland Abbey, Yelverton 01822 853607

National Trust and Plymouth City Council. Primarily a 20th-century creation in the grounds of 30-metre-long medieval barn and abbey. Box hedge parterre with over 50 different herbs. Magnolias, starting an Elizabethan style garden and thyme area. Walks; lovely views of Devon and Cornwall. 6m S of Tavistock off the A386 - clearly signed from the A386. *Open: Fri-Weds late Mar-Oct, 10.30-5.30; Sat-Sun Nov-Dec 2-5 (last admission 45 minutes before closing). Entrance: £2.30 (children £1.10); abbey extra.*

Antony, Torpoint 01752 812191 (NT); 812364 (Woodland Garden office)

National Trust and Trustees of Carew Pole Garden Trust. Set in a landscape designed by Reginald Pole Carew, after consultation with Humphry Repton. Commanding views to the River Lynher; terraces, formal courtyard, knot garden and ornamental Japanese pond. Adjacent 100-acre established woodland garden and natural woods. 2m W of Torpoint on the A374. *Open: Tues-Thurs and Bank Hol Mon April-Oct, 1.30-5.30 (last admission 4.45); also Sun June-Aug, same times. Woodland garden Mon-Sat Mar-Oct 11-5.30. Entrance: Woodland Garden only £3.00; house and formal garden £4 (children £2, groups £3.40).*

STEWARTS COUNTRY GARDEN CENTRE
GOD'S BLESSING LANE, BROOMHILL, HOLT, NR WIMBORNE, DORSET BH21 7DF
TEL: 01202 882462 FAX: 01202 842127

Stewarts Country Garden Centre occupies a picturesque greenfield site in rural Dorset. It covers a large area of 25 acres. Great gardening ideas are to be found in the Plantaria and Garden Shop, with its attractive Gift shop featuring many individual craft items, crystal, pottery, silk flowers and more. As with Stewarts other site, there is an extensive range of outdoor furniture on display. The light and airy Le Jardin Coffee Shop restaurant serves breakfast, lunch and afternoon tea.

From small beginnings in Forfarshire, Scotland, way back in 1742, the company, acknowledged as the first garden centre in the UK, has always been at the forefront of Garden Centre innovation. With its attention to detail and range of items for every garden and gardener, the Country Garden Centre has a special ambience that brings visitors back again and again.

The Centres nursery produces around 250,000 plants annually. Also here for the visitor is the informative Nature Trail, which provides an insight into the flora and fauna of the Dorset countryside, with information boards at various points along the trail highlighting particular features or items of special interest.

Regular informative talks are held in the purpose-built Phoenix Centre, where highly knowledgeable guest speakers can guide you through a variety of garden related topics. Guided tours of the site are also available.

Stewarts also produces its own range of informative leaflets on various aspects of gardening. Technical and specialist information on any gardening topic is available from the highly skilled staff. There is also an attractive children's play area. *Open: Monday - Saturday 9-5.30, Sunday 10-4.*

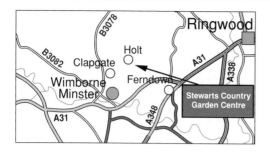

Directions:

From Wimborne Minster take the B3078 towards Cranborne. After about a mile take a right turn towards Holt. Turn right in Holt and Stewarts Country Garden Centre lies on the right at the end of God's Blessing Lane.

Barbecues	Fencing	Information Desk
Books & Stationery	Fruit Trees	Large Car Park
Childrens Play Area	Garden Furniture	Plant Guarantee
Christmas & Seasonal Displays	Garden Products	Plants
Credit Cards Accepted	Giftware	Restaurant/Coffee Shop
Disabled	Greenhouses & Sheds	Seeds & Bulbs
Dried & Artificial Flowers	Houseplants	Trees

LOCAL GARDENS

Deans Court, Wimborne Minster 01202 886116

13 acres of parkland and partly wild garden, with water features, specimen trees (including swamp cypress, Wellingtonias, blue cedars, Japanese pagoda tree and 28-metre tulip tree), free-roaming peacocks. Also herb garden with more than 250 species and walled kitchen garden. Chemical-free produce and plants for sale. In centre of Wimborne off the B3073. *Open: May 30th - June 30th - open for sculpture in garden; Closed Mon 7, 14, 21 and 28 June; otherwise phone for advice. House open by written appointment. Entrance: £2 (OAPs £1.50, children 50p).*

Edmondsham House, Cranborne 01725 517207

Large walled kitchen garden with lots of interest: herbs, fruit cage, Jerusalem artichokes, Russian comfrey, rhubarb, asparagus - all grown without chemical fertilisers or pesticides. Sunken greenhouse, spring bulbs, good spring-flowering shrubs, trees. Grass cockpit - thought to be one of the few 'naturalised' areas of the sort in the nation. 1m S of Cranborne off the A354 and B3081. *Open: Apr-Oct Weds and Sun 2-5 (also by appointment). For house opening please check. Entrance: £1 (children 50p); house and garden £2.50 (children £1, under-fives free).*

Stapehill Abbey Gardens, 276 Wimborne Road, Stapehill 01202 861686

Gardens of early 19th-century Cistercian Abbey, recently renovated and restored. Rose garden, large rock garden with waterfall and pools. Lawns, herbaceous borders, lake, tropical house. Victorian cottage garden and greenhouse, wisteria walk. Fine mature trees; woodland walk. Also on site, craft centre, licensed coffee shop, Country World museum with National Tractor Collection and farmyard where pony rides are available. On old A31 Wimborne-Ferndown road. *Open: April-Sept daily 10-5; Oct-20th Dec and 3rd Feb-Mar Weds-Sun 10-4. Entrance: £5.00 (OAPs/students £4.50, children 4-16 £3.50).*

STEWARTS GARDEN-LANDS

LYNDHURST ROAD, SOMERFORD, CHRISTCHURCH, DORSET BH23 4SA
TEL: 01425 272244 FAX: 01425 279723

Stewarts Garden-Lands must be one of the most comprehensive Garden Centres in the country. Garden-Lands is the most complete of Garden Centres with everything beautifully displayed. Its ideal location on the edge of the New Forest and close to the historic town of Christchurch, makes it the perfect place to visit at any time of the year.

Encompassing an extensive Plantaria, Stewarts can boast a wonderful range of top-quality trees, shrubs and plants from all over the world. Garden-Lands has one of the biggest outdoor furniture show areas in the country, with a great selection of bamboo and cane furnishings. Every area is filled with garden products and produce, much of it from Stewart's other distinguished site in Holt.

From small beginnings in Forfarshire, Scotland, way back in 1742, the company, acknowledged as the first garden centre in the UK, has always been at the forefront of Garden Centre innovation. This centre specialises in conservatories, summerhouses, huts, garden sheds etc., offering a huge range of these structures, to fit every garden and pocket.

There is an attractive Gift Shop, where many individual craft manufacturers' work is represented including pottery, crystal, silk flowers and more. The Garden Shop can supply all your gardening requirements from gift and fun items to equipment for the more serious gardener.

Stewarts also produce its own range of informative leaflets on various aspects of gardening. Technical and specialist information on any gardening topic is available from the higly skilled staff. The marvellous Four Seasons Coffee Shop restaurant serves breakfast, lunch and afternoon tea. *Open: Monday to Saturday 9-6, Sunday 10-4.*

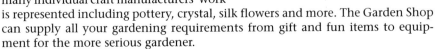

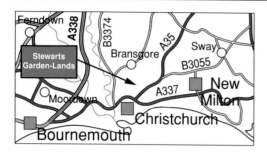

Directions:

At the junction of the A337 and A35 take the Lyndhurst road and at the first roundabout turn left. Stewarts Garden Lands lies opposite Sainsbury's.

Aquatics	Dried & Artificial Flowers	Houseplants
Barbecues	Fencing	Information Desk
Books & Stationery	Fruit Trees	Large Car Park
Christmas & Seasonal Displays	Garden Design	Plant Guarantee
Conservatories	Garden Furniture	Plants
Credit Cards Accepted	Garden Products	Restaurant/Coffee Shop
Cut Flowers	Giftware	Seeds & Bulbs
Disabled	Greenhouses & Sheds	Trees

LOCAL GARDENS

Apple Court, Hordle Lane, Hordle, Lymington

1½ acres within former walled late 19th-century kitchen garden. White garden, modern grassary, herbaceous borders lined with pleached limes, fern path. National Collections of hostas and display borders of daylilies - beds of red, yellow, pink and yellow at their peak in July and August. Specialist nursery. 200 metres N of A337 between New Milton and Lymington. *Open: Mar-end Oct daily except Weds 10-1, 2-5; Entrance: £2 (children 25p).*

Spinners, School Lane, Boldre 01590 673347

Informal woodland garden interplanted with wide range of herbaceous plants and bulbs as well as hydrangeas, azaleas, rhododendrons, camellias, maples, magnolias etc. Plants for sale in nursery, which specialises in less common hardy plants and shrubs. National Collection of trilliums. Autumn interest provided by good trees, particularly Nyssa sinensis. 1½m N of Lymington off the A337. *Open: April-mid-Sept Tues-Sat 10-5, Sun-Mon by appointment; mid-Sept-Mar nursery and part of garden open Tues-Sat (telephone for details). Entrance: £1.50.*

Artsway, Station Road, Sway, Nr Lymington 01590 682260

Visual arts centre funded by the National Lottery. Formerly a coach house, it has been landscaped by Sue Sutherland. The boules court created by Johnny Woodford and Cleve West is what they term 'an outdoor installation' more than a garden. West designs show gardens at Hampton Court, and has here developed a very practical and achievable creation, visited by more than 200 people a week. 4m NW of Lymington. *Open: Daily all year. Gallery open Weds-Sun all year noon-4. Entrance: free.*

ALTONS GARDEN CENTRE
ARTERIAL ROAD, WICKFORD, ESSEX SS12 9JG
TEL: 01268 726421 FAX: 01268 590825

Altons Garden Centre first opened on Decimilisation day, 1971. This family-run concern is conveniently laid out, with specific areas each naturally flowing into the next. The Centre offers an A-Z range of species of flowering and foliage plants, shrubs and trees, including grasses, bamboos, fruit trees and alpine plants. Each comes with detailed information on its preferred siting (shade-loving, etc.), soil conditions and care regime. The viewing garden areas feature superb topiary - a footballer and skier are just two of the whimsical and expertly produced examples. Throughout the Centre, the informed and informative staff provide attentive, conscientious advice and service to all customers, and are able to help both the novice and experienced gardener.

The Garden Centre specialises in large plants and also has a good range of trees and shrubs for small gardens. Here visitors will find everything they need to plant and maintain a beautiful and healthy garden, including a range of composts and top soils, gardening tools, ornaments and sundries. For the indoor gardener, there's a superb range of houseplants on offer.

The well-stocked, attractive gift shop offers a range of pictures, candles, posters and prints, frames, games, silk flowers, basketware, games and toys, and CDs and cassette tapes. In the Bookshop, visitors will find a wide variety of gardening titles.

The coffee shop will satisfy the appetite with a good selection of sandwiches, salads, cakes and other snacks, teas, coffees and soft drinks, in a large heated wooden building - or, when the weather is fine, guests can sit out in the attractive patio area. There is a separate but complementary pool supplies and maintenance department. *Open: Mon-Sat 9-6, Sun 10.30-4.30; reduced hours Jan-Feb - phone for details.*

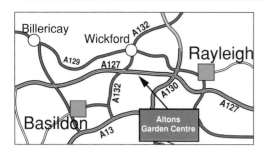

Directions:

Altons Garden Centre is on the westbound A127 between the A130 junction to Chelmsford and the A132 to Wickford and Basildon.

Aquatics	Dried & Artificial Flowers	Greenhouses & Sheds
Barbecues	Fencing	Houseplants
Books & Stationery	Fireworks	Information Desk
Childrens Play Area	Fruit Trees	Large Car Park
Christmas & Seasonal Displays	Garden Construction	Paving
Clothing	Garden Design	Plant Guarantee
Conservatories	Garden Furniture	Plants
Credit Cards Accepted	Garden Machinery	Restaurant/Coffee Shop
Disabled	Garden Products	Seeds & Bulbs
Display Gardens	Giftware	Trees

LOCAL GARDENS

Volpaia, 54 Woodlands Road, Hockley 01702 203761

1-acre garden for plant lovers, with rhododendrons, camellias, other shrubs, magnolias and many exotic trees. Springtime wood anemones and bluebells; Davidia involucrata, eucryphia and cornus. Paths lead to lovely natural woodland of mature oak, birch and hornbeam, uvularias, erythroniums, Solomon's seal, disporums and trilliums, underplanted with ferns and liliaceous plants. Bog garden with ferns, hostas, gunneras, primulas and skunk cabbage. Teas. 2¼m NE of Rayleigh off the B1013. *Open: by appointment. Entrance: £1 (children 30p).*

RHS Garden Hyde Hall, Rettendon 01245 400256

8-acre magnificent hilltop garden of flowering trees, perennials, shrubs, spring bulbs. Small alpine house and temperate glasshouse, the latter with white Cobaea scandens, daturas and other tender plants. Good collection of modern and shrub roses; National Collection of viburnum and malus. Large formal pond, lower pond and new bridge, broad planting of half-hardy salvias and alliums. Also 12-acre field replanted with new trees. Thatched Barn licensed restaurant. 7m SE of Chelmsford off the A130. *Open: 24th Mar-Aug daily 11-6, Sept-Oct daily 11-5. Entrance: £3 (children 6-16 70p; pre-booked groups of 10 or more £2.50 per person).*

Cameo Cottage, Chapel Lane, Purleigh 01621 828334

Surrounding a partly 17th-century cottage, this ¾-acre cottage garden is filled with plants for all seasons. The seemingly informal layout is regulated into particular colour schemes, creating the 'cameos' that give the cottage its name. Interest is also provided by the variation in levels. Also bog garden, herbaceous varieties including many rare treasures. 9m SE of Chelmsford between the B1010/B1012. *Open: by appointment. Entrance: £1.00.*

FRINTON ROAD NURSERIES
FRINTON ROAD, KIRBY CROSS, ESSEX CO13 0PD
TEL: 01255 674838 FAX: 01255 850032

Frinton Road Nurseries is a family business now established for over 50 years. With a reputation for friendly and helpful service, it occupies a site in Frinton-on-Sea which has been used for growing plants and produce for over 100 years. Recently the Nurseries have acquired additional land at nearby Thorpe-Le-Soken, and production has now increased to supply plants to garden centres throughout East Anglia and the Home Counties.

Over the years the professional and knowledgeable staff have participated in competitions, winning numerous awards at the Tendring Show and Suffolk Show - and, in 1996, exhibited two winning baskets at the Chelsea Flower Show. On several occasions the plant area and the flower house have been voted the best in East Anglia. The Nurseries boast an enormous selection of plants, shrubs and trees - everything needed to create or enhance a thriving and beautiful garden.

In addition to all the gardening essentials one of the other highlights of this Nursery is the Outdoor Living Showroom, displaying a wide range of garden furniture, including a selection of tasteful rattan garden seats, tables and other furnishings. During the Christmas season this showroom is transformed into a themed seasonal display of ideas and inspiration for decorating your home with beautiful and imaginative foliage, winter-flowering plants and more.

The delightful Applegarth coffee shop serves light lunches and home-made cakes and other treats in pleasant and comfortable surroundings. Other facilities include the fine gift shop, outdoor clothing section, food shop and, for children, a 'Young in the Country' department. A recent addition is the floristry shop 'Frinton Road Flowers', where a trained florist prepares arrangements using a wide range of fresh, dried and silk flowers. *Open: Mon-Sat 8.30-5.30.*

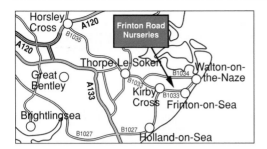

Directions:

Frinton Garden Centre lies on the left of the B1033 about half way between Kirby Cross and Frinton-on-Sea.

Aquatics	Dried & Artificial Flowers	Houseplants
Barbecues	Farm Shop	Information Desk
Books & Stationery	Fencing	Large Car Park
Childrens Play Area	Floristry	Paving
Christmas & Seasonal Displays	Fruit Trees	Pet Products and/or Pets
Clothing	Garden Design	Plant Guarantee
Conservatories	Garden Furniture	Plants
Credit Cards Accepted	Garden Products	Restaurant/Coffee Shop
Cut Flowers	Giftware	Seeds & Bulbs
Disabled	Greenhouses & Sheds	Trees
Display Gardens		

LOCAL GARDENS

Lower Dairy House, Little Horkesley 01206 262220

1½-acre plantsman's garden, a riot of colour. Rockery and raised beds, natural stream with waterside plantings and bog gardens. Lawns, herbaceous borders, many different varieties of ground cover and shrubs. Roses. Spring bulbs, perennials and old-fashioned annuals - larkspur, marigolds, geraniums. Good range of diascias and cistus; pond with hostas, primulas, mimulus. Woodland dell. 7m N of Colchester off the A134. *Open: phone for details. Entrance: £1.50 (children 50p).*

Beth Chatto Gardens, Elmstead Market 01206 822007

5-acre landscaped garden by acclaimed designer Chatto. Many unusual plants, in a wide variety of conditions from hot and dry to water garden. Gravel garden, herbaceous border. Every gardener will learn valuable lessons from this garden, particularly on how to show both flower and leaf to best advantage. The Unusual Plants nursery adjacent is also open to the public. ¼m E of Elmstead Market off the A133. *Open: Mar-Oct Mon-Sat 9-5; Nov-Feb Mon-Fri 9-4. Closed Suns & Bank Holiday Mondays. Entrance: £3 (children free).*

Melford Hall, Long Melford 01787 880286

Park and formal gardens of magnificent 16th-century Hall. Sunken garden, good specimen trees including rare Oriental Xanthoceras sorbifolium. The oak avenue is currently being replanted, and the herbaceous borders restored to their original Victorian and Edwardian planting and design. Clipped box hedges, bowling green terrace, topiary, pond and fountain. 3m N of Sudbury off A134. *Open: April Sat-Sun and Bank Holiday Mon 2-5.30; May-Sept Weds-Sun and Bank Holiday Mon 2-5.30; Oct Sat-Sun 2-5.30. Hall open (features special Beatrix Potter exhibition). Entrance: garden and principal rooms of hall £4.20.*

THURROCK GARDEN CENTRE
SOUTH ROAD, SOUTH OCKENDEN, ESSEX RM15 6DU
TEL: 01708 851991 FAX: 01708 859138

Established in 1978, the award-winning **Thurrock Garden Centre** occupies a 6-acre site which is surrounded by fields and woodland near the Lakeside Shopping Centre. This family business specialises in hanging baskets and has won many awards from the Chelsea Flower Show, with a First in 1994, 1995 and 1998 for the Plantaria section and also a First for Foliage in 1994 and 1995. The Garden Centre hosts regular demonstrations during the Spring season.

Along with an excellent range of outdoor and indoor plants, trees and shrubs, this traditional Centre has a pleasant atmosphere where you can browse for every item for the garden. There is never any pressure from the informed and helpful staff. There is a wide range of displayed garden furniture and other outdoor features as well as an Aquatic Centre and for the children an interactive animal area.

The comprehensive Gift Shop stocks a large selection of ceramics, candles, glassware, cards, ornaments and much more. The Book Shop has an extensive range of gardening, children's and cookery books and many other subjects of interest. There's also an extensive selection of silk flowers.

Another unique feature of this superior Centre is the miniature landscapes on display, together with paving, walling and fencing, which offer an at-a-glance appreciation of the way different plants and hard landscaping can benefit the garden. In addition to all this there is a Clothing Department with a wide range of outdoor wear and accessories. The Centre's well-appointed Coffee Shop offers sandwiches, home-made cakes and pastries in a relaxing environment. *Open: Monday to Saturday 9-5.30 (6 p.m. in summer), Sunday 10.30-4.30.*

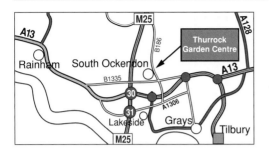

Directions:

Thurrock Garden Centre lies no more than ten minutes from Lakeside Shopping Centre. From Junction 31 of the M25 follow signs for South Ockendon A1306. After 1 mile turn left towards South Ockendon on the B186. Go straight over junction at the top of the hill. Thurrock Garden Centre can be found after 1 mile on the right.

Aquatics	Fencing	Houseplants
Barbecues	Fireworks	Information Desk
Books & Stationery	Floristry	Large Car Park
Christmas & Seasonal Displays	Fruit Trees	Paving
Clothing	Garden Construction	Plant Guarantee
Credit Cards Accepted	Garden Furniture	Plants
Disabled	Garden Products	Restaurant/Coffee Shop
Display Gardens	Giftware	Seeds & Bulbs
Dried & Artificial Flowers	Greenhouses & Sheds	Trees

LOCAL GARDENS

West Ham Park, Upton Lane, Forest Gate, London

Well-cultivated land since the mid-14th century, these gardens were developed primarily in the mid- to late 1700s, when Upton House and its 30-acre garden were fostered. Sixty-seven-metre long glasshouse filled with over 3,000 exotic species, rivalling the collections at Kew Gardens. One of the UK's earliest true rock gardens, with alpines. One of the oldest gingko trees in the country. Imaginative Victorian bedding, some good hollies. *Open: daily all year 7.30-dusk. Entrance: free.*

The Magnolias, 18 St Johns Avenue, Brentwood 01277 220019

Informal and interesting plantsman's garden covering half an acre - a shining example of what can be achieved in a relatively small area. Good ground cover, trees and shrubs including magnolias, maples, camellias, pieris and rhododendrons. Collection of spring bulbs. Seven ponds including Koi ponds, raised pools, other water features. Large swathes of hostas; unusual and rare bamboos. Interesting all year round. *Open: telephone for details. Entrance: £1.50 (children 50p).*

Ingatestone Hall, Ingatestone 01277 353010

Grounds of 16th-century manor house. Large stewpond bordered by enormous gunnera. Nut walk, grass walk and other walks, including lime walk said to be haunted by Bishop Benjamin Petre's dog since the night in 1740 when Petre was set upon and the dog saved his life. Pristine lawns with Magnolia grandiflora, weeping beeches, mulberries and other specimen trees. Walled garden with lily pond and marvellous standard roses. 7m SW of Chelmsford off the A12. *Open: early April-end Sept weekends and Bank Holiday Mon 1-6; mid-July-end Aug also Weds-Fri 1-6. House open. Entrance: £3.50 (OAPs/students £3, children £2).*

BRAMBRIDGE PARK GARDEN CENTRE
KILN LANE, BRAMBRIDGE, EASTLEIGH, HAMPSHIRE SO50 6HT
TEL: 01962 713707 FAX: 01962 714985

Brambridge Park Garden Centre occupies the old walled garden of the imposing 18th-century Brambridge House. Much of the original building was destroyed by fire and rebuilt in 1892. The fine original walled garden is now the outside display area, with a massive range of trees, shrubs and foliage and flowering plants for home and garden.

The original estate buildings are complemented by the garden centre's main building. The centre's magnificent central structure is done in reproduction Victorian wrought iron work. This houses palms, bamboos, bananas and other exotica. The central Rotunda is a shop within a shop, home to the majority of gift items and gardening extras available.

Within the walled garden area is a display called World Gardens, which allows visitors to take a trip 'round the world' without leaving English soil. Just cross the moat to enter these special gardens. The mystical Eastern Garden has bubbling cascades and a bamboo grove set around an enchanting pagoda. Year-round colour and interest are provided by the rhododendrons, azaleas, acers and pines. The Southern Garden has a Doric sun temple, classical features and a rock wall set amongst bold, colourful and textured planting in the Mediterranean style. The Western Garden has a cottage corner, lovers' seat, pavilion and orchard where attractive paving edges and features combine with mixed shrubs and herbaceous borders to capture the charm of an English garden.

The garden centre also owns the surrounding woods and meadows of Brambridge Park Conservation area. Many improvements have been put into place to encourage wildlife. There is a wonderful nature trail which has been developed to help visitors explore nature at close quarters. The 'Country House' coffee shop lunches home-made cakes, cream teas, specials and roasts. *Open: Monday to Saturday 9-6, Sunday 10.30-4.30.*

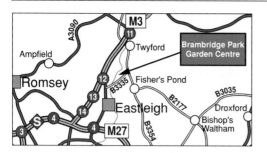

Directions:

From junction 12 of the M3 take the A335 towards Eastleigh and at the first roundabout turn left onto the B3335. At the second crossroads turn left and Brambridge Garden Centre can be found on the left.

Aquatics	Dried & Artificial Flowers	Houseplants
Barbecues	Fencing	Information Desk
Books & Stationery	Fruit Trees	Large Car Park
Childrens Play Area	Garden Design	Pet Products and/or Pets
Christmas & Seasonal Displays	Garden Furniture	Plant Guarantee
Clothing	Garden Machinery	Plants
Conservatories	Garden Products	Restaurant/Coffee Shop
Credit Cards Accepted	Giftware	Seeds & Bulbs
Disabled	Greenhouses & Sheds	Trees
Display Gardens		

LOCAL GARDENS

The Tudor House Museum, Tudor House, Bugle Street, Southampton 01703 332513

A tranquil garden in the heart of the city. Designed by Dr Sylvia Landsberg, this garden has many features of a Tudor garden such as a knot garden with germander, box and santolina, heraldic beasts on poles, fountain encircled by hyssop and camomile, camomile seat, arbour, many herbs. Delightful museum here as well. *Open: all year Tues-Fri 10-noon, 1-5, Sat 10-noon, 1-4, Sun 2-5. Museum open. Entrance: free.*

Sir Harold Hillier Gardens and Arboretum, Jermyns Lane, Ampfield 01794 368787

Hampshire County Council-managed 184-acre gardens containing the finest collection of hardy trees and shrubs in the UK, with about 12,000 different species and cultivars. Home to 11 National Collections, including hamamelis and quercus. Wonderful spring and autumn colours. Winter Garden said to the largest of its kind in Britain. Guided tours take place first Sunday of each month (except Jan) and other Suns during May to Oct. Plants for sale and shop in adjacent nursery. 3m NE of Romsey off the A3090. *Open: April-Oct weekdays 10.30-6, weekends and bank holidays 9.30-6, Nov-Mar (except 25th-26th Dec)10.30- dusk. Entrance: Apr-Oct £4.25 (OAPs £3.75); Nov-Mar £3.25 (OAPs £2.75).*

Broadlands, Romsey 01794 505010

The elegant work of Capability Brown, the landscaping here epitomises the 18th-century English Landscape School. Pristine lawns from the steps of the porticoed west front run to the River Test. The impressive parkland is filled with cedar and beech trees. 18th-century mansion once home to Viscount Palmerston and then to Lord Mountbatten. S of Romsey on the A31. *Open: 14 June-3 Sept noon-5.30 (last admission 4). Entrance: £5.50 (OAPs and concessions £4.70, children 12-16 £3.85, under 12's free).*

REDFIELDS GARDEN CENTRE

EWSHOT LANE, CHURCH CROOKHAM, FLEET, HAMPSHIRE GU13 0UB
TEL: 01252 624444 FAX: 01252 624445

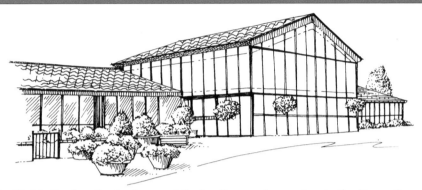

Redfields Garden Centre is one of the leading garden centres in the Home Counties. Shopping here is an enjoyable experience, as the centre offers seasonal and themed displays and promotions as well as a selection of special offers all year round. The centre's recently revamped and improved layout has made for an exciting new shopping environment. Founded in 1977, the centre has remained very much a family business. Covering 10 acres, it comprises a definitive garden centre and shop, plus a licensed restaurant.

There is always a large selection of seasonal plants in stock for year-round colour in your garden. From large specimen plants, trees, shrubs, bedding, annuals, perennials - whatever you are seeking, you will find here. They also provide a Plantfinding Service for obtaining out-of-the-ordinary plants.

The fast-growing conservatory department includes greenhouses, sheds and summerhouses and provides a complete service from start to finish, including surveying, electrics - everything you need to create the perfect outdoor room. A garden design service is another of the features of this superb garden centre, where the motto is 'Service and Value'. Everything you need to keep your garden in top condition is here. There is a fine range of quality brand names in tools, garden machinery, shredders, mowers, hedgecutters and more. There are garden machinery specialists who can answer your questions and offer sound and helpful advice.

The centre's shop offers an amazing selection of top-quality cane, resin, wood and metal garden furniture, gifts such as ornaments, china, books, pictures and stationery, together with houseplants, silk flowers and all associated floristry equipment. Their truly exceptional restaurant 'The Bunnery' is open for morning coffee, snacks, hot lunches and afternoon teas. *Open: daily Monday-Saturday 9-6, Sunday 10.30-4.30*

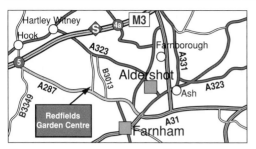

Directions:

From junction 5 of the M3 take the A287 towards Farnham. After about 5 miles turn left into Redfield Lane and Redfields Garden Centre can be found on the right.

Aquatic Products	Dried & Artificial Flowers	Greenhouses & Sheds
Barbecues	Fencing	Houseplants
Books & Stationery	Fireworks	Information Desk
Childrens Play Area	Floristry	Large Car Park
Christmas & Seasonal Displays	Fruit Trees	Pet Products
Clothing	Garden Construction	Plant Guarantee
Conservatories	Garden Design	Plants
Credit Cards Accepted	Garden Furniture	Restaurant/Coffee Shop
Cut Flowers	Garden Machinery	Seeds & Bulbs
Disabled	Garden Products	Trees
Display Gardens	Giftware	

LOCAL GARDENS

The Vyne, Sherborne St John 01256 881337

National Trust. 17 acres of classic English parkland. Extensive lawns, lake. Herbaceous borders, fine oaks, cedars, clipped yews. Galleried Tudor chapel house with historic stained glass windows. Summerhouse garden, wild garden, woodlands walk. Occasional garden tours start at 2.30. Gardeners available to answer queries. 4m N of Basingstoke off the A340. *Open: April-Oct Weds-Sun 12.30-5.30; Bank Holiday Mon 11-5.30. House open as garden but 1.30-5.30. Entrance: £2.50; house and garden £5.00.*

West Green House Garden, West Green, Hartley Wintney, Hook 01252 844611

Ruined walled garden that has recently been restored under the direction of well-known Australian gardener Marilyn Abbott. Approached through topiaried Alice in Wonderland garden. Herbaceous borders in purples, mauves, blues and black; outer borders in reds and pinks. Box borders. Potager with two fruit cases. Green theatre, parterre, orangery. Quinlan Terry lake has been recently restored and within the grounds you can find follies designed by Quinlan Terry. 10m NE of Basingstoke off the A30. *Open: May-Aug Weds-Sun and Bank Holiday Mon 11-4. Entrance: £3.*

Hinton Ampner, Hinton Ampner, Bramdean 01962 771305

National Trust. 12-acre 20th-century shrub garden, designed by Ralph Dutton. Box and yew topiary with strong architectural elements and marvellous views. Scented plants, unexpected vistas. Dramatic bedding; orchard with bulbs and wildflowers in spring; formal box hedges. Philadelphus and magnolia walks. Dell garden. Shrub rose border. Plants for sale. 8m E of Winchester off the A272. *Open: April-Sept Tues-Weds and Sat, Sun and Bank Holiday Mon 1.30-5.30 (last admission 5); Entrance: £3.20 (children 5-16 £1.60). Groups of 15 or more must book in advance.*

AYLETT NURSERIES
NORTH ORBITAL ROAD A414, LONDON COLNEY, ST ALBANS AL2 1DH
TEL: 01727 822255 FAX: 01727 823024

Aylett Nurseries is an independent family owned garden centre, established in 1955. Specialising in dahlias we offer a wide selection in a vast range of colours, sizes and forms. The welcome show of colour dahlias can provide when summer bedding plants start to fade, make them a must for the all-year-round garden. The nursery also produces bedding plants, geraniums, fuchsias and hanging baskets. During spring our glasshouses are a mass of colour.

Our extensive plant area contains a profusion of shrubs, trees, alpines, herbs, azaleas, climbers, roses, herbaceous and much more. As well as an A to Z of plants, if you are looking for ideas we have plenty of display beds, and demonstration gardens. In the garden shop you will find all the sundries that you would associate with a first class garden centre and we also have a range of garden furniture and barbeques.

Houseplants are another of our specialities; there is always a vast selection to suit all tastes from the traditional favourites to the more exotic specimens. The houseplant department also displays a range of planted bowls created by the Aylett's experienced team, and a superb selection of flowering plants.

Our flower shop offers a wonderful range of fresh and artificial flowers, china and glass vases. The gift shop has a bevy of interesting and unusual gifts from scented candles, stationary items and jigsaws to toiletries and sundials. Our coffee shop provides a welcome stop while visiting the garden centre, serving a selection of home-made cakes, light lunches and snacks

All these facilities combined with our reputation for customer service makes Aylett Nurseries a one-stop centre for every gardener. *Open: Monday to Friday 8.30-5.30, Saturday 8.30-5, Sunday 10.30-4.*

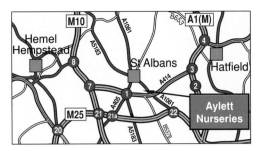

Directions:

From Junction 21A of the M25 signed St Albans, join the A405 for Hatfield. At the roundabout junction with the M10 take the A414 for Hatfield. Aylett Nurseries are just over 1 mile on the left.

Aquatics	Dried & Artificial Flowers	Houseplants
Barbecues	Fencing	Information Desk
Books & Stationery	Floristry	Large Car Park
Childrens Play Area	Fruit Trees	Paving
Christmas & Seasonal Displays	Garden Design	Plant Guarantee
Clothing	Garden Furniture	Plants
Credit Cards Accepted	Garden Products	Restaurant/Coffee Shop
Cut Flowers	Giftware	Seeds & Bulbs
Disabled	Greenhouses & Sheds	Trees
Display Gardens		

LOCAL GARDENS

Knebworth House, Knebworth 01438 812661

Historic former home of author Bulwer Lytton. Wonderful gardens laid out by Lutyens in 1908, restored and embellished over the past 20 years. Gertrude Jekyll herb garden, yew hedges, rose beds, lily ponds and herbaceous borders. Gold garden, many fine trees. Twin pollarded lime avenues, newly restored maze, tranquil woodland walks. Direct access off Ai(M) at junction 7 (Stevenage South). *Open: 1999 weekends 17 Mar - 26 Sep; Daily 29 Mar - 11 Apr, 29 May - 3 Sep. Closed 6 Jun. Entrance £5.00 (including house & Raj Exhibition £6.00, OAP's & Children £5.50)*

Cheslyn House, 54 Nascot Wood Road, Watford 01923 235946

Watford Council-managed 3½-acre garden with bog garden, rock garden, lawns, herbaceous borders with a good collection of hemerocallis, pond, aviary. Woodland haven for wildlife with camellias, mature rhododendrons, pieris and azaleas. Fine trees including Sequoiadendron giganteum, Eucryphia x nymansensis 'Nymansay', Catalpa bignoniodes and Diospyros kaki. Renovation programme presently underway. In north Watford off the A411. *Open: daily dawn-dusk (except 25th-26th Dec, 1st Jan). Entrance: free.*

Gardens of the Rose, Chiswell Green, St Albans 01727 850461

Royal National Rose Society's gardens with one of the world's most important and best collections of roses. Trial grounds for roses from the world over. Original red rose of Lancaster and white rose of York. Over 1,700 varieties and 30,000 rose trees. 2m S of St Albans off the B4630. *Open: early 4 Apr-31 May 10-4, 5 Jun-26 Sep weekends 9-5, weekdays 10-6. Entrance; Apr/May £2.50 (disabled £2, children 6-16 £1); Jun-Sep £4 (disabled £3.50, children £1.50).*

THE VAN HAGE GARDEN COMPANY
BRAGBURY LANE, BRAGBURY END, STEVENAGE, HERTFORDSHIRE SG2 8TJ
TEL: 01438 811777 FAX: 01438 815485

A series of old barns linked together form **The Van Hage Garden Company** in Bragbury End. Each barn retains many of its original features and individuality. Here you will find quality garden plants and products in a historic farmhouse setting, with lots of added attractions to interest the whole family. A trip here is more than just shopping for the garden - it's a pleasant outing for grown-ups and children alike. Stroll among delightful displays of nursery-fresh shrubs, trees, roses, heathers and many other hardy garden plants, all guaranteed to grow in your garden. The trained staff will be delighted to answer your questions and offer advice.

From silk flowers and gardening books to seeds, garden buildings and patio furniture to garden machinery and barbecues, you will find it here, together with bold displays of bedding plants and bulbs in season. The houseplant conservatory has thousands of plants. Among tried and tested favourites there are also some unusual plants. Most spectacular is the indoor area featuring a rock face with water cascading into a pond brimming with an assortment of fish. Outdoors there is a superb farmhouse complete with display garden. This life-size demonstration area is completely authentic in every detail.

The cosy coffee shop, appropriately called the Dutch Coffee House, has exposed beams and a fine assortment of farm implements. Hot and cold light lunches, teas and coffees are served here, with an emphasis on wholesome home-made food. The Children's Corner has a large adventure climbing frame amid plenty of open space with picnic tables. Here too are a collection of animals and pets, including guinea pigs and ducks. *Open: Monday 9.30-6, Tuesday-Saturday 9-6, Sunday 10.30-4.30. Closed on Easter Sunday.*

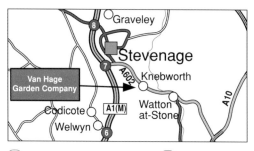

Directions:

From junction 7 of the A1(M) take the A602 towards Hertford and Hoddesdon. The Van Hage Garden Centre lies on the right in the village of Knebworth.

Aquatics	Dried & Artificial Flowers	Houseplants
Barbecues	Fencing	Information Desk
Books & Stationery	Fireworks	Large Car Park
Childrens Play Area	Floristry	Paving
Christmas & Seasonal Displays	Fruit Trees	Pet Products and/or Pets
Clothing	Garden Construction	Plant Guarantee
Conservatories	Garden Design	Plants
Credit Cards Accepted	Garden Furniture	Restaurant/Coffee Shop
Cut Flowers	Garden Products	Seeds & Bulbs
Disabled	Giftware	Trees
Display Gardens	Greenhouses & Sheds	

LOCAL GARDENS

Hatfield House, Hatfield 01707 262823

Dating from the 17th century, transformed over the past 30 years by the Marchioness of Salisbury. 42 acres, gardened organically. New pond (originally dates from 1607) and wild garden; scented garden with varied knot gardens and herb garden, all with plants used from the 15th to 17th centuries. Annual festival at midsummer. 2m from junction 4 of the A1(M) off the A1000 and A414. *Open: 25 Mar-end Sept; Park daily 10.30-8, Fris 11-6; West Garden Tues-Sun 11-6; East Garden Fri 11-6; House Tue-Thur 12-4, Sat & Sun 1-4.30, Bank Holidays 11-4.30. Connoisseurs Day every Friday. Entrance: Park £1.50 (children 5-15 80p); House, Park and West Gardens £6 (children 5-15 £3); Connoisseurs Day £5.*

Benington Lordship, Benington 01438 869668

Hilltop garden on the site of the ruins of the castle with Norman keep and moat, overlooking lakes. Early spring scillas. Rock/water garden, newly planted rose garden, ornamental kitchen garden with gold and silver border and penstemons. Spectacular double herbaceous borders. Wildflowers in the grass. Nursery, Victorian folly, wonderful views. 5m E of Stevenage off the A119. *Open: Jan-Mar (ring for opening days and times), April-Sept Weds and Bank Holiday Mon noon-5, also certain charity days. Entrance: £2.80 (children free).*

Wrest Park, Silsoe 01525 860152

English Heritage. Over 90 acres of early 18th-century formal garden. Woodland, statues and giant vases, artificial river, impressive canal. Columns, temples, Cascade Bridge, Palladian-style Bowling Green House, Orangery. Italianate terraces with parterres. Deep mixed borders, turf alley. 10m S of Bedford off the A6. *Open: 1 April-30 Sep 10-6 , 1 Oct - 31 Oct 10-5. Entrance: £3.20 (OAPs £2.40, children 5-15 £1.60).*

THE VAN HAGE GARDEN COMPANY
CHENIES, NR RICKMANSWORTH, HERTFORDSHIRE WD3 6EN
TEL: 01494 764545 FAX: 01494 762216

Situated on the border of Buckinghamshire and Hertfordshire, in the midst of beautiful countryside in the village of Chenies is this superior garden centre. Established over 23 years ago it has built up an enviable local reputation over the years for quality and service. Since becoming part of the **Van Hage Group** in 1997, many improvements to the existing site have been made, including a newly designed Plant Nursery, which provides customers with an extensive range of plants and other gardening essentials.

Advice and comprehensive information are always at hand from the Centre's knowledgeable, conscientious and friendly-staff. The garden centre is full of inspirational ideas, from fun topiary animals in large terracotta pots to a wide selection of large and small statues. There is also an unrivalled choice of plants, shrubs, trees, climbers, ferns and herbaceous - something to add a special touch to any garden.

Inside you can lose yourself amongst glossy leaves and exotic blooms in the houseplant area and wander at your leisure through this delightful garden centre. The gift department will provide you with plenty of ideas for your home with a lovely range of candles, glass and pottery, a tempting selection of preserves and a large selection of books with titles for both young and old. The furniture department offers distinctive furniture for your garden, terrace, patio or conservatory. Or browse in the aquatics department - where everything can be found from ponds to fountains, aquatic plants to fish!

So whether you are shopping for trees, shrubs, baskets or pots and containers The Van Hage Garden Company is well worth a visit. Van Hage also has its own Garden Club, and all visitors are welcome to join. *Open: Monday 9.30am-6.00pm; Tuesday-Saturday 9.00am-6.00pm; Sunday 10.30am-4.30pm; Closed on Easter Sunday*

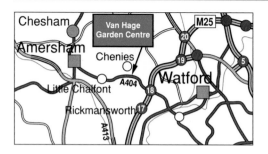

Directions:

At Junction 18 from the M25 take the A404 towards Amersham. After about a mile the Van Hage Garden Centre can be found on the right in the village of Chenies.

Aquatics	Dried & Artificial Flowers	Information Desk
Barbecues	Fencing	Large Car Park
Books & Stationery	Fruit Trees	Paving
Christmas & Seasonal Displays	Garden Furniture	Plant Guarantee
Clothing	Garden Products	Plants
Conservatories	Giftware	Seeds & Bulbs
Credit Cards Accepted	Greenhouses & Sheds	Trees
Disabled	Houseplants	

LOCAL GARDENS

Campden Cottage, 51 Clifton Road, Chesham Bois 01494 726818

This ½-acre garden offers year-round interest. Fine collection of rare and unusual plants; interesting contrasts of colours, foliage and shapes. Formal area with walled border, yew hedge and extended lawns. Magnificent weeping ash; attractive York stone terrace filled with terracotta pots, planted for seasonal colour. Popular open day in March for the renowned collection of hellebore species and hybrids. Off the A416 between Amersham on the Hill and Chesham. *Open: phone for details. Entrance: £1.50 (children free).*

Chenies Manor House, Chenies, nr Rickmansworth 01494 762888

In keeping with the 15th- to 16th-century manor house, a series of linked and decorative gardens. Cottage plants, old-fashioned roses. 'White' garden with formal topiary; kitchen garden; 'physic' garden with poisonous and medicinal plants. Parterre, historic turf maze. The 'Royal Oak', said to be Queen Elizabeth's favourite tree here, is still extant. Off the A404 between Amersham and Rickmansworth. *Open: Bank Holiday Monday afternoons. Entrance: £2.20 (children £1.00); house and garden £4.50.*

Cliveden, Taplow, Maidenhead 01628 605069

National Trust-owned grounds of house designed by Sir Charles Barry, with handsome balustrade brought back from the Villa Borghese in Rome in the 1890s by the 1st Viscount Astor. A series of separate gardens first laid out in the 1700s. Rose garden (by Jellicoe), water garden, topiary, herbaceous borders. Parterre. Long Garden, statuary, fountains. Woodland walks and nice views of the River Thames and the mansion itself. 2m N of Taplow off A4094. *Open: 13th Mar–1st Nov daily 11–6; Nov–Dec daily 11–4. Woodlands open all year; house open April–Oct Thurs and Sun 3–6 (last admission 5.30). Entrance: £5 (house £1 extra).*

THE VAN HAGE GARDEN COMPANY
GREAT AMWELL, NR WARE, HERTFORDSHIRE SG12 9RP
TEL: 01920 870811 FAX: 01920 871861

The Van Hage Garden Company has built up a prestigious reputation over the years for quality and service, since it was established back in 1953. The Centre has been a consistent award-winner since 1986, not just for excellence and achievement but for specific areas or specialities, including its outstanding House Plant Department. Superlatives can be used up very quickly to describe the range of this Centre, one of Europe's top gardening emporiums, with an amazing selection of products to meet all gardening requirements. Its extensive range of plants, tools, ornaments, furniture and other gardening essentials, including trees, shrubs, baskets, or pots and containers, foliage or flowering houseplants, will grace any garden, home, office or conservatory.

This is quality on a large scale, and in terms of design, presentation and service this Centre is very hard to beat. It is a complete home, garden and lifestyle outlet, offering unrivalled product selection within an exciting and ideas-filled environment.

Voted Garden Centre of the Year for 1998, there's advice and comprehensive information on hand from the Centre's knowledgeable, conscientious and friendly staff. The garden centre is a leisure destination for the whole family with a children's zoo as one of the major attractions. Children can also enjoy rides on the Miniature Steam Railway (weekends only) with tunnels, bridges and a station laid out in a beautiful setting - both are firm favourites with adults and children alike! The 250 seater restaurant, Café VH serves breakfast, appetising lunches, teas and a selection of tasty snacks in comfortable and pleasant surroundings. Special displays at Christmas and throughout the year demonstrate the magical effects that can be achieved in any garden. With all this and more, this top-quality Centre well repays a visit. Group visits are welcome and gardening/topical demonstrations can be arranged for parties of 20 or more - bookings only. *Open: Monday 9.30am-6.00pm; Tuesday-Saturday 9.00am-6.00pm; Sunday 10.30am-4.30pm; Closed: Easter Sunday*

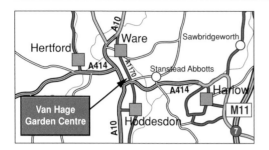

Directions:

From the A10 take the A414 towards Harlow. At the first roundabout turn left on the A1170 towards Ware South and the Van Hage Garden Centre is on the left.

🍖 Barbecues	Fireworks	Houseplants
📖 Books & Stationery	Floristry	ℹ️ Information Desk
Christmas & Seasonal Displays	Fruit Trees	Ⓟ Large Car Park
Clothing	Garden Construction	Paving
Conservatories	Garden Furniture	Plant Guarantee
CC Credit Cards Accepted	Garden Machinery	) Plants
Cut Flowers	Garden Products	Restaurant/Coffee Shop
Disabled	Giftware	Seeds & Bulbs
Dried & Artificial Flowers	Greenhouses & Sheds	Trees
Fencing		

LOCAL GARDENS

Marriott Hanbury Manor Hotel and Country Club, Ware 01920 487722

Grounds of Jacobean-style mansion on the site of the much older previous house. The newer house was built in the 1890s and designed by Sir Ernest George for the Hanbury family, all expert horticulturists. Herb garden, fruit houses, pre-Victorian walled garden with listed moon gate. Herbaceous borders, original pinetum with ancient sequoias. Period rose gardens and bulb-filled orchard. Secret garden in a woodland setting. 2m N of Ware on the A10. *Open: all year. Entrance: free (apart from charity days).*

Hopleys, Much Hadham 01279 842509

4-acre plantsman's garden, with well-established pool and bog garden. Borders of shrubs and hardy plants. Conifer bed, one of the largest ash trees in the UK. Newer colourful borders. Many of the garden's plants are on sale in the nursery. 5m SW of Bishop's Stortford off the B1004. *Open: Mar-Dec Mon, Weds-Sat 9-5, Sun 2-5 (also on special charity days). Entrance: £1.50 (children under 16 free).*

Benington Lordship, Benington 01438 869668

Hilltop garden on the site of the ruins of the castle with Norman keep and moat, overlooking lakes. Beautiful early spring display of scillas. Hidden and colourful rock/water garden, newly planted rose garden, ornamental kitchen garden with two borders one filled with penstemons. Spectacular double herbaceous borders. Wildflowers in the grass - garlics, scillas, snowdrops and cowslips. Nursery, Victorian folly, wonderful views. 5m E of Stevenage off the A119. *Open: April-Sept Suns 2-5 and Bank Holiday Mon 12-5, also certain charity days. Entrance: £2.80 (children free) - very poor disabled access.*

WOODS OF BERKHAMSTED
THE OLD IRONWORKS, HIGH STREET, BERKHAMSTED, HERTFORDSHIRE HP4 1BJ
TEL: 01442 863159 FAX: 01442 384333

Since it opened in 1974, **Woods of Berkhamsted** is a most unusual garden centre situated on the High Street in the centre of Berkhamsted. The largest independently owned shop in the town, it fronts the High Street where there is a country-style gift shop containing an ever-changing collection of presents and novelties. Beyond this deceptively modest frontage lies a vast expanse cleverly laid out so that there is a lot to choose from in a relatively small area. With space at a premium, this distinguished Centre uses every square metre to best advantage. A conservatory at the front houses a profusion of flowering pot plants and foliage houseplants, arranged in colourful displays in this ideal environment.

One special feature of this attractive garden centre is the comprehensive display of water plants and features, including fountains, ponds and pumps. The gift department offers ranges of clocks, pictures, ornaments and other items with a horticultural flavour, as well as cards, gifts and novelties.

This traditional garden centre suffers from none of the distractions found in others - it remains resolutely unlike a supermarket, focusing instead on a carefully selected range of high-quality plants, gardening supplies and equipment. There are carefully selected collections of plants, including herbs, alpines and climbers and a range of scented plants for the garden.

The friendly uniformed staff can offer helpful advice on all aspects of buying for the home or garden. The Centre also supply a range of more than 30 helpful and comprehensive easy-to-follow leaflets on all manner of gardening jobs, offering tips and advice on topics such as shady corners, weeding, summer-flowering bulbs, window boxes, climbing plants, lawns, gardening for children, hanging baskets and much more. *Open: daily Mon-Sat (incl Bank Holidays) 9-5.30; Sun 10.30-4.30*

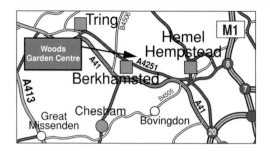

Directions:

From the Tring turning off the A41 take the A4251 towards Berkhamsted. Woods of Berkhamsted lies on the left just after the turning to Aldbury.

Aquatics	Fruit Trees	Information Desk
Barbecues	Garden Construction	Large Car Park
Christmas & Seasonal Displays	Garden Design	Pet Products and/or Pets
Credit Cards Accepted	Garden Furniture	Plant Guarantee
Disabled	Garden Products	Plants
Dried & Artificial Flowers	Giftware	Seeds & Bulbs
Fencing	Greenhouses & Sheds	Trees
Floristry	Houseplants	

LOCAL GARDENS

Ashridge Management College, Berkhamsted 01442 843491

Run by Ashridge (Bonar Law Memorial) Trust. Approximately 200 acres, with 90 acres of pleasure gardens and the rest woodland. Gardens designed by Repton and modified by Wyatville. Italian garden, orangery, Rosarie, grotto, Armorial garden. Skating pond, avenues of Victorian trees, including a large oak planted by Princess (later Queen) Victoria, rhododendron walk. 1864 conservatory. Arboretum with specimen trees. 3m N of Berkhamsted off the A41. *Open: April-Sept Sat-Sun and Bank Holiday Mon 2-6. Entrance: £2 (OAPs/children £1).*

Waddesdon Dairy Water Garden, Waddesdon 01296 651211

National Trust gardens around Lord Rothschild's late-Victorian chateau. Grand park with intricate planting, cascades, still ponds. Flamboyant bedding, exotic pines, cypresses, Wellingtonias, cedars; also native yews, chestnuts, limes. Parterre and fountains. 6m NW of Aylesbury on the A41. *Open: 3rd Mar-24th Dec Weds-Sun and Bank Holiday Mon 10-5. House (including the wine cellar) open April-June and Sept-Oct Thurs-Sun and Bank Holiday Mon 11-4; July-Aug Weds-Sun and Bank Holiday Mon 11-4; timed tickets, recommended last admission 2.30). Entrance: £3 (children £1.50); house and grounds £10 (children £7.50).*

Hughendon Manor, High Wycombe 01494 755573

National Trust-owned high-Victorian gardens created by Disraeli's wife Mary Anne in the 1860s, recently restored. Striking colour schemes, unusual conifers. Old English apple orchard (not always open - please check opening times and days), beech woodland walks. Victorian flower beds, new sub-tropical planting scheme. 1m N of High Wycombe on the A4128. *Open: Mar, Sat-Sun noon-5; April-Oct Weds-Sun and Bank Holiday Mon noon-5 (last admission 4.30). House open as garden, but 1-5. Park and woodland open all year. Entrance: £1.50 (children 75p). Parties must pre-book; no parties Sat, Sun or Bank Hol.*

BYBROOK BARN GARDEN CENTRE
CANTERBURY ROAD, ASHFORD, KENT TN24 9JZ
TEL: 01233 631959 FAX: 01233 635642

Taking its name from the barn opposite its present site, **Bybrook Barn Garden Centre** has in its 25-year history outgrown its original premises in the barn and moved here, where the owners have developed the landscape to include an ornamental lake and a large and decorative bridge. With 45,000 square feet of covered heated indoor display area, plus a massive covered outdoor area, a one acre lake, plus some 5 acres of outdoor space, this is the largest and by far the best traditional garden centre in the area. Despite the other franchises on-site, the centre remains faithful to providing high-quality plants and garden supplies to its customers.

Everywhere you turn, this distinctive centre offers something special. Pride of place goes to the centre's Victorian Vinery, now used as a water feature/fountain display area. Queen Victoria is known to have used this Vinery many times. Another fascinating structure is an original Burmese Cart, once used as a gun carriage but now converted to more pacifist use.

The displays of plants are unique in that they are presented in a most natural way, to show you exactly what can be achieved in the average garden. The beds are slightly raised for maximum effect and easy access. Each small area is enclosed by different styles of brickwork and other materials. The gift shop stocks items too varied to list, including a most impressive display of quality objets d'art and ornaments. Together with the kitchen shop, furniture centres, picture gallery, array of silk and dried flowers, craft shop and probably the finest selection and display of marine fish and aquaria in southern England, this centre supplies everything you need to beautify home, garden and conservatory. *Open: Monday to Saturday Summer, 9-6; Winter, 9-5.30; Sunday 10.30-4.30.*

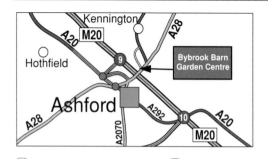

Directions:

From junction 9 of the M20 turn left at the first roundabout and then left again to cross the motorway. Turn first left and Bybrook Barn Garden Centre is on the left opposite the Harvester pub.

Aquatics	Farm Shop	Greenhouses & Sheds
Barbecues	Fencing	Houseplants
Books & Stationery	Fireworks	Information Desk
Camping Equipment	Floristry	Large Car Park
Christmas & Seasonal Displays	Fruit Trees	Paving
Clothing	Garden Construction	Pet Products and/or Pets
Conservatories	Garden Design	Plant Guarantee
Credit Cards Accepted	Garden Furniture	Plants
Cut Flowers	Garden Machinery	Restaurant/Coffee Shop
Disabled	Garden Products	Seeds & Bulbs
Dried & Artificial Flowers	Giftware	Trees

LOCAL GARDENS

Godinton Park, Ashford 01233 620773

Formal gardens laid out in around 1900 by Reginal Blomfield. Topiary, wild gardens, walled kitchen garden. Under restoration in 1998, today this programme of repairs and renovation is continuing. The boundary hedge, planted to Blomfield's original design, is being cut back to the yew trunks, in a process that takes in one side at a time and leaves two years in between. It is estimated that the hedge will be re-established by 2003. 1½m W of Ashford on the A20. *Open: April-Sept Thurs-Sat 2-5. Entrance: house and garden £4 (children £2). Coaches by appointment only.*

Beech Court Gardens, Challock 01233 740735

An 10-acre oasis of peace and beauty, 150 metres above sea level. Woodland garden surrounding medieval farmhouse, with large collection of viburnums, hydrangeas, azaleas, rhododendrons, roses, summer borders. Fine collection of trees including acers. Small sunken area with moisture-loving plants. Picnic area, children's trail, area for visually impaired visitors and craft shop. 5m N of Ashford off the A251/A252. *Open: end Mar-mid-Nov Mon-Thurs 10-5, Fri-Sun and Bank Holiday Mon noon-6; other times by appointment. Entrance: £2.50 (OAPs £2.30, children £1).*

Church Hill Cottage Gardens, Charing Heath 01233 712522

1½-acre garden developed and planted since 1981, with a strong sense of design. Distinct areas containing borders and island beds, planted with huge range of perennials, spring bulbs, hostas, ferns and shrubs. Established birches; large collection of violas and dianthus. Woodland area. 16th-century cottage. Plants for sale in nursery. ½m W of Charing off the A20. *Open: mid-Mar-Sept Tues-Sun and Bank Holiday Mon 10-5. Entrance: £1.50 (children free).*

COOLING'S NURSERIES LTD
RUSHMORE HILL NURSERIES, KNOCKHOLT, SEVENOAKS, KENT TN14 7NN
TEL: 01959 532269 FAX: 01959 534092

Cooling's Nurseries Ltd began life as a small family-run concern between the wars. Still family-run, it maintains a strong tradition of quality and service. It has been at its present location since 1990. The very loyal customers attest to the superior advice and expert help offered by the educated and friendly staff.

A gardener's garden centre, it emphasises the traditional basics of gardening: most plants are produced onsite, and the range offered is truly comprehensive. No glitz or gimmicks, just a well-laid-out and vast array with growing and propagation areas, and a relaxed atmosphere of conscientious assistance and support. No matter the aspect or soil conditions you have to work with, the staff can help you choose the best plants to suit your individual needs, tastes and budget.

Winner of Retail Nursery of the Year in 1997 (and a finalist in 1998), this fine nursery sells over 1 million plants a year, and offers all manner of trees, shrubs, conifers, climbers, perennials and bedding plants, and the tools and supplies to ensure that they thrive in your garden, home, office or conservatory.

The superb restaurant and coffee shop offers a good selection of snacks and light meals, and has been a winner of a Healthy Food Award and Clean Food Award. From the windows guests gaze out over the rose garden, herbaceous border, lawn, hedges, mixed borders and woodland garden surrounding the restaurant - and perhaps providing a few more ideas about what can be achieved in your garden.

Another special feature of the Nurseries is the hundred seater lecture room for talks and demonstrations, a list of which is available on request. *Open: Mon-Sat 9-5, Sun 10-4.30, Bank Holidays 10-5.*

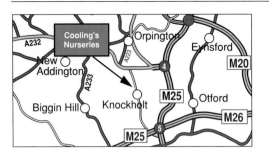

Directions:

From junction 4 of the M25 take the A21 towards Croydon. At the second roundabout turn left towards Knockholt. Cooling's Nurseries is on the left after about 1 mile.

▤ Books & Stationery	🛆 Garden Products	⑂ Plants
Credit Cards Accepted	ⓘ Information Desk	🍴 Restaurant/Coffee Shop
♿ Disabled	Ⓟ Large Car Park	◔ Seeds & Bulbs
✿ Display Gardens	Plant Guarantee	🌴 Trees
ℂ Fruit Trees		

LOCAL GARDENS

Chartwell, nr Westerham, Kent 01732 866368

12-acre National Trust garden on a hill with, as former owner Winston Churchill put it, 'that view' - over Weald of Kent. Avenue of golden roses, fishpools and lakes, walled rose garden, well-established trees. Hostas, penstemons, peonies and other herbaceous plants. Hydrangea petiolaris and Magnolia grandiflora. Self-service restaurant. 2m S of Westerham off B2026. *Open: garden 27th Mar-Jun and Sept-Oct Weds-Sun and Bank Holiday Mon, and July-Aug Tues-Sun and Bank Holiday Mon 11-5 (last admission 4.15); house open all year daily. Entrance (garden only): £2.50 (children £1.25); house and garden £5.50 (children £2.75).*

Crystal Palace Park, Crystal Palace Road, London 0181 313 4407

Borough of Bromley public park where Sir Joseph Paxton's Crystal Palace was re-erected, though unfortunately burnt down in 1936. Paxton also created these fine gardens which once surrounded his 'glass cathedral'. The terraces remain, as do many other of the 200-acre park's best features, including the 29 life-sized statues of prehistoric creatures. Also large maze, farmyard with animals. Summer symphony concerts and fireworks. Junction of Thicket Road and Crystal Palace Road. *Open: all year daily 7.30-dusk. Entrance: free (charge for farmyard).*

Priory Gardens, Orpington, Kent 0181 464 3333 ext. 4471

Borough of Bromley public park adjacent to Bromley Museum (the museum is housed in an attractive mediaeval priory building). Dating back to 1634, extended in the formal Arts and Crafts style. Recently replanted herbaceous garden, marvellous patterned annual bedding, fine mature shrubs and trees, rose garden and refurbished lake. Beautifully maintained and tasteful public space. Off Orpington High Street. *Open: all year daily 7.30-dusk (Sat, Sun and Bank Holidays 9.30-dusk). Entrance: free.*

THE MILLBROOK GARDEN COMPANY
STATION ROAD, SOUTHFLEET, GRAVESEND DA13 9PA
TEL: 01474 331135 FAX: 01474 331152

With an established garden centre business in Crowborough dating back some 20 years, **Millbrook Garden Centre** was opened by the same owners here in Southfleet in 1993. The original site was a rotting cabbage field, completely transformed for the Centre's premises. Easy to get to, the site is also historic: it is an important archaeological site and home to an ancient Roman settlement. Books detailing this fascinating history can be purchased at the Centre.

The huge covered and outside areas are filled with shrubs, seedlings, roses, small trees, herbaceous plants, herbs, bedding and ericaceous (peat-loving plants). In addition, the Centre's Houseplants Help Desk can help you choose from the extensive range available.

Garden equipment, tools and items for sale include pots, ceramics and statuary, wooden tubs, sundials, wind chimes, garden furniture, and fencing. The Centre's landscaping team can help you design and plan the perfect outdoor room.

The Centre specialises in water features and aquatics, with a separate area devoted to a good range of 'Swallow' brand aquatics, rock-effect cascades and helpful leaflets on how to set up an indoor aquarium, with full advice on filtration systems, plants and fish, fish food and other supplies.

There are many other features of this comprehensive Garden Centre, including a wild bird care centre, stock of 'Stormafit' outdoor clothing and accessories, giftware department and book shop. Close to the Thames Estuary, this link with the sea is highlighted in the onsite Liners Restaurant (open weekdays 9.30-4.30, Sun 10.30-4, hot food from noon each day). Its rails, decking and nautical flavour are superbly evocative - when the weather permits, guests can sit outdoors on the promenade deck and admire the view. *Open: daily summer Mon-Sat 9-6, Sun 10.30-4.30; winter Mon-Sat 9-5, Sun 10.30-4.30.*

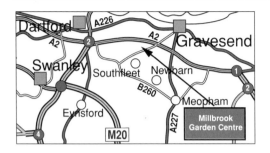

Directions:

Take the exit from the A2 marked Gravesend (West) and Northfleet At the roundabout follow signs to Southfleet. Millbrook Garden Centre is on the right.

Aquatics	Fencing	Information Desk
Barbecues	Floristry	Large Car Park
Books & Stationery	Fruit Trees	Paving
Christmas & Seasonal Displays	Garden Furniture	Pet Products and/or Pets
Clothing	Garden Machinery	Plant Guarantee
Conservatories	Garden Products	Plants
Credit Cards Accepted	Giftware	Restaurant/Coffee Shop
Disabled	Greenhouses & Sheds	Seeds & Bulbs
Dried & Artificial Flowers	Houseplants	Trees

LOCAL GARDENS

Stoneacre, Otham, Maidstone (01622) 862871

One-acre cottage garden of timber-framed 13th-century Hall house restored in the 1920s, with small potager and low box hedging, herbaceous borders and framework of yew hedges. Gingko, Staphylea colchica, mulberry trees. Path to summerhouse within the 2-acre wild garden which also features two ponds and apple orchard. Garden trail. 4m SE of Maidstone off the A20. *Open: house daily all year; garden 27th Mar-Oct Weds and Sat 2-6 (last admission 5; parties by arrangement). Entrance: house and garden £2.50 (children £1.25).*

Great Comp Charitable Trust, Platt, Borough Green, Sevenoaks (01732) 882669/886154

7-acre imaginatively-planted garden with year-round interest: spring hellebores, including H. orientalis; summer herbaceous plants, rose garden, Mediterranean garden; autumn colour with young dawn redwood and Californian redwood (Sequoia sempervirens 'Cantab'); winter heathers. Long grass walks between the different beds and borders. Statuary, temple, woodland areas. Scene for annual music festival. Teas on Sun and Bank Holiday Mon or for parties by arrangement. 2m E of Borough Green off A20/B2016. *Open: April-Oct daily 11-6. Entrance: £3 (children £1).*

Hall Place, Bourne Road, Bexley (01322) 562574

Superb Bexley Council-managed public garden surrounding Jacobean mansion. Two borders of herbaceous plants, large classical rose garden. Yew hedge, topiary gardens, rock garden, patterned herb garden, heather garden, evergreen and deciduous trees. N of A2 near A2/A223 junction. *Garden open all year Mon-Fri 7.30-dusk, Sat-Sun and Bank Holiday Mon 9-dusk. House open summer Mon-Sat 10-5, Sun 2-6; winter Mon-Sat 10-4.15. Model allotment, glasshouses and parts of nursery Mon-Fri 9-6 (4 in winter) except 25th Dec. Entrance: free.*

POLHILL GARDEN CENTRE
LONDON ROAD, BADGERS MOUNT, SEVENOAKS, KENT TN14 7BD
TEL: 01959 534212 FAX: 01959 532777

Polhill Garden Centre is a welcoming family-run garden centre which was established 30 years ago by Jim Novell, who used to grow tomatoes to be sold in Covent Garden. Latterly his son David and David's wife Allison, together with managing director Colin Cross, have helped to increase and improve the centre's prestige and popularity, by ensuring that it provides a complete shopping experience. With the motto 'The Centre that Grows on You', this comprehensive centre enjoys a very relaxed atmosphere. Many shoppers come for the day and find it stimulating from the moment they drive in past the windmill at the entrance and as they browse throughout the distinct areas and associated franchise outlets. The garden furniture department is extensive. With a full range of cane, resin, teak, cast aluminium and others your furniture needs in the garden will be taken care of.

A unique feature of this centre is the scale models of Easter Island carvings. Imaginative and exciting, they reflect Allison Novell's passion for the place, which is revealed in every corner of this fascinating centre. There is something for every garden and all tastes and pockets here - the railway sleepers in the fencing department are an example of the contemporary range of both traditional and more innovative products on offer.

The garden furniture department is extensive, with a full range of cane, resin, wood and metal leisure furniture. There are also many onsite franchises here, including furniture outlets, a landscaping service, bakery, butcher's shop, sporting goods shop, children's clothing shop, Rolawn Turf Growers, tile outlet and specialist giftwear shop. The spacious and very comfortable restaurant serves morning coffee, lunches, daily specials, roasts and afternoon tea. *Open: Monday to Saturday 9-5.30 (open till 8 p.m. on Thursdays), Sunday 10.30-4.30.*

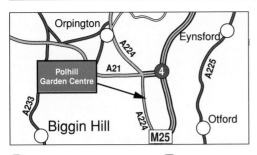

Directions:

From junction 4 of the M25 take the link road towards Orpington. At the roundabout turn left on the A224 towards Sevenoaks and Polhill Garden Centre can be found on th left.

Aquatics	Dried & Artificial Flowers	Greenhouses & Sheds
Barbecues	Farm Shop	Houseplants
Books & Stationery	Fencing	Information Desk
Childrens Play Area	Floristry	Large Car Park
Christmas & Seasonal Displays	Fruit Trees	Paving
Clothing	Garden Construction	Pet Products and/or Pets
Conservatories	Garden Design	Plant Guarantee
Credit Cards Accepted	Garden Furniture	Plants
Cut Flowers	Garden Machinery	Restaurant/Coffee Shop
Disabled	Garden Products	Seeds & Bulbs
Display Gardens	Giftware	Trees

LOCAL GARDENS

Emmetts Garden, Ide Hill 01732 750367

National Trust. 5-acre hill top garden, one of the highest gardens in Kent with fine views over the Weald of Kent. Fine plantsman's collection of rare shrubs and trees. Rose garden, rock garden. Lovely autumn colour from acers, spring colour from bluebells and flowering shrubs. Especially noted for its azaleas and rhododendrons. 1½m S of A25. *Open: 11-5.30 (last admission 4.30) late Mar-May Weds-Sun and Bank Holiday Mon; June-Oct Weds, Sat-Sun and Bank Holiday Mon. Entrance: £3 (children £1.50).*

Penshurst Place, Penshurst 01892 870307

10 acres of gardens dating back to the 14th century, divided into a series of rooms by more than 1 mile of yew hedge. Year-round interest. Masses of spring bulbs; formal rose garden; herbaceous borders; famous peony border. Planting of 640-metre double line of oaks completed in 1995. Garden for the blind. Small wooden gazebo, Italian garden. SW of Tonbridge on the B2176. *Open: weekends in Mar, then daily late Mar-Oct 11-6. House open noon-5.30 (last admission 5). Garden tours for groups of 20 or more. Entrance: £4.20 (OAPs/students £3.70, children £2.80); house and grounds £5.70 (OAPs/students £5.30, children £3.20).*

Ightham Mote, Ivy Hatch 01732 810378

National Trust. 14-acre garden and medieval manor in wooded cleft of the Kentish Weald. Mixed borders of many unusual plants. Courtyard, lawns. Newly planted orchard. Water features including moat and small lakes, which lead to six acres of woodland walks with shrubs and rhododendrons. 6m E of Sevenoaks off the A25. *Open: daily except Tues & Sats 11-5.30 (last admission 4.30). Entrance: £5 (children £2.50, family ticket £12.50).*

RUXLEY MANOR GARDEN CENTRE
MAIDSTONE ROAD, SIDCUP, KENT DA14 5BQ
TEL: 0181 300 0084 FAX: 0181 302 3879

Ruxley Manor Garden Centre has been in the same family for four generations. Owner Richard Evans' great-grandfather began a nursery business in Lee Green, southeast London, in 1876. The centre moved to its present 23-acre site in 1960. The retail side of the business was up and running by 1964, and continues to grow and thrive. Today Richard, together with his brother and other family members, continues to uphold the proud family tradition of quality and service.

This extensive centre comprises both wholesale and retail sections, with a very large range of plants, garden supplies and more covering a wide area, with plenty of room for visitors to browse at their leisure. The comprehensive selection of products available includes seeds and seedlings, bulbs, trees and shrubs (including some unusual varieties), and all manner of flowering and foliage plants. Houseplants are the speciality here, as the centre boasts a superb range of hundreds of different species and varieties to brighten every home, conservatory or office.

Other features of this centre include very large displays of high-quality garden furniture, terracotta pots and tubs, compost and other garden sundries, tools and a range of attractive garden features such as self-contained fountains. Customers will always find something different here, to inspire and help them to create the garden they desire. The Giftshop stocks an exciting range of cards, books, ornaments, dried and silk flowers and more, to provide the perfect present or attractive addition to the home or garden. The licensed Italian restaurant enjoys a very good reputation and serves excellent lunches and dinners. The extensive menu features a number of tempting specialities, all home-cooked and home-prepared by the Italian chef (open for lunch Mon-Sat, dinners Tues-Sat, closed on Suns). *Garden Centre Open: Monday to Saturday 9-5.30, Sunday 10-4.*

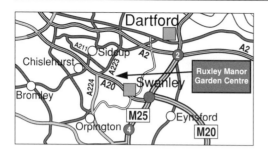

Directions:

From junction 3 of the M25 take the A20 towards London. At the first exit turn on the A223 towards Bexley and at the first roundabout take the B2173 to Swanley. Ruxley Manor Garden Centre is 800 yds on the right.

Aquatics	Farm Shop	Houseplants
Barbecues	Fencing	Information Desk
Books & Stationery	Fruit Trees	Large Car Park
Christmas & Seasonal Displays	Garden Construction	Paving
Clothing	Garden Design	Pet Products and/or Pets
Conservatories	Garden Furniture	Plant Guarantee
Credit Cards Accepted	Garden Products	Plants
Disabled	Giftware	Seeds & Bulbs
Display Gardens	Greenhouses & Sheds	Trees
Dried & Artificial Flowers		

LOCAL GARDENS

Avery Hill Park, Eltham 0181 850 3217

Gardens with three huge conservatories: cold house with camellias, tropical house with coffee and ginger plants and bananas, domed temperate house with staghorn ferns and bougainvillea. Rose gardens; aviary. What remains of the 50-room mansion, which was damaged in the Blitz, has been used as a teacher training college since 1906. *Open: daily all year (except 25th-26th Dec, 1st Jan) 7.30-dusk. Winter garden open Mon-Thurs 1-4, Fri 1-3, weekends 10-4. Entrance: free.*

Eltham Palace Gardens, Court Road, Eltham 0181 294 2548

Approached across a medieval bridge over a moat dotted with small islands and water lilies, and entered via covered culverts, these lovely gardens were laid out in the 1930s for Mr and Mrs Stephen Courtauld. Flower gardens at the east terrace, rose garden, orangery, mature trees leading to rectangular pool. Clipped lawns and laurel bank. Informal garden area, glasshouses. Little remains of the Palace but for the wonderful Art Deco Hall. *Open: telephone (0171) 973 3434 for information on opening dates, times and entrance price.*

Hall Place, Bourne Road, Bexley 01322 562574

Superb Bexley Council-managed public garden surrounding Jacobean mansion. Two borders of herbaceous plants, large classical rose garden. Yew hedge, topiary gardens, rock garden, patterned herb garden, heather garden, evergreen and deciduous trees. N of A2 near A2/A223 junction. *Garden open all year Mon-Fri 7.30-dusk, Sat-Sun and Bank Holiday Mon 9-dusk. House open summer Mon-Sat 10-5, Sun 2-6; winter Mon-Sat 10-4.15. Model allotment, glasshouses and parts of nursery Mon-Fri 9-6 (4 in winter) except 25th Dec. Entrance: free.*

ALL-IN-ONE GARDEN CENTRE
ROCHDALE ROAD, MIDDLETON, MANCHESTER M24 2RB
TEL: 01706 711711 FAX: 01706 759759 WEBSITE: www.allinone.co.uk

All-in-One Garden Centre aims always to develop a greater understanding of what the gardener needs, and to stock new plants and products, including the latest in garden accessories and finishing touches such as furnishings, garden lighting, aquatics, seeds and more. Originally a foundry tip covering 5 acres, this centre started as a small shop selling shrubs and garden accessories, with a staff of 10. Today joint partners Beryl and David Stafford oversee a staff of 50 strong, who are on hand to provide advice and information to all customers.

Roses are the speciality of this superior garden centre. In recognition of this, the GCA has presented the centre with a climbing red rose named 'All in One'. Beryl is current chairperson of the GCA; David held office as chair in 1987.

Specialising in conservatories for over 20 years, with a vast range of leisure buildings together with a dedicated advice centre to help make planning a pleasure rather than a chore, the centre has a massive selection of plants in stock to brighten up the home, garden or conservatory. Experienced advisors are always on hand to help with your gardening decisions.

Many garden displays are in evidence, featuring statuary and water gardens. The attractive and comfortable 80-seat restaurant has recently been refurbished. As with the rest of the garden centre, the choice available varies to suit the season. It overlooks many of the centre's interesting and attractive displays. In summer there is outdoor seating.

The patio displays change monthly, as part of the centre's continued effort to provide ideas, inspiration and help to every gardener. All-in-One is also home to hanging basket planting specialists, and there are regular seasonal demonstrations, promotions and displays. *Open: Monday to Friday 9-5.30 (summer hours 9-8), Saturday 9-5.45, Sunday 10.30-4.30.*

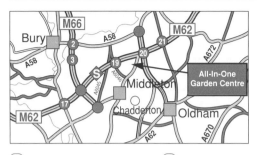

Directions:

From Junction 20 of the M62 take the A672(M) towards Oldham and turn first right onto the A664 towards Rochdale. The All-in-One Garden Centre is on the left.

Aquatics

Barbecues

Books & Stationery

Christmas & Seasonal Displays

Clothing

Conservatories

Credit Cards Accepted

Disabled

Display Gardens

Dried & Artificial Flowers

Fencing

Fireworks

Floristry

Fruit Trees

Garden Construction

Garden Furniture

Garden Products

Giftware

Greenhouses & Sheds

Houseplants

Information Desk

Large Car Park

Paving

Pet Products and/or Pets

Plant Guarantee

Plants

Restaurant/Coffee Shop

Seeds & Bulbs

Trees

LOCAL GARDENS

Land Farm, Colden, Hebden Bridge 01422 842260

North-facing 4-acre expanse at an elevation of 1,000 feet in the Pennines. Designed as a low-maintenance garden, yet with a wide range of herbaceous plants, alpines and shrubs. Herbaceous garden, formal garden and newly developed woodland garden with cornus and rhododendrons. As featured on Gardeners' World, this expanse also features *tropaeolum speciosum*. Art gallery in the former barn. Map available from Hebden Bridge Visitors' Centre. 3½m NE of Todmorden off the A646. *Open: May-Aug Sat-Sun and Bank Holiday Mon 10-5. Entrance: £2.50. Parties welcomed but pre-booking necessary.*

Towneley Park, Todmorden Road, Burnley 01282 424213

16th-century Hall with a mostly early 19th-century exterior. Pond to the front, then a ha-ha leading to open parkland laid out in the late 1700s. Formal beds with annuals, herbaceous plants and shrubs. Small lime walk, extensive woodland with large rhododendrons and interesting walks. Nature centre, aquarium, museum of local crafts. 1½m SE of Burnley off the A671. *Open: daily all year during daylight hours. Hall open Mon-Fri 10-5, Sun noon-5. Closed Christmas week. Entrance: free.*

Heaton Hall, Heaton Park, Prestwich, Manchester 0161 773 1085

A 650-acre park landscaped in the late 16th-early 17th centuries, surrounding Heaton Hall, designed by Wyatt in 1772. The grounds contain several neo-classical structures. Formal, brightly coloured Edwardian gardens. Small heather garden, large formal rose garden, lovely dell of rhododendrons and mature trees. A stream with pools and waterfalls leads to a boating lake. The Prestwich side of the park features small demonstration gardens. 4m N of city centre on A576. *Open: all year, daylight hours. Entrance: free (parking charge Sat, Sun and Bank Holidays during summer).*

BARTON GRANGE GARDEN CENTRE
WIGAN ROAD, DEANE, BOLTON, LANCASHIRE BL3 4RD
TEL: 01204 660660   FAX: 01204 62525

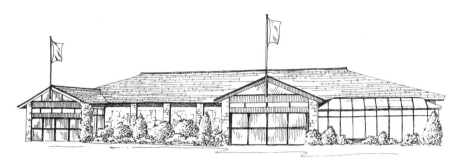

Established in 1963, **Barton Grange Garden Centres**, comprising this Centre, one in Preston and another in Woodford, has an enviable reputation as a leader in the field of gardening and outdoor leisure. Having developed its own wholesale plant growing division, Barton Grange can offer a high quality range of trees, shrubs, seasonal bedding plants and houseplants. To complement this range of plants, the Centre can supply you with everything from tools and fertilisers to garden furniture, tropical and coldwater fish and a range of pets and accessories. After a million-pound refurbishment, this award-winning centre now boasts a huge range of services, quality products and expertise.

Much of the hardy nursery stock is home grown, as are many of the flowering houseplants for the home, conservatory or office. The Pets and Aquatics department has also been extensively refurbished, so that it now offers a comprehensive range of pet accessories and water gardening products, including both cold-water and tropical fish. The gift shop is also well worth a visit providing a good day out for all the family.

The Colliers Kitchen restaurant serves a selection of light meals, snacks, and home-made cakes and deserts in surroundings with a mining theme, adorned with an abundance of old photographs of the former Victoria Colliery. The centrepiece of this distinguished eatery is a manual winding wheel. Seasonal events and promotional days are held throughout the year, consisting of children's weekends, workshops and classes demonstrating the techniques behind various planting schemes, floristry and creating the perfect hanging basket. An October fireworks festival and special Christmas event,in 1997, at the Centre won the GCA Best Christmas Display Award. *Open: Mon-Sat 9-5.30, Sun 10.30-4.30; also Thurs (April-Dec) 9-8.*

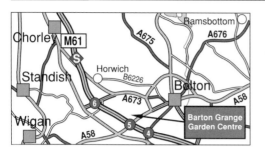

Directions:

From junction 5 of the M61 take the A58 towards Bolton. Barton Grange Garden Centre lies just of the junction.

Aquatics	Fireworks	Information Desk
Barbecues	Floristry	Large Car Park
Books & Stationery	Fruit Trees	Pet Products and/or Pets
Christmas & Seasonal Displays	Garden Design	Plant Guarantee
Conservatories	Garden Furniture	Plants
Credit Cards Accepted	Garden Products	Restaurant/Coffee Shop
Disabled	Giftware	Seeds & Bulbs
Display Gardens	Houseplants	Trees
Dried & Artificial Flowers		

LOCAL GARDENS

Lyme Park, Disley, Stockport 01663 762023/766492

National Trust 17 acre garden of Palladian-style Lyme Hall. Foremost NT garden for high-Victorian-style bedding. Many rare and old-fashioned plants. Two 150 year-old camellias; Dutch garden, Gertrude Jekyll-style herbaceous border, wooded ravine garden with stream, rhododendrons, azaleas, ferns, shade-loving plants. 300 year-old lime avenue, rose garden. Teas. 6m SE of Stockport just W of Disley on A6. *Open: 26th March-Oct, Fri-Tues 11-5; Wed/ Thurs 1-5; Nov-20th Dec Sat/Sun noon-3. Guided tours by arrangement. Entrance: garden £2 (park: pedestrians free, car £3.50 includes occupants).ildren 50p).*

Haigh Hall Gardens, Haigh Country Park, Haigh, Wigan 01942 832895

A grand hall surrounded by mature parkland. Oval pool, specimen shrubs, rose beds. Three walled gardens, one with shrubs and young specimen trees; one with good herbaceous border and well-stocked shrub border. Wild garden; landscaped area with conifers and heathers. Formal area with lawns, yew hedges, roses. Arboretum with good acers. Craft gallery, model village and railway, children's rides. 2m NE of Wigan off the B5238. *Open: Daily all year during daylight hours. Entrance: free (parking charge in summer).*

Rivington Terraced Gardens, Bolton Road, Horwich, Bolton 01204 691549

Remains of gardens built in the early 1900s by Lord Leverhulme and designed by Thomas Mawson. Woodland set on steep west-facing hillside overlooking Rivington reservoirs. Rocky ravine; mature trees and a wealth of rhododendrons. Remains of Japanese garden, restored pigeon tower. Trail leaflet (25p) available explaining the various features. 1m N of Horwich off the A673. 10-minute walk from Rivington Hall and Great House Barn. Refreshments available at Hall Barn. *Open: daily all year. Entrance: free.*

BARTON GRANGE GARDEN CENTRE
GARSTANG ROAD, BARTON, PRESTON, LANCASHIRE PR3 5AA
TEL: 01772 864242 FAX: 01772 863480

Established in 1963, **Barton Grange Garden Centres**, comprising this Centre, one in Bolton and another in Woodford, has an enviable reputation as a leader in the field of gardening and outdoor leisure. Having developed its own wholesale plant-growing division, Barton Grange can offer a high quality range of trees, shrubs, seasonal bedding plants and houseplants. This 7-acre Centre features many specimen trees and shrubs imported from Italy, together with home-grown houseplants fresh from their own nursery and is one of very few to offer a five year plant guarantee for all outdoor hardy plants. To complement this range of plants, the Centre can supply you with everything from tools and fertilisers to garden furniture, water features and a range of pets and pet care products.

The Centre's knowledgeable and conscientious staff includes highly qualified horticulturists and trained florists. The Centre also boasts a complete and professional landscape gardening service - from back garden rockeries and patios to major parkland schemes, the Centre is well equipped to provide a comprehensive service to suit your individual tastes, requirements and budget.

The Centre's aquatics and pet centre now offers a comprehensive range of pet and water gardening products, including cold-water fish. The household goods department and gift shop are also well worth a visit, providing a good day out for all the family.

The Walled Garden Cafe Bar Restaurant serves a selection of breakfasts, snacks, light and full meals, cakes, teas and coffees in a relaxed and pleasant surroundings. Seasonal events and promotional days are held throughout the year, consisting of children's weekends, workshops demonstrating the techniques behind various planting schemes and creating the perfect hanging basket, an October fireworks festival and special Christmas events. *Open: January to November Monday to Saturday 9-5.30 (Thursdays until 8 p.m. April to November), Sun 10.30-4.30; December Monday to Friday 9-8, Saturday 9-5.30, Sunday 10.30-4.30.*

Directions:
Barton Grange Garden Centre is located 4 miles north of Preston on the A6. After passing through the village of Broughton the centre can be found on the right hand side.

Aquatics	Floristry	Information Desk
Barbecues	Fruit Trees	Large Car Park
Books & Stationery	Garden Construction	Pets and Pet Products
Christmas & Seasonal Displays	Garden Design	Plant Guarantee (5 years)
Credit Cards Accepted	Garden Furniture	Plants
Disabled	Garden Products	Restaurant/Coffee Shop
Dried & Artificial Flowers	Giftware	Seeds & Bulbs
Fencing	Houseplants	Trees
Fireworks		

LOCAL GARDENS

Catforth Gardens, Roots Lane, Catforth 01772 690561/690269

Catforth Gardens comprise three country gardens. The Bungalow Garden is a 1-acre informal garden providing year-round colour and interest with rare herbaceous plants including dicentras, pulmonarias and euphorbias, unusual shrubs and trees, azaleas, rhododendrons, National Collection of hardy geraniums, large rockery, woodland garden, two ponds with bog gardens. The Farmhouse Garden is a ¼-acre cottage garden with a variety of herbaceous perennials. Paddock Garden is a 1½-acre summer flower garden with rose garden, climbing roses and three natural clay-lined water-lily ponds. Plants for sale in adjacent nursery. 5m NW of Preston off the B5269. *Open: mid-Mar-mid-Sept daily 10.30-5. Entrance: combined price £2.50 (accompanied children 50p).*

Ashton Memorial, Williamson Park, Lancaster 01524 33318

Cited by Pevsner as 'the grandest monument in England', Ashton Memorial was designed in 1906 by John Belcher and looks down on Lancaster from the highest point in Williamson Park. Beautifully landscaped parkland with broad paths, woodland underplanted with rhododendrons and a variety of other shrubs. Stone bridge spanning small lake. E of Lancaster town centre. *Open: daily April-Sept 10-5, Oct-Mar (except 25th-26th Dec and 1st Jan) 11-4. Entrance: park and ground floor of memorial with exhibition free; memorial viewing gallery 50p; butterfly house, mini-beast house, conservation garden and free-flying bird enclosure Entrance; Adult £2.95, £2.50 OAPs & concessions, £1.50 children 5 and over.*

Salmesbury Hall, Crofton New Road, Salmesbury, Preston 01254 812010

Owned by a charitable trust, pleasant grounds of a 14th-century house. Year-round interest provided by fine range of venerable trees, shrubs and plants. House is interesting historically, is open and run by the trust. 3m E of Preston off the A59/A677 (junction 31 of the M6 towards Blackburn). *Open: Tuesday-Sunday 11-4.30. Entrance charge - please phone for details.*

DAISY NOOK GARDEN CENTRE
MEDLOCK HALL, DAISY NOOK, FAILSWORTH, LANCASHIRE M35 9WJ
TEL: 0161 681 4245 FAX: 0161 688 0822

Founded in 1973, **Daisy Nook Garden Centre** was the brainchild of a local doctor, Mr Richard Calder. Working as manager of the Centre, he took over as owner in 1985, and has totally rebuilt, refurbished and expanded the Centre over the intervening years. Today, in addition to the excellent range of trees, shrubs, flowering and foliage plants, groundcover, herbs and more, the Centre also boasts an unusual range of alpines and dwarf conifers.

The Centre prides itself on its wide selection of roses, which includes miniatures and shrub roses. All roses come with a two-year guarantee. Covering 5 acres and set in picturesque countryside, with the River Medlock running through it, the Centre features extensive display gardens including professionally-designed water features.

The handsome furniture department has a comprehensive range of wood, resin and plastic furniture for the garden or conservatory. The new houseplant department was awarded Winner of the 1998 Houseplant Competition for the Northwest region by the GCA.

This welcoming and interesting garden centre also features a dedicated patio department, while the onsite coffee shop is just the place to relax and enjoy a hot drink and a hot or cold snack or meal, all freshly prepared.

Outdoor garden centre manager Paul Tyler gives regular talks on-site on a variety of topics of interest to every gardener, from the novice to the most experienced. *Open: spring/summer Monday to Friday 9-7, Saturday 9-5, Sunday 10.30-4.30; winter Monday to Saturday 9-5, Sunday 10.30-4.30.*

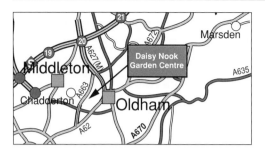

Directions:

Take Junction 20 from the M62 towards Oldham and at the first set of lights turn right into Ashton Road East. Daisy Nook Garden Centre is about 1 mile down on the left.

🟡 Aquatics	🟦 Fencing	🟦 Houseplants
🟦 Barbecues	🟦 Fireworks	ⓘ Information Desk
🟦 Books & Stationery	🟦 Floristry	ⓟ Large Car Park
🟦 Childrens Play Area	🟦 Fruit Trees	🟦 Paving
🟦 Christmas & Seasonal Displays	🟦 Garden Construction	🟦 Plant Guarantee
ⓒⓒ Credit Cards Accepted	🟦 Garden Furniture	⟩ Plants
🟦 Disabled	🟦 Garden Products	🟦 Restaurant/Coffee Shop
🟦 Display Gardens	🟦 Giftware	🟦 Seeds & Bulbs
🟦 Dried & Artificial Flowers	🟦 Greenhouses & Sheds	🟦 Trees

LOCAL GARDENS

Fletcher Moss Botanical & Parsonage Gardens, Didsbury 0161 434 1877

Well-maintained garden on a steep south-facing bank. Variety of heathers, bulbs, azaleas, shrubs, alpines and small trees. Water garden and lawned area. Moisture-loving plants, including gunneras, by the rocky streams. Grassy area with specimen trees. The nearby formal Victorian Parsonage Gardens contain herbaceous borders, rhododendrons, camellias and lawns. Orchid house (open: Mon-Fri 9-4) and a wonderful swamp cypress and mulberry tree. 5m S of Manchester, off A5145. *Open: daily, 9-dusk. Entrance: free.*

Heaton Hall, Heaton Park, Prestwich, Manchester 0161 773 1085

A 650-acre park landscaped in the late 16th-early 17th centuries, surrounding Heaton Hall, designed by Wyatt in 1772. The grounds contain several neo-classical structures. To the front of the Hall are formal, brightly coloured Edwardian gardens. Also a small heather garden, large formal rose garden, and a lovely dell of rhododendrons and mature trees. A stream with pools and waterfalls leads to a boating lake. The Prestwich side of the park features small demonstration gardens. 4m N of city centre on A576. *Open: all year, daylight hours. Entrance: free (parking charge Sun and Bank Holidays).*

Daisy Nook Country Park, Failsworth 0161 308 3909

This beautiful country park is a haven for a variety of flora and fauna. It offers people of all ages the chance to enjoy a peaceful walk and to observe wildlife amidst varied countryside. The park includes a lake, woodland areas, a canal and flower-filled meadows, with bridleways and footpaths linking to other countryside areas. 4m NE of Manchester off the A62. *Open: telephone for details. Entrance: telephone for details.*

GATEACRE GARDEN CENTRE

E. H. WILLIAMS LTD., ACREFIELD ROAD, GATEACRE, LIVERPOOL L25 5JW
TEL: 0151 428 6556 FAX: 0151 428 9388

Developed over more than 60 years, since 1935, **Gateacre Garden Centre** once occupied the countryside, but urban spread has meant that it is now within Liverpool itself. Necessarily small due to the constraints of the surrounding houses, this garden centre nevertheless uses all space to best effect and offers a comprehensive range of plants, tools, gardening supplies and more. Gateacre Garden Centre offers exceptional service from the conscientious and knowledgeable staff together with an excellent quality of nursery stock coming from its long tradition in retail horticulture. The centre began life as a nursery owned and run by the grandfather of current owner Sally Cornelissen. The staff are more than haooy to assist with choosing the best plants, shrubs, trees, composts, fertilisers and furniture for the garden.

The centre is well-known locally and has built up a reputation for quality and service. The terraced display areas boast numerous raised long and rectangular beds. There is a range of outdoor pots and terracotta ornaments, gazebos and pergolas enhancing the viewing area, along with tables with inbuilt irrigation and a good selection of statuary. The outdoor area is fitted with all-weather flooring; the flower beds are edged with logs for a lovely rustic effect. There is a wide selection of specimen stock and unusual plants such as tree ferns and palms which should enable you to find appropriate plants for any garden.

There's a fine selection of quality garden implements, and a houseplant area brimming with foliage and flowering plants and hanging baskets. The Gift Shop offers cards and a range of glassware in unusual colours, shapes and designs. *Open: daily Mon-Sat 9-5.30(winter 5pm close) Sun 10.30-4.30; Late nights Apr-Jun, Mon-Fri 9-7.30*

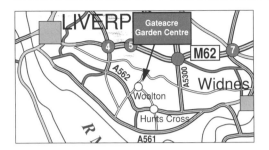

Directions:

Take the A561 from Liverpool city centre and at the crossroads in Hunts Cross turn left towards Woolton. Gateacre Garden Centre can be found on the right after about 2 mile, just after the village.

🎅 Christmas & Seasonal Displays		👁 Fruit Trees		℗ Large Car Park	
ℂℂ Credit Cards Accepted		🌿 Garden Products		🏺 Plant Guarantee	
🌼 Dried & Artificial Flowers		🏬 Giftware		⎰ Plants	
▥ Fencing		☘ Houseplants		☻ Seeds & Bulbs	
🌸 Floristry		ⓘ Information Desk		🌴 Trees	

LOCAL GARDENS

Reynolds Park Walled Gardens, Church Road, Woolton, Liverpool 0151 724 2371

As its names suggests, a walled garden - in very good condition and with large dahlia beds, herbaceous borders and wonderful wall climbers. Also a large grassy area with mature trees, a small rose garden and an unusual clipped yew garden. With only two staff, this Liverpool City Council garden (controlled by the city's Environmental Services department) is maintained beautifully. 4½m SE of Liverpool city centre off the A562. *Open: Mon-Fri all year 9-4. Entrance: free.*

Walton Hall Gardens, Walton Lea Road, Walton 01925 601617

Warrington Borough Council-managed gardens with impressive rockery featuring birch trees, rhododendrons, azaleas and other small shrubs and trees. Large pool with terrapins and carp, water features, gunneras, water lilies, series of formal gardens with tulips and annuals. Formal beds of modern roses, large beech trees, light woodland with acers, magnolias, camellias. Plants for sale on various Sundays in summer. Also children's zoo, play area, heritage centre, pitch and putt, crazy golf. 2m SW of Warrington off the A56. *Open: daily 8-dusk. Entrance: free. Charge for car parking.*

Calderstone Park, Liverpool 0151 225 4835

Large landscaped park managed by Liverpool Council Development and Environmental Services. Lake and rhododendron walk, mature trees, shrubs. At centre an old walled garden surrounded by: a flower garden of grasses, perennials and annuals, with a long greenhouse; Old English Garden with formal paths, pergolas with climbers including vines and clematis, circular pond; Japanese Garden with pools and rocky streams, acers, bamboo and pines. National Collection of aeachmeas. 4m SE of city centre off the A562. *Open: Old English Garden and Japanese Garden April-Sept daily 8-7.30; Oct-Mar daily (except 25th Dec) 8-4. Park open daily all year. Entrance: free.*

LADY GREEN NURSERIES & GARDEN CENTRE
LADY GREEN LANE, INCE BLUNDELL, FORMBY, LIVERPOOL L38 1QD
TEL: 0151 929 3635 FAX: 3778 EMAIL: ladygreengardencentre@btinternet.com

Lady Green Garden Centre was opened in 1985 by owners Philip and Sue Allison. Philip, a trained landscape designer, has developed the Centre grounds from small beginnings as a ploughed field to its present status as a successful and prosperous business with a growing reputation for the variety and quality of its plants. Set in 9 acres, it boasts a successful garden design business. Philip and his wife Sue have used their flair for design to develop a beautiful mature landscape of trees, pools and gardens to set off and complement the Garden Centre plantaria, offering a wealth of ideas to every gardener. Many interesting reclaimed stone items, saved from destruction by City of Liverpool redevelopers, are available to buy, including stone troughs and York stone flags and finials.

Frequent medal-winners at the acclaimed Southport Flower Show, the Centre offers a wide selection of top-quality shrubs, trees and conifers, while the plant stock ranges from small alpine varieties to mature shrubs and conifers, all container-grown for planting throughout the year. The trained and knowledgeable staff can offer advice on the most suitable plants for any position. There's also a good selection of garden furniture, for that finishing touch to any garden. Garden tools, hardware, fertilisers and chemicals are also available.

For the home, the Centre stocks a range of silk and dried flowers, house plants and seasonal pot plants, books, cards and attractive gift items. 'Teasels' Coffee Shop has a welcoming, friendly atmosphere and serves a variety of freshly prepared meals and home-made cakes. Evening events include enlightening garden talks, demonstrations and dinner soirees. Approved members of the Garden Centre Association. *Open: Mon-Sat 9-5.30, Sun 10.30-4.30.*

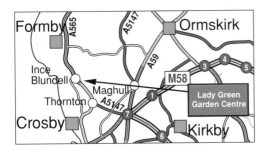

Directions:

From the M57/M58 junction take the A5207 towards Formby. After passing through the village of Thornton and joining the A565 Lady Green Garden Centre lies in the small village of Ince Blundell.

Aquatics	Dried & Artificial Flowers	Houseplants
Barbecues	Fencing	Information Desk
Books & Stationery	Fireworks	Large Car Park
Childrens Play Area	Fruit Trees	Paving
Christmas & Seasonal Displays	Garden Construction	Plant Guarantee
Clothing	Garden Design	Plants
Credit Cards Accepted	Garden Furniture	Restaurant/Coffee Shop
Disabled	Garden Products	Seeds & Bulbs
Display Gardens	Giftware	Trees

LOCAL GARDENS

Calderstone Park, Liverpool 0151 225 4835

Large landscaped park managed by Liverpool Council Development and Environmental Services. Lake and rhododendron walk, mature trees, shrubs. At centre an old walled garden surrounded by: a flower garden of grasses, perennials and annuals, with a long greenhouse; Old English Garden with formal paths, pergolas with climbers including vines and clematis, circular pond; Japanese Garden with pools and rocky streams, acers, bamboo and pines. National Collection of aechmea. 4m SE of city centre off the A562. *Open: Old English Garden and Japanese Garden April-Sept daily 8-7.30; Oct-Mar daily (except 25th Dec) 8-4. Park open daily all year. Entrance: free.*

Croxteth Hall and Country Park, Croxteth Hall Lane, Liverpool 0151 228 5311

Liverpool Council Leisure Services 500-acre parkland. Rhododendrons and large woodland areas. Large walled garden laid out as a Victorian kitchen garden, with organically-grown vegetables, fruits and decorative plants. Herbaceous borders with ornamental grasses and perennials. Small herb garden, greenhouses, mushroom house. NE of city centre off A5058. *Open: April-Sept daily 11-5; please ring for winter dates and times. Hall and Victorian Farm also open. Entrance: house, farm and walled garden £3.60 (OAPs/children £1.80); walled garden £1.05 (OAPs/children 55p); grounds free.*

Worden Park, Leyland 0177) 421109

Gardens surrounding craft and theatre workshops in the former stable block and section of old house. Unusual hornbeam circular maze, big conservatory. Rockery, herbaceous border. Formal sunken lawn area. Swathes of open parkland with mini golf, model railway, children's adventure playground, arboretum and ice-house. Regular events - ring for details. 4m S of Preston off B5253. *Open daily 8-dusk. Entrance: free (except for the first Sat in June).*

SEFTON MEADOWS GARDEN & HOME CENTRE

SEFTON LANE, MAGHULL, MERSEYSIDE L31 8BT
TEL: 0151 531 6688 FAX: 0151 527 1868

Sefton Meadows began in 1988 with one building selling plants and compost, and a small nursery. Developed and added to over the years, it now has several departments over 4½ acres. This garden centre continues to grow, with new innovations all the time - a large extension to the nursery is currently underway.

This thriving family business has both open and covered areas, with all walkways under cover. It is renowned for its seasonal displays. In summer and spring there are barbecue displays on the large patio, with demonstrations on the best barbecue to buy for the size of your garden, the kinds of meals you'd like to prepare outdoors, and how much you'd like to spend. Other demonstrations by the knowledgeable staff feature tips on flower arranging, preparing hanging baskets and much more. From mid-October until December Sefton Meadows hosts its superb Christmas promotion, with fully animated grotto and displays covering over 7,000 square feet of floor space.

There is a large range of marine fish on offer, accompanied by expert advice in the specialist pets and aquatics centre. Here are also sold pond fish, with a speciality of large Koi carp. Pets available include rabbits, hamsters and other small domestic animals, as well as a great variety of exotic birds.

Winner of the Diamond Award at the Southport Flower Show for landscaping and design, this garden centre stocks a superb range of trees, shrubs and flowering and foliage plants, as well as a selection of gardening tools and implements.

The onsite coffee shop serves hot and cold snacks, lunches and teas in relaxed and attractive surroundings. There's also a comprehensive gift shop. *Open: Monday to Saturday 9-6, Sunday 10.30-4.30; Late night opening during spring and over the Christmas period.*

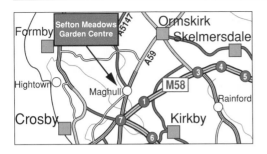

Directions:

From the M58/M57 junction take the A59 towards Ormskirk. Turn first left into Liverpool Road South and again first left into Sefton Lane. Sefton Meadows is on the right over the bridge.

Aquatics	Fireworks	Information Desk
Barbecues	Floristry	Large Car Park
Books & Stationery	Fruit Trees	Paving
Christmas & Seasonal Displays	Garden Construction	Pet Products and/or Pets
Credit Cards Accepted	Garden Design	Plant Guarantee
Disabled	Garden Furniture	Plants
Display Gardens	Garden Products	Restaurant/Coffee Shop
Dried & Artificial Flowers	Giftware	Seeds & Bulbs
Fencing	Houseplants	Trees

LOCAL GARDENS

Rufford Old Hall, Rufford 01704 821254

Impressive 16th-century timber-framed house with gardens covering 14 acres laid out by the National Trust in the style of the 1820s. Informal garden with wonderful spring-flowering azaleas and rhododendrons. Two large topiary squirrels. Cottage garden to the north side of the house. Woodland walks, lawns and gravel paths. Teas. 7m NE of Ormskirk off the A59. *Open: 27th Mar-Oct Sat-Weds noon-5.30. Hall open 1-5.30 (last admission 4.30). Entrance to garden: £2 (children £1); house and garden £3.80 (children £1.90).*

Speke Hall, Liverpool 0151 427 7231

National Trust 35-acre estate of grand Elizabethan hall. Formal garden with rose garden, herbaceous border with a variety of perennials. Rhododendrons, ferns, camellias and hollies. Moated area with recently opened stream garden and formal lawns. Wild wood. Teas. 8m SE of Liverpool off the A561. *Open: Tues-Sun and Bank Holiday Mon 27th Mar-Oct (except 2nd April) noon-5.30; Nov-Mar (except 1st Jan, 24th-26th and 31st Dec) Tues-Sun noon-4. Hall open as garden 27th Mar-Oct; then Nov-mid-Dec Sat-Sun 1-4.30. Entrance: £1.50 (children 80p); house and gardens £4.10 (children £2.10).*

Windle Hall, St Helens

18th-century walled garden surrounded by 5 acres of lawns. Water and rock garden, tufa stone grotto, herbaceous borders, rose gardens containing exhibition blooms, greenhouses, thatched summer house. Pergola. Also ducks, miniature ornamental ponies. N of E Lancs Rd, St Helens. 5m W of M6 via East Lancs Rd, nr Southport junction. Entrance by bridge over E Lancs Rd. *Open: certain weekends in aid of the National Gardens Scheme; telephone for details. Entrance: £1 (children 50p).*

WORSLEY HALL GARDEN CENTRE
LEIGH ROAD, BOOTHSTOWN, WORSLEY, MANCHESTER M28 2LJ
TEL: 0161 790 8792 FAX: 0161 790 2305

Worsley Hall Garden Centre began life as "New Hall Nurseries" the Victorian walled garden of Worsley New Hall, residence of the Earl of Ellesmere who was the nephew of the famous Duke of Bridgewater, known as "The Canal Duke."

The walled gardens have now evolved into a thriving popular garden centre and many of the original garden features can still be seen. The large hollow walls were once heated through hot air ducts and used to produce exotic fruits such as pineapples, grapes and melons. The head gardener's house with gothic spire designed by Edward Bloore remains a major landmark and feature of the garden centre.

Photographs and oil paintings of the hall are on display in the cosy café where visitors enjoy coffee, tea and a range of nice fayre. Newly opened, the aviary and aquarium boasts a large range of tropical and cold water fish, accessories etc. and are located adjacent to the café .

Specialising in garden plants, especially fruit trees, the Centre offers a vast array of plants suitable for large or small gardens and also a well-stocked shop. Advice and assistance is both free and freely given. You will always be given a warm welcome at the Centre by the friendly knowledgeable staff.

The Centre holds the Salford & Bolton fuchsia society's annual show and exhibition and also holds demonstrations for the gardening enthusiasts.*Open: summer Mon-Sat 8-5.30, Sun 10.30-4.30; winter Mon-Sat 8-5, Sun 10.30-4.30.*

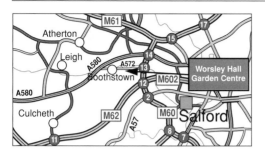

Directions

From junction 13 on the M60 (formerly junction 13 of the M62) take the A572 towards Boothstown. After 1/2 mile Worsley Hall Garden Centre lies on the left and is well signposted.

🄰 Aquatics		🄳 Dried & Artificial Flowers		🄿 Large Car Park	
🄱 Barbecues		🄲 Fruit Trees		🄿 Paving	
🄱 Books & Stationery		🄶 Garden Furniture		🄿 Pet Products and/or Pets	
🄲 Childrens Play Area		🄶 Garden Machinery		🄿 Plant Guarantee	
🄲 Christmas & Seasonal Displays		🄶 Garden Products		🄿 Plants	
🄲 Credit Cards Accepted		🄶 Giftware		🄿 Restaurant/Coffee Shop	
🄲 Cut Flowers		🄷 Houseplants		🄿 Seeds & Bulbs	
🄳 Disabled		🄸 Information Desk		🄳 Trees	
🄳 Display Gardens					

LOCAL GARDENS

Heaton Hall, Heaton Park, Prestwich, Manchester 0161 7731085

A 640-acre park landscaped in the late 16th-early 17th centuries, surrounding Heaton Hall, designed by Wyatt in 1772. The grounds contain several neo-classical structures. To the front of the Hall are formal, brightly coloured Edwardian gardens. Also a small heather garden, large formal rose garden, and a lovely dell of rhododendrons and mature trees. A stream with pools and waterfalls leads to a boating lake. The Prestwich side of the park features small demonstration gardens. *4m N of city centre on A576. Open: all year, daylight hours. Entrance: free (parking charge Sun and Bank Holidays).*

Alexandra Park, Oldham

These municipal gardens are being restored and restructured by local residents, over 85 per cent of whom have no garden of their own at home. The terraced houses some of them live in, built for cotton workers during the 19th century, can be seen nearby. Millennium funds are helping these residents rework these gardens. Very much a work in progress, planned plantings include herbaceous borders, roses, and specimen trees. *6m NE of Manchester off the A62.*

Fletcher Moss Botanical & Parsonage Gardens, Mill Gate Lane, Didsbury 0161 4341877

Well-maintained garden on a steep south-facing bank. Variety of heathers, bulbs, azaleas, shrubs, alpines and small trees. Water garden and lawned area. Moisture-loving plants, including gunneras, by the rocky streams. Grassy area with specimen trees. The nearby formal Victorian Parsonage Gardens contain herbaceous borders, rhododendrons, camellias and lawns. Orchid house (open: Mon-Fri 9-4) and a wonderful swamp cypress and mulberry tree. *5m S of Manchester, off A5145. Open: daily, 9-dusk. Entrance: free.*

WOODLANDS NURSERIES

ASHBY ROAD, STAPLETON, LEICESTERSHIRE LE9 8JE
TEL: 01455 291494 FAX: 01455 292152

Woodlands Nurseries started as a one-acre Tomato Nursery in the 1970s. Today, the biggest garden centre in the East Midlands occupies an 18-acre site and boasts one of the largest covered sales areas in the UK. As the name suggests, there is more to this business than simply selling garden products. A modern, 4½-acre production facility supplies quality plant material which is always nursery fresh. This means there is a wide range of plant varieties, in plentiful supply and grown by an enthusiastic team. Plants abound the moment customers enter the large car park.

Woodlands has developed a strong business in plant sales. Hardy outdoor plants, herbaceous perennials and annuals are major lines. Hanging baskets and seasonal plants are a speciality. There is an all-year-round houseplant department which creates superb planted arrangements. Gardening sundries and accessories include composts, fertilisers, containers, tools, stoneware and other ornamental items. Seasonal lines include bulbs, seeds and birdcare. Recently introduced is a range of quality timber products.

One of the newest areas to be included is for conservatory, patio and garden furniture, plus barbecues. Gardening should be relaxing as well as enjoyable, and there is a wide range to suit all tastes. A selection of gas and charcoal barbecues will inspire al fresco dining with family and friends. Carefully chosen ceramics, glassware, candles and basketware are amongst the popular gift items. A recently introduced bookshop offers a wide choice for all ages. The floral art department boasts superb replicas of flowers, fruits and foliage plants, together with accessories to create stunning arrangements and displays. Perhaps the most interesting feature of this centre is the annual Christmas decorations display. Every year the skilled staff create a magical spectacle which appeals to all ages. In the autumn of 1999, a new restaurant is due to open on the site. This will complete a shopping experience which is not to be missed.

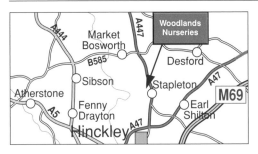

Directions:

From Leicester take the A47 towards Coventry. At the A447 junction turn right and, after 3 miles, Woodlands Nurseries can be found on the left just past the village of Stapleton.

Barbecues	Fruit Trees	Plant Guarantee
Books & Stationery	Garden Furniture	Plants
Christmas & Seasonal Displays	Garden Products	Restaurant/Coffee Shop - Opening Autumn 1999
Credit Cards Accepted	Giftware	
Disabled	Houseplants	Seeds & Bulbs
Dried & Artificial Flowers	Information Desk	Trees
Floristry	Large Car Park	

LOCAL GARDENS

Gaddesby Hall, Gaddesby, Leicestershire LE7 4WG

6-acre well-laid-out gardens of a Queen Anne house. The gardens have been restored and replanted over the years since 1987 by the current owners. Landscaped to a grand design, with rare specimen trees, Wellingtonia and cedars. Lily pond within a yew enclosure, dingle walk, silver pear walk. New border in pinks, yellows and blues; swathes of spring bulbs including fritillaries, snowdrops, aconites, anemones. Hellebores underplanted with tulips. Fine 13th-century church for a backdrop. 8m NE of Leicester off the A607. *Open: by written appointment. Entrance: £2 (children 50p) in aid of church.*

Beeby Manor, Beeby 01162 595238

Charming, traditional English garden in fine cottage style. Mature gardens covering three acres, divided into a series of magical rooms and encircled by venerable yew hedges. Rose towers, box parterre, walled herbaceous borders, formal lily ponds. An arboretum is currently under development. Featured in Homes and Gardens 1996 and TV Surprise Gardens 1998. 8m E of Leicester off the A47. *Open: by appointment. Entrance: £1.80.*

Long Close, 60 Main Street, Woodhouse Eaves, Loughborough 01509 890616

Long and rectangular 5-acre garden of daffodils, bluebells, snowdrops and bulbs in spring; azaleas, flowering shrubs, many varieties of rhododendrons, camellias, many rare shrubs, magnolias, mature trees, lily ponds. Also herbaceous borders, a good penstemon collection, wildflower meadow walk and terraced lawns. Winding paths leading to an informal pool. Courtyard provides shelter for many tender wall-covering plants rarely found this far north. Teas. Plants for sale. S of Loughborough off the B591. *Open: daily Mar – Jul, Mon-Sat 9.30-1 and 2-5.30; Entrance: £2 (children free) - tickets from craft shop opposite, parties welcome – catering by arrangement.*

BAYTREE NURSERIES AND GARDEN CENTRE
HIGH ROAD, WESTON, SPALDING, LINCOLNSHIRE PE12 6JU
TEL: 01406 370242 FAX: 01406 371665

Begun as a modest small-holding in 1970, **Baytree Nurseries and Garden Centre** is the place where both the specialist and beginner can explore every aspect of gardening and garden life in an impressive complex ranging over 30 acres. The sheer scale and diversity of this garden centre and nursery are truly impressive. It is laid out as a series of delightful surprises, with changing exhibitions and attractions of interest to all the family.

Baytree is famous for its roses, with over 250 varieties, from Hybrid Teas to Floribundas, ramblers, climbers, miniatures, ground cover, patio and standards.

The Owl Centre boasts one of Britain's largest and most varied collections of owls from around the world. The undercover flying arena is one of Europe's largest, with seating for more than 100 people, where visitors can enjoy an educational and exciting display of these noble birds. Recognised as a breeding centre for the Republic of South Africa, the Owl Centre now includes a hospital unit for the treatment of sick and injured owls and birds of prey, funded by donations from the public and businesses. Falconry accessories and books, videos and more are available from the 'Tu Whit Tu Whoo' gift shop. Owl Centre open daily 9.30-5.30 (winter 9.30-4); admission £2.50 (OAPs and children 4-16 £2).

Among this superlative Centre's many other features are its extensive pets and aquatic centre, bulbland (with the most comprehensive range of bulbs in the country), florist shop, mower sales and service centre, nature garden, display garden and play garden. Among the many quality items for sale are garden tools, garden furniture, outdoor plants and a range of barbecues.

The licensed Hop In Restaurant serves wholesome country food, from sandwiches to full roast dinners. *Open daily, summer 9-6; winter 9-5.*

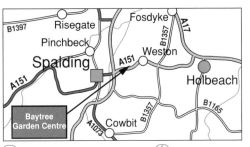

Directions:

From Spalding take the A151 towards Holbeach. Baytree Garden Centre can be found after about a mile after crossing the A16 on the left.

Aquatics	Dried & Artificial Flowers	Houseplants
Barbecues	Fencing	Information Desk
Books & Stationery	Floristry	Large Car Park
Childrens Play Area	Fruit Trees	Paving
Christmas & Seasonal Displays	Garden Design	Pet Products and/or Pets
Clothing	Garden Furniture	Plant Guarantee
Conservatories	Garden Machinery	Plants
Credit Cards Accepted	Garden Products	Restaurant/Coffee Shop
Cut Flowers	Giftware	Seeds & Bulbs
Disabled	Greenhouses & Sheds	Trees
Display Gardens		

LOCAL GARDENS

Ayscoughfee Hall and Gardens, Churchgate, Spalding 01775 725468

Set in 5 acres of walled garden, on the east bank bordering the River Welland, lovely gardens of medieval wool merchant's house enclosed by handsome old walls. Built in 1420, originally as a wool merchants house. Formal gardens date from the 17th century. Good bedding displays. The Hall is home to the Museum of South Holland Life and Spalding Tourist Information Centre, within easy walking distance of Spalding town centre. *Open: daily all year; weekdays 9-5, Sats 10-5, Suns and Bank Holidays 11-5. Entrance: free.*

Burghley House, Stamford 01780 752451

Magnificent Elizabethan house with huge art collection. Small formal rose garden with lavender, fountain, urns and oval pond. Scuplture garden with specimen trees, shrubs abd mature trees featuring contemporary works of art. The house is surrounded by a splendid example of Capability Brown's parkland design. ½m E of Stamford close to A1. *Open: garden and parkland April-3rd Oct (except 4th Sept) daily 11-4.30. House open: daily Apr 1 - Oct 3 11:00 - 4:30; closed Sep 4. Sculpture Garden open: Apr 1 - Oct 3 11:00 - 4:00: Main garden open: apr 1 - Apr 25 11:00 - 4:00. Entrance: £1; house, garden and parkland £6.10 (OAP's £5.85, Children 1 free with fee paying adult otherwise £3.00).*

Spalding Tropical Forest, Glenside North, Pinchbeck 01775 710882

Forest designed by David Stevens and enclosed by half an acre of glass. Arranged into four zones - tropical, dry tropics, temperate and oriental - each with pertinent plantings and landscaping. Dramatic water features, including a waterfall that can be walked through and ponds, streams and cascades. Particularly beautiful orchids and flowering climbers. Plants for sale in Rose Cottage water garden centre. 2m N of Spalding off theA16. *Open daily, summer 10-5.30; winter (except 25th-26th Dec) 10-4. Entrance charge to the Tropical Forest only : £2.45 (OAPs £1.99, children 5-16 £1.40).*

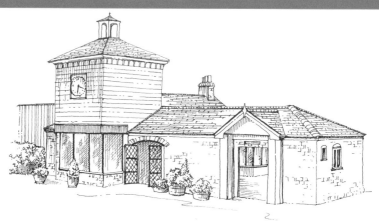

CROWDERS GARDEN CENTRE
LINCOLN ROAD, HORNCASTLE, LINCOLNSHIRE LN9 5LZ
TEL: 01507 525252 FAX: 01507 527888

Crowders Garden Centre occupies an ideal setting in rural countryside on 300 acres of growing land. One of the largest privately owned garden centres in the country, it has transformed the existing farm buildings into different departments and areas devoted to various aspects of gardening. The former stables, for instance, have been converted into the Centre's attractive information office and gift shop. The Centre is unique in having a proud history of over 200 years in the trade, always in the capable hands of the Crowder family.

Renowned throughout the UK, in 1997 Crowders was awarded two prestigious contracts: one to supply trees, shrubs and herbaceous plants to the new Number One Court at Wimbledon, the other to supply container-grown shrubs totalling 132 different varieties in a range of colours to be planted at 23 stations along the new Midland Metro line from Birmingham to Wolverhampton.

The Centre's Tree Nursery is its major feature, with a wonderful variety of fruit trees (including apple and cherry varieties), ornamental, rowan, hawthorn, native and specimen trees. Another specialisation is the large cacti selection. The locally renowned Bott's Coffee Shop/Restaurant, open Monday to Saturday 9.30-5.00 and Sunday 10.00-4.30, boasts a superb menu of home-made foods prepared onsite. Fresh produce from the gardens is used in many of the dishes, which include traditional favourites such as home-made soup, toasted sandwiches, filled baguettes and jacket potatoes, as well as a changing choice of specials like roast chicken with stuffing; steak, onion and mushroom pie; and fennel, leek and cauliflower bake. The Centre is happy to host a variety of special events throughout the year, such as tours for groups, talks and meals, annual fireworks displays and more. *Open: Mon-Fri 9.30-5, Sunday 10-5*

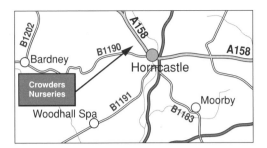

Directions:

Take the A158 out of Horncastle towards Wragby and Lincoln and Crowders Nurseries lies on the left after about 1 mile.

🔲 Barbecues	🔲 Dried & Artificial Flowers	ⓘ Information Desk
▮ Books & Stationery	◗ Fruit Trees	Ⓟ Large Car Park
🔲 Christmas & Seasonal Displays	🔲 Garden Design	🔲 Plant Guarantee
◣ Clothing	🔲 Garden Furniture	） Plants
▦ Credit Cards Accepted	🔲 Garden Products	🔲 Restaurant/Coffee Shop
⛓ Disabled	🔲 Giftware	● Seeds & Bulbs
🔲 Display Gardens	🔲 Houseplants	🔲 Trees

LOCAL GARDENS

Gunby Hall, Gunby, Spilsby (01909) 486411

The setting for Lord Tennyson's 'Haunt of Ancient Peace', National Trust 7-acre grounds surrounding 1700 hall built by Sir William Massingberd. Formal and walled gardens, herb garden, wild garden, kitchen garden with fruit trees and vegetables. Wonderful pergola garden and apple tree walkway. Old roses, herbaceous borders. Parkland with avenues of horse chestnuts and limes. 2½ m NW of Burgh-le-Marsh S of the A158. *Open: 31st Mar- 30th Sep; Garden and House Wed 2-6; Garden only Wed & Thurs 2-6; House and Garden Tues, Thurs & Fri by written arrangement with Mr J Wrisdale of Gumby Hall. Entrance: £2.50 (children £1.25); house and garden £3.50 (children £1.75).*

83 Halton Road, Spilsby (01790) 752361

Small and impressive scented cottage garden of ¼ acre and ¼-acre hardy plant nursery. Gravel walk with deep borders either side through a garden divided into a series of smaller units. Densely planted mixed borders, summerhouse, colour-themed garden. Many unusual spring bulbs, shrub roses, hardy geranium collection with over 120 varieties supplied by owners' specialist nursery. 10m W of Skegness on B1195. *Open: mid-Mar-mid-Oct Weds-Sun and Bank Holiday Mon 10-5. Entrance: collection box for charity.*

The Lawn, Union Road, Lincoln (01522) 560306

Exotic and interesting Lincoln City Council parkland with a botanic collection representing Lincoln's ties to other cities and countries throughout the world.. Sir Joseph Banks conservatory with plants arranged by areas Banks visited during his three-year voyage with Captain Cook. Water features. Off Burton Road beside Lincoln Castle. *Open: summer Mon-Fri 9-5, Sat-Sun 10-5; winter Mon-Thurs 9-5, Fri 9-4, Sat-Sun 10-4. Entrance: free (charge for parking).*

PENNELLS GARDEN CENTRE
NEWARK ROAD, SOUTH HYKEHAM, LINCOLN LN6 9NT
TEL: 01522 880033/880044 FAX: 01522 870320

Founded by Richard Pennell in 1780, **Pennells Nurseries** are among the oldest in the country. Still in the same family, the nursery developed from humble beginnings. By the 1880s, clematis species, for which the nursery remains justly famous, first started to appear in quantity in the company's catalogue. Pennells Nursery continues to supply other GCA members and trade, and has developed a deserved reputation as a leading supplier not only of clematis but also of climbers, shrubs, conifers, roses and perennials. It grows over 300,000 clematis for garden centres, making it one of the largest UK growers. It backs up the quality of its plants by a strong emphasis on service, and has recently received an Investors in People Award.

Both the nursery and its associated Garden Centre aim to maintain their tradition of excellence of product, with knowledgeable staff, professional service and advice, and a commitment to satisfying customer needs. The garden centre boasts 40,000 square feet of covered and heated shop area, with a wide selection of trees, conifers, shrubs, climbers and herbaceous perennials including herbs, rockery and alpine plants, and a range of gardening tools, seeds, bulbs and garden sundries. Houseplants and conservatory plants are very much in evidence, together with a great variety of bedding plants and garden accessories such as hanging baskets, tubs, urns and containers - whatever you require, for any season, you'll probably find it here.

The garden centre also features a range of barbecues, and its rattan wicker furniture will enhance any garden or conservatory. The Gift Shop is the place to find ceramics, books, candles and other gift ideas. The welcoming and attractive Coffee Shop serves breakfasts, lunches, snacks, cakes, pastries and drinks. *Open: Monday to Saturday 8.30-5; Sunday 10.30-4.30.*

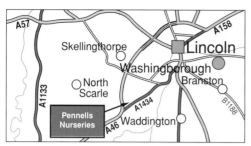

Directions:

From Lincoln take the A1434 towards Newark-on-Trent. Pennells Nurseries can be found on the right, at the junction with the A46.

- Aquatics
- Barbecues
- Books & Stationery
- Christmas & Seasonal Displays
- Conservatories
- Credit Cards Accepted
- Disabled
- Display Gardens
- Dried & Artificial Flowers

- Fencing
- Fruit Trees
- Garden Design
- Garden Furniture
- Garden Products
- Giftware
- Greenhouses & Sheds
- Houseplants

- Information Desk
- Large Car Park
- Pet Products and/or Pets
- Plant Guarantee
- Plants
- Restaurant/Coffee Shop
- Seeds & Bulbs
- Trees

LOCAL GARDENS

Aubourn Hall, Aubourn 01522 788270

Handsome gardens of 15th-century Hall, covering about 3 acres. Lawns, mixed borders, mature trees, shrubs, roses. Secluded areas include a newly planted rose garden, woodland dell, 'Golden Triangle' planted with crab apple trees. A pergola covered with late-flowering roses and clematis surrounds the swimming pool. On the grounds there is also a lovely 11th-century church, one of the smallest in Lincolnshire. 7m SW of Lincoln between the A607 and A46. *Open: Weds July-Aug 2-5. Entrance: £3 (OAPs £2.50).*

Doddington Hall, Doddington 01522 694308

Excellent walled gardens with parterres of iris, roses and clipped box edging, herbaceous borders, fountains and flag iris; wild gardens with walks leading to a turf maze, stream, ancient cedar, holly, yew and sweet chestnuts. Formal yew alley; pleached hornbeams; thousands of spring bulbs; herb garden; mature trees, all in grounds of Elizabethan manor house. 5m W of Lincoln on the B1190. *Open: Sun only Mar-April, 2-6; Weds, Sun and Bank Holiday Mon May-Sept, 2-6. House open as garden but May-Sept only. Groups by arrangement at other times. Entrance: £2.10 (children £1.05); house and garden £4.20 (children £2.10).*

Mill Hill Plants and Gardens, Elston Lane, East Stoke 01636 525460

½-acre country garden made up of a series of small gardens with many unusual hardy and half-hardy varieties. Year-round interest. This garden is a fine example of what can be achieved in an exposed north-sloping site. Adjacent nursery. 5m SW of Newark off the A46. *Open: Weds-Sun April-Sept, 10-6; Fri-Sun Oct, 10-6. Groups and individuals welcome by appointment. Entrance: £1.20 (donation to collecting box); children free.*

SQUIRE'S GARDEN CENTRE, SHEPPERTON
HALLIFORD ROAD, UPPER HALLIFORD, SHEPPERTON, MIDDLESEX TW17 8RU
TEL: 01932 784121 FAX: 01932 780569

Founded in 1935, the Squire's group is a family business which comprises seven garden centres, a rose nursery and herbaceous and bedding plant nurseries. The company seeks to maintain high standards combining quality plants and gardening products with the best service to gardeners and a tradition of working with the local community. The **Squire's Garden Centre at Shepperton** is located on the site of Squire's award-winning rose nurseries within easy reach of Hampton Court and the River Thames. This extensive Centre has a large tree and shrub area which holds a vast selection of trees, shrubs and bedding plants, and in the shop you will find a wide range of houseplants including specimen subjects, gardening products and gifts. Knowledgeable advice is available from trained staff in all departments and at the information desk.

In the rose fields a varied selection of climbing, patio, bush, standard and shrub roses are grown. Expert rose-grower Jim Phillips has over 40 years experience, and the nursery exhibits annually at the Hampton Court and Chelsea Flower Shows where they are regular medal winners. Groups are welcome to be shown around the nurseries by prior arrangement between June and August. The Centre hosts The Royal National Rose Society's Annual Southern Show during the last weekend of June in every year and exhibitors come from as far afield as Cornwall and the Midlands. In addition there are a number of individual shops on site comprising: Farm Shop, Aquatics Centre, Craft Shop, Wool Shop, Mower Shop and service centre and  Cornhill Conservatories. The licenced Orangery Tearooms serve a variety of delicious hot and cold snacks and meals. There is a children's play area at the garden centre, and baby changing and disabled facilities are available.

Special Customer Evenings are held each year offering a mixture of talks and demonstrations as well as the opportunity to wander around the Centre, browse and chat over a glass of wine. *Opening Times: Monday to Saturday 9.00 am - 6.00 pm; Sunday 10.30 am - 4.30 pm; Spring late-night opening Friday and Saturday to 7 pm. until end of June.*

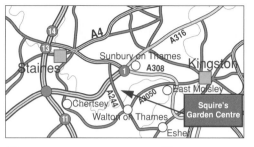

Directions:

From Junction 1 of the M3 take the Windsor road and at the first main junction turn left on the A244towards Walton-on-Thames. At the first roundabout take the left turn and then turn left into Halliford Road. Squire's Garden Centre can be found on the right.

Aquatics	Dried & Artificial Flowers	Houseplants
Barbecues	Farm Shop	Information Desk
Books & Stationery	Fencing	Large Car Park
Childrens Play Area	Fruit Trees	Paving
Christmas & Seasonal Displays	Garden Furniture	Plant Guarantee
Conservatories	Garden Machinery	Plants
Credit Cards Accepted	Garden Products	Restaurant/Coffee Shop
Disabled	Giftware	Seeds & Bulbs
Display Gardens	Greenhouses & Sheds	Trees

LOCAL GARDENS

Hampton Court Palace, East Molesey 0181 781 9500

Mixture of tastes and styles over 66 acres plus over 600 acres of informal deer park. Great Vine planted in 1768 (grapes for sale every September); world-famous maze. Fabulous bedding plants, knot garden, fountain garden, wilderness garden. Laburnum walk, rose garden, pond garden and largest herbaceous border in the south of England. Privy Garden with parterres, 17th-century plants. On A308 at junction of A309. *Open: Daily all year, dawn - dusk. Entrance: Park free; Maze £2.10 (children £1.30); Rose Gardens, Wilderness and East Front Gardens free; King William III Privy Garden, Sunken Garden and Great Vine £2 (children £1.30) - free to Palace ticket-holders.*

Royal Botanic Gardens, Kew, Richmond 0181 940 1171

This famous botanic gardens covers 300 acres and holds the finest plant collection in the world with over 35,000 different types of plants. Features include six spectacular glass-houses including the Victorian Palm House and the innovative Princess of Wales conservatory with ten different climatic zones ranging from rainforest to desert. Saesonal features include magnolias and flowering cherries in spring, bluebells and rhododendrons in early summer and beatiful autumn colour from Kew's collection of over 9,000 tree. *Open: daily 9.30 (except 25th Dec, 1st Jan). Closing times vary according to season. Glasshouses close earlier than gardens. Entrance: £5 (last hour £3.50; OAPs/students £3.50, children 5-16 £2.50, under 5's free, blind/partially sighted and wheelchair occupants free).*

The Walled Garden, Sunbury Park, Sunbury-on-Thames 01784 451499

Spelthorne Borough Council-maintained grounds of a 16th century house built for a courtier of Elizabeth I. The walled garden was developed in 1985. Knot gardens with lavender and box, modern roses, parterres, attractive climbers. Pergola leading to Victorian rose beds. Island beds of plants from all over the world. Summertime art exhibitions and band con-certs. On Thames Street in Sunbury via the B375. *Open: all year daily (except 25th Dec) 8-8 or 30 minutes after sunset whichever is the earlier. Entrance: free.*

SQUIRE'S GARDEN CENTRE, TWICKENHAM
SIXTH CROSS ROAD, TWICKENHAM, MIDDLESEX TW2 5PA
TEL: 0181 977 9241 FAX: 0181 977 9241

Founded in 1935, the Squire's group is a family business which comprises seven garden centres, a rose nursery and herbaceous and bedding plant nurseries. The company seeks to maintain high standards combining quality plants and gardening products with the best service to gardeners and a tradition of working with the local community.

The **Squire's Garden Centre at Twickenham** is the flagship of the company. It was the national winner of the Garden Centre of the Year Award 1998/99. The Centre was totally rebuilt in 1993 on the site of the original Squire's Garden Centre which opened in 1964. It has one of the finest selections of trees, shrubs and garden plants in southwest London. Its plant area is an oasis amid the bustling urban sprawl. There is a dedicated advice desk in the plant area manned by qualified staff, as well as the information desk situated in the large shop. Inside the shop there is an enormous range of gardening products, pet products, gifts, garden furniture and cane furniture.

On the site you will also find a DIY Department, Conservatories, a Conservatory Blind Shop, a Mower Shop and Service Centre, Chair Caning and a specialist Florist Shop.

The licenced Plantation Cafe serves delicious hot and cold food, often to the accompaniment of live music played on a grand piano. The Centre also has baby changing and disabled facilities. The Centre is host to many horticultural shows, demonstrations and talks throughout the year. Special Customer Evenings are held each year, offering a mixture of talks and demonstrations as well as the opportunity to wander around the Centre, browse and chat over a glass of wine. *Opening Times: Monday to Saturday 9.00 am - 6.00 pm; Sunday 10.30 am - 4.30 pm; Spring late-night opening Wednesday to Saturday to 7 pm. until end of June.*

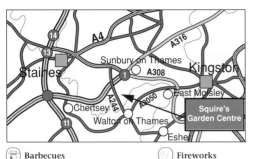

Directions:

From Junction 1 of the M3 take the A316 towards London and at the third slip road take the A305 towards Twickenham. Turn right at Sixth Cross Road and Squire's Garden Centre can be found on the right.

Barbecues	Fireworks	Information Desk
Books & Stationery	Floristry	Large Car Park
Christmas & Seasonal Displays	Fruit Trees	Paving
Clothing	Garden Furniture	Pet Products and/or Pets
Conservatories	Garden Machinery	Plant Guarantee
Credit Cards Accepted	Garden Products	Plants
Cut Flowers	Giftware	Restaurant/Coffee Shop
Disabled	Greenhouses & Sheds	Seeds & Bulbs
Dried & Artificial Flowers	Houseplants	Trees
Fencing		

LOCAL GARDENS

Hampton Court Palace, East Molesey 0181 781 9500

Mixture of tastes and styles over 66 acres plus over 600 acres of informal deer park. Great Vine planted in 1768 (grapes for sale every September); world-famous maze. Fabulous bedding plants, knot garden, fountain garden, wilderness garden. Laburnum walk, rose garden, pond garden and largest herbaceous border in the south of England. Privy Garden with parterres, 17th-century plants. On A308 at junction of A309. *Open: Daily all year, dawn - dusk. Entrance: Park free; Maze £2.10 (children £1.30); Rose Gardens, Wilderness and East Front Gardens free; King William III Privy Garden, Sunken Garden and Great Vine £2 (children £1.30) - free to Palace ticket-holders.*

Royal Botanic Gardens, Kew, Richmond 0181 940 1171

This famous botanic gardens covers 300 acres and holds the finest plant collection in the world with over 35,000 different types of plants. Features include six spectacular glass-houses including the Victorian Palm House and the innovative Princess of Wales conservatory with ten different climatic zones ranging from rainforest to desert. Saesonal features include magnolias and flowering cherries in spring, bluebells and rhododendrons in early summer and beatiful autumn colour from Kew's collection of over 9,000 tree. *Open: daily 9.30 (except 25th Dec, 1st Jan). Closing times vary according to season. Glasshouses close earlier than gardens. Entrance: £5 (last hour £3.50; OAPs/students £3.50, children 5-16 £2.50, under 5's free, blind/partially sighted and wheelchair occupants free).*

Ham House, Richmond 0181 940 1950

National Trust restored 17th-century garden. Paths divide eight large square lawns. Parterres of lavender, box and cotton lavender. Replicas of 17th-century garden furniture. Gravel terrace, hibiscus, pomegranate trees, clipped yew cones. The orangery, dating back to the 1600s, thought to be the oldest surviving example of its type in the UK. S bank of Thames W of A307. *Open: Sat-Weds all year, 10.30-6 or dusk except 25/26 Dec and 1 Jan. Entrance: £1.50 (Children £0.75). House open Apr-Oct 1-5 at additional charge of £3.50*

BAWDESWELL GARDEN CENTRE
A1067 FAKENHAM - NORWICH ROAD, EAST DEREHAM, NORFOLK NR20 4ST
TEL: 01362 688387 FAX: 01362 688504

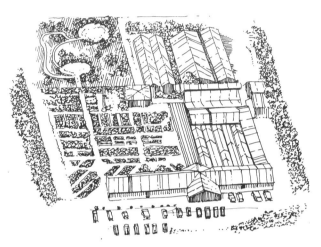

Bawdeswell Garden Centre began as a nursery back in 1973, and has evolved into a specialist conifer nursery and thriving gardening centre. Since the early 1990s owners Peter and Judy Underwood have expanded the plant production side, growing an increasing range of pot plants, patio plants, shrubs and perennials. The Centre places great emphasis on providing full and helpful information on each plant, which is ably backed up by the staff's knowledge and courteous attention. In addition, the Centre boasts an experienced team of landscape designers who can advise on both hard and soft landscaping. The impressive landscaped area on-site highlights some of the unusual and appealing plants available. Other attractive features include seasonal displays, such as the special Christmas display from October onwards, demonstrating many good ideas for decorating home and garden.

A specialist feature of this Garden Centre is its range of garden furniture. It sells all types including cane, wrought-iron and resin furnishings, offering one of the largest selections in the region. Be it loungers, tables, patio furniture, hammocks or deck chairs, the centre can provide a range of choices to suit every taste and pocket.

There's also a comprehensive selection of garden materials and tools, outdoor wear and pet supplies. The Plant Guide is a detailed book produced by the Centre - a must for every gardener, from the novice to the professional, available from the wonderful bookshop. The Centre's small and cosy coffee shop serves snacks and light meals as well as teas, coffees and soft drinks. The Gift Shop has a range of body-care products, craftware, ornaments, cards and more. Home-made treats for sale include preserves, pickles and other tempting traditional favourites. *Open: Mon-Sat 8-5.30(Summer), 8-5 (Winter); Sun 10.30-4.30; Bank Holidays 10-5*

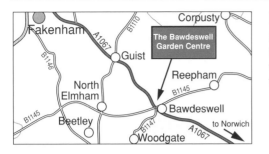

Directions:

Bawdeswell Garden Centre lies on the A1067 half way between Norwich and Fakenham in the small village of Bawdeswell.

Aquatics	Fencing	Information Desk
Barbecues	Fruit Trees	Large Car Park
Books & Stationery	Garden Construction	Paving
Christmas & Seasonal Displays	Garden Design	Pet Products and/or Pets
Clothing	Garden Furniture	Plant Guarantee
Conservatories	Garden Products	Plants
Credit Cards Accepted	Giftware	Restaurant/Coffee Shop
Disabled	Greenhouses & Sheds	Seeds & Bulbs
Display Gardens	Houseplants	Trees
Dried & Artificial Flowers		

LOCAL GARDENS

Blickling Hall, Aylsham, Norwich 01263 738030

Large National Trust gardens, with features from the 17th-20th centuries. Rhododendrons, azaleas, herbaceous borders, surrounding historic Jacobean house. Samuel Wyatt orangery (1782), massive yew hedges, parterre (1870, planned by Wyatt and Nesfield). Topiary pillars, pool with 17th-century fountain. Doric temple dating to 1730, cedars of Lebanon, magnolias, parkland beyond. Gothic Tower (1773) and Mausoleum (1796). Cream teas and lunches. 1½ mile NW of Aylsham off the B1354. *Open: house 27th Mar-Oct, Weds-Sun 1-4.30; gardens 27th Mar-July and Sept-Oct Weds-Sun, Bank Holiday Mon, Aug daily; all 10.30-5.30; Nov-Mar Sat-Sun 11-4. Entrance: £3.50 (house and gardens £6.20).*

Castle Acre Priory, Castle Acre, King's Lynn 01760 755394

Interesting walled herb garden in four divisions: medicinal, strewing, culinary and decorative herbs. Three 16th-century apple trees, lavenders. The central circular bed features an attractive bay tree. ¼m W of Castle Acre, 5m N of Swaffham, off A1065. *Open: summer daily 10-6; winter Weds-Sun 10-1, 2-4. Entrance: £3.10 (concs £2.30, children £1.60, under 3's free).*

Mannington Hall, Saxthorpe, Norwich 01263 584175

20-acre garden with shrubs, trees, roses, lake, surrounding moated 15th-century manor house (not open to the public). Daffodil-lined drive, lawns down to the moat with drawbridge. Secret scented garden, flowering shrubs, herbaceous borders, rose gardens featuring 1,500 varieties, highlighting types popular from medieval times to the present. Lake, woods, meadowland, extensive country trails and walks. Saxon church ruins on the grounds, as well as 19th-century follies. Teas and lunches. 18m NW of Norwich off the B1149. *Open: May-Sept Sun noon-5; June-Aug Weds-Fri 11-5. Entrance: £3 (concs £2.50, children free).*

PODINGTON GARDEN CENTRE
HIGH STREET, PODINGTON, WELLINGBOROUGH, NORTHAMPTONSHIRE NN29 7HS
TEL: 01933 353656 FAX: 01933 410332 WEBSITE: www.podington.co.uk

Podington Garden Centre is set in rolling countryside, approached through a leafy driveway that leads into the vast expanse of this purpose-built *'Plant Persons' paradise'*. Established in 1977 by the Read family, it remains a family-run organisation, inspired by the enthusiasm and dedication of the Reads. They take pride in the centre's dedication to quality, choice and presentation. There is something for every gardener here, with an exceptional range of plants for the garden and home complemented by an impressive selection of garden furniture, ornamental fish - everything you need to make the most of your garden.

The award-winning plant area boasts an enormous selection of thousands of finest quality garden plants. Presented on raised beds for easy access, there are over 1,000 species of shrubs, more than 450 species of conifers and over 250 species of ornamental trees, together with herbaceous plants, alpines, heathers and bedding plants. The centre's all-weather covered area is home to ever-changing and colourful displays of seasonal favourites. The garden shop stocks seeds, chemicals, hose fittings, tools, ceramics, books, beautiful giftware, pots, trays, compost and more.

In the houseplant conservatory you will find old favourites and more unusual flowering and foliage plants in an exciting range of varieties and colours. The displays are changed weekly, and also feature planted bowls, bottled gardens, cacti and air plants. In addition to all this there are landscaping materials - paving and walling, rockery stone, statuary, trellises, fencing and more - and a comprehensive aquatics and pet department.

Another delightful feature of this garden centre is The Gnomes' Kitchen, where you can stop and recharge your batteries over elevenses, meals, snacks, cakes and beverages in charming and comfortable surroundings. *Open: Monday to Saturday 9.00-6.30 (9.00-5.30 during winter), Thursday 9.00-8.00, Sunday 10.30-4.30.*

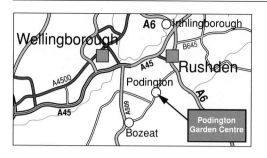

Direction:

Take the road to Podington from the A6 just south of Rushden and Podington Garden Centre is in Podington High Street after about 2 miles. The route from the A509 is reasonably well signposted from Bozeat.

Aquatics	Floristry	Information Desk
Barbecues	Fruit Trees	Large Car Park
Books & Stationery	Garden Construction	Paving
Christmas & Seasonal Displays	Garden Design	Pet Products and/or Pets
Clothing	Garden Furniture	Plant Guarantee
Credit Cards Accepted	Garden Machinery	Plants
Disabled	Garden Products	Restaurant/Coffee Shop
Display Gardens	Giftware	Seeds & Bulbs
Dried & Artificial Flowers	Greenhouses & Sheds	Trees
Fencing	Houseplants	

LOCAL GARDENS

Cottesbrook Hall Gardens, Cottesbrook 01604 505808

Grounds of handsome Queen Anne house. Gardens are notable for their great variety of trees, shrubs and plantings, including herbaceous borders and fine old cedars and specimen trees. Wild garden, water garden. 'Dilemma' garden, Statue Walk. 10m N of Northampton between the A508 and A5199. *Open: Easter -End Sept Tues-Fri and Bank Holiday Mon, also Sept Tues-Sun, 2-5.30 (last admission 5). Parties by appointment other weekdays. House open Easter - End Sept Thurs and Bank Holiday Mon, Sept Thurs/Sat/Sun/Bank Holiday Mon, hours as for gardens. Entrance: £2.50 (children £1.25); house and gardens £4 (children £2).*

Delapre Abbey, London Road, Northampton 01604 761704

Northampton Borough Council 500-acre parkland with walled former kitchen garden, rose beds, annual and perennial beds, lawns, wilderness garden, lily ponds, good trees and shrubberies. 18th-century thatched game larder. Lakes and golf course. Near the entrance stands one of the Queen Eleanor Crosses marking the 1290 funeral route of Edward I's queen. 1m S of Northampton on the A508. *Open: daily Mar-Sept 10-dusk. Park open all year. Entrance: free.*

Castle Ashby Gardens, Castle Ashby 01604 696696

Parkland (not open to the general public) including an avenue planted at the suggestion of King William III in 1695. Capability Brown landscaping includes the lakes. Extensive lawns and trees, nature trail. Matthew Digby Wyatt Italian gardens with orangery, terrace and arboretum. Topiary. 5m E of Northampton between A428 and A45. *Open: daily 10-dusk, though ring for details because house and gardens sometimes hired out. Entrance: £2.50 (OAPs £1, children over 10 £1) - when entrance is unattended, tickets from machine.*

HEIGHLEY GATE GARDEN CENTRE
MORPETH, NORTHUMBERLAND NE61 3DA
TEL: 01670 513416 FAX: 01670 510013 EMAIL: office@heighley-gate.co.uk

Heighley Gate Garden Centre boasts the largest and best-stocked plant areas in the northeast. This combined with fully trained staff and competitive prices make it a plant-lover's paradise. The centre buys plants from throughout Europe to offer the best quality and choice, with large conifers and shrubs from Italy, trees and shrubs from Holland and, of course, an enormous amount of British plant material. One of the only garden centres in the area providing its own quality nursery-grown plants, it produces over 1 million home-grown plants every year, including an impressive range of large and small herbaceous plants, annual bedding and dwarf conifers. The conifer section is second to none, having recently been recognised in a national competition as being the best in the UK.

To complement the range of plants the centre - a Thai and Vietnamese terracotta specialist - displays a large selection of pots, tubs and urns. The large selection of stone fountains, statues and ornaments by Henri Studio ranges from the smallest animal or wall fountain to the beautiful three- and four-tiered fountains, all of which can be seen up and running at the centre.

There is also a beautiful and varied choice of silk, fabric and dried flowers, and a fabulous selection of seedlings available. The attractive coffee shop commands magnificent views overlooking fields, woods and moors for miles around. All this and a superb Pets and Aquatics centre, range of tools and garden accessories, garden buildings, conservatory and garden furniture, paving and fencing, cut flowers, fruit and vegetables, and large display of gifts and books makes this a one-stop shop for all your gardening needs. *Open: summer Monday to Friday 9-5.30; winter Monday to Friday 9-5; all year Saturday and Bank Holidays 9.30-5, Sundays 10.30-4.30.*

Directions:
From the A1/A697 junction take the A697 towards Longhorsley. Heighley Gate Garden Centre is on the left hand side.

Aquatics	Dried & Artificial Flowers	Houseplants
Barbecues	Farm Shop	Information Desk
Books & Stationery	Fencing	Large Car Park
Childrens Play Area	Floristry	Paving
Christmas & Seasonal Displays	Fruit Trees	Pet Products and/or Pets
Clothing	Garden Furniture	Plant Guarantee
Conservatories	Garden Machinery	Plants
Credit Cards Accepted	Garden Products	Restaurant/Coffee Shop
Cut Flowers	Giftware	Seeds & Bulbs
Disabled	Greenhouses & Sheds	Trees
Display Gardens		

LOCAL GARDENS

Alnwick Castle, Alnwick 01665 510777; Sat-Sun 01665 603942

Plans are afoot, under the direction of the Duchess of Northumberland, for an amazing high-tech water garden here amid the existing Capability Brown landscape, with its 12-acre Italianate walled garden (now sadly derelict) designed by Nesfield and its towering yew hedges, beech, oak and hornbeam. The water garden will have a cascade through the centre of the garden and a spiral wall of ice growing and disintegrating throughout the day. Educational facilities and a garden for the blind will also feature. Fusiliers Museum in castle. 30m N of Newcastle off the A1. *Open: daily April-Sept 11-5 (last admission 4.15). Castle opens at noon. Entrance: £5.95 (OAPs £5.45, children £3.50, family £15).*

Cragside House, Rothbury, Morpeth 01669 620333

Formal 'High Victorian'-style garden created by the first Lord Armstrong. Fully restored orchard house, dahlia walk, carpet bedding with displays. Fernery, 3½-acre rock garden. Further extensive grounds of more than 1,000 acres famous for its beautiful lakes and excellent rhododendrons. 13m SW of Alnwick off the A697. *Open: Tues-Sun and Bank Holiday Mondays April-end Oct 10.30-7 (last admission 5); Nov-Dec weekends and selected days 10.30-4. House open as for grounds, 1-5.30 (last admission 4.45). Entrance: garden, grounds and exhibition £3.95 (house, garden and grounds £6.20).*

Ashfield, Hebron 01670 515616

5-acre garden that's a real showpiece, with colourful herbaceous borders, woodland plantings with acer, betula, sorbus. Interesting shrub and tree groupings. Alpines, many bulbs, dwarf conifers. Woodland walks pass hellbores, hostas and other shade-lovers. 3m N of Morpeth off the C130. *Open: all year by appointment. Entrance: £1.50.*

DUKERIES GARDEN CENTRE
WELBECK, WORKSOP, NOTTINGHAMSHIRE S80 3LT
TEL: 01909 476506 FAX: 01909 482047

Dukeries Garden Centre is set in 11 acres of the beautiful walled garden of Welbeck Abbey, where an ongoing programme of refurbishment has seen it grow into one of the most popular garden centres in the East Midlands. Established in 1985 on the vast Welbeck Estate (the largest working estate in the country), the historic greenhouses, which once grew all the produce for the Duke of Portland's estate, were installed by the 5th Duke in 1876. They have been restored and make an elegant backdrop for the centre's vast range of shrubs and plants, and are themselves crammed with every type of plant and flower. These greenhouses (all original and carefully restored) are linked by one long glass gallery which is 100 yards long.

The range and quality of the plants on sale here are second to none. The centre grows the majority of its bedding plants on site. All staff are horticulturally trained, and are on hand not only to help you find exactly what you want, but also to give you expert advice and answer any questions. The centre also hosts topical demonstrations to help you get the most enjoyment from the plants you buy.

In addition to its superb range of plants, the centre also has an extensive selection of garden ornaments, garden furniture, conservatories and garden sheds. The licenced Welbeck Restaurant, housed in one of the glass lean-to greenhouses, serves morning coffee, home-made lunches, afternoon teas and all-day snacks. All food is home-made on the premises. The restaurant is recommended by the Egon Ronay Lite Bite Guide. The centre's Gift Shop is a cornucopia of ceramics, glass, pictures, candles, dried and silk flowers together with a tempting range of specialist foods. *Open: Mar to Oct daily 9-6; Nov to Feb daily 9.30-5.*

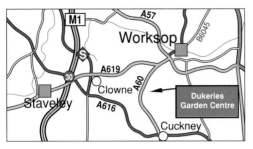

Directions:

From junction 30 of the M1 take the A619 towards Worksop. After 5 miles turn right onto the A60 and Dukeries Garden Centre can be found on the left.

🍴 Barbecues	🌿 Floristry	ⓘ Information Desk
📕 Books & Stationery	🌳 Fruit Trees	🧍 Plant Guarantee
🎄 Christmas & Seasonal Displays	🪑 Garden Furniture	) Plants
👕 Clothing	🌲 Garden Products	🍴 Restaurant/Coffee Shop
ECO Credit Cards Accepted	🏛 Giftware	☀ Seeds & Bulbs
♿ Disabled	🌱 Houseplants	🌳 Trees
💐 Dried & Artificial Flowers		

LOCAL GARDENS

Clumber Park, Clumber Estate Office, Clumber Park, Worksop 01909 476592

National Trust. Pleasure gardens and Lincoln terrace laid out by W Sawrey Gilpin early in the 19th century. 3,800 acres of parkland. Vinery and palm house; the extensive (138-metre) glasshouses are the longest and best in the Trust's properties. Walled kitchen garden with herb border, vegetable and fruit border, old apple tree varieties and Victorian apiary still in working order. Kitchen garden exhibition of late 19th- and early 20th-century gardening tools. Handsome cedar avenue. 4½m SE of Worksop off the A1/A57. *Open: daily all year during daylight hours. Garden, Vineries and Tool exhibition open April-Sept weekends and Bank Holiday Mondays 11-5 (last admission 4.30). Entrance: 70p (children 30p, under-8s free); cars £3, coaches £7 (£14 weekends and Bank Holidays).*

Brodsworth Hall, Brodsworth 01302 722598

15 acres of grounds of Italianate house being restored to their original Victorian grandeur. Mixed borders of ferns, fuchsias, Japanese anemones, aconites, daylilies; evergreen shrubberies. Marble fountain, folly temples. Flower dell, rose garden, thyme garden with nearly 100 varieties. The only complete collection of the Portland group of roses; other historic roses as well. 6m NW of Doncaster off the A635. *Open: April-Oct Tues-Sun and Bank Holiday Mon noon-5. House open as gardens, but 1-5. Entrance: £2.60 (concessions £2.00, children £1.30). Hall and gardens £4.70 (concessions £3.50, children £2.40).*

Rufford Country Park, Ollerton 01623 823148

Nottinghamshire County Council. Mature cedars, lime avenues, lakes. Within the formal gardens there are 8 themed gardens. New rose garden in front of Abbey ruins. Arboretum with good collection of birches and oaks. 2m S of Ollerton on the A614. *Open: Daily all year, Country Park open dawn-dusk. After 5.30 parking only available at Rufford Mill. Please phone for details. Rufford Abbey Cistercian area also open. Entrance: free. Car park charge weekends April-Oct, Bank Holidays and school summer holidays.*

THE BURFORD GARDEN COMPANY
SHILTON ROAD, BURFORD, OXON OX18 4PA
TEL: 01993 823117/3285/2502 FAX: 01993 823529 WEBSITE: www.bgc.co.uk

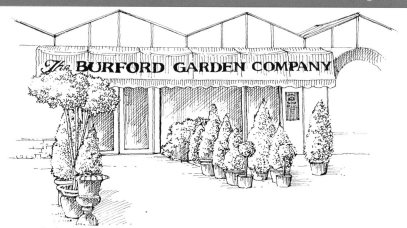

Set on a slight rise, with wonderful views around of Cotswolds, **The Burford Garden Company** began as a small family concern in 1977, as a nursery growing plants and vegetables. Over the years it has grown into a thriving business, and now boasts a total of 40,000 square feet of purpose-designed indoor and covered sales area. This winner of prestigious awards at the Chelsea Flower Show and the Royal Show, this environmentally-conscious Centre features an outdoor Plantarea accommodating large stocks of a great variety of plants and trees - including 460 different roses, 75 types of clematis and 300 species of herbaceous plants. There is also a dedicated section of garden leisure buildings and other wood structures.

Other special departments, all staffed by horticulturalists or other experts in their particular field, include those devoted to house and conservatory plants, including palms and citrus fruit trees, garden sundries, ornamental stoneware and terracotta, gifts - including a full range of wax jackets and fleeces, wellies, scarves and gloves, as well as many attractive and luxury products not usually seen elsewhere - pets, aquatics,

foodworks - for fresh and gourmet foods and wines - and the Bookshop, with over 1,800 gardening books and a comprehensive range of video cassettes. There's a very exciting toy shop - if you can lure the children away from the super outdoor and indoor play areas.

English home cooking can be enjoyed in the acclaimed terraced Planters Restaurant; other services offered include a baby changing room, wheelchairs for customer use, and delivery within a range of 30 miles. *Open: Jan-Feb Mon-Weds 9-5.30, Thurs-Sat 9-6, Sun 11-5; Mar-Dec Mon-Weds and Sats 9-6.00, Thurs, Fri 9-7, Sun 11-5; closed 25th-26th Dec.*

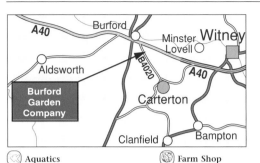

Directions:

Take the A40 towards Oxford from the centre of Burford and immediately turn right onto the B4020 towards Carterton. Burford Garden Centre is on the left.

(⊙) Aquatics	(🐷) Farm Shop	(⌒) Greenhouses & Sheds
(🍖) Barbecues	(▥) Fencing	(✿) Houseplants
(📖) Books & Stationery	(✳) Fireworks	(ⓘ) Information Desk
(T) Childrens Play Area	(🌼) Floristry	(Ⓟ) Large Car Park
(☀) Christmas & Seasonal Displays	(🌳) Fruit Trees	(▦) Paving
(⌐) Clothing	(✄) Garden Construction	(🐾) Pet Products and/or Pets
(⌐) Conservatories	(✿) Garden Design	(🌱) Plant Guarantee
CC Credit Cards Accepted	(▤) Garden Furniture	(}) Plants
(🌸) Cut Flowers	(🚜) Garden Machinery	(¶¶) Restaurant/Coffee Shop
(♿) Disabled	(🪓) Garden Products	(☁) Seeds & Bulbs
(❄) Display Gardens	(📷) Giftware	(🌴) Trees
(🍾) Dried & Artificial Flowers		

LOCAL GARDENS

Blenheim Palace, Woodstock, Oxford 01993 811325

Grounds and gardens originally planned by Henry Wise, Queen Anne's master gardener, with landscaping, lake and cascade created by 'Capability' Brown. Herb and lavender garden, kitchen garden, Italian garden, maze (planted 1991). Formal gardens by Achille Duchene, with two Versailles-style water terraces. Cedar grove. Butterfly house, restaurant and cafeteria. 8m NW of Oxford off A44. *Open: mid-Mar-Oct 10.30-5.30 (last admission 4.45). House open as garden; park open all year except 25th Dec from 9. Entrance: gardens only £3; house and gardens £7.80 (OAPs £5.80, children £3.80); park only £1 (child 50p, cars inc occupants £5).*

Buscot Park, Faringdon 01367 240786

Surrounding late 18th-century house, 20th-century established garden. Avenues of weeping oak, lime and beech, water garden. Large walled kitchen garden, Judas tree tunnel and pleached avenue of hop hornbeam (ostrya). Old roses and climbing vegetables mixed to great effect. A417 between Lechlade and Faringdon. *Open: April-Sept Mon-Fri and second and fourth Sat and following Sunday every month 2-6 (last admission 5.30); house closed Mon-Tues. Entrance: £3.30 (children £1.65); house and grounds £4.40 (children £2.20).*

Kelmscott Manor, Kelmscott, Lechlade 01367 252486

A treat for anyone interested in the Pre-Raphaelites and in particular Willilam Morris. Morris planted this garden, seeking to capture the feel and romantic appeal of nature untamed, and the sense that a garden is a place filled with and meant for magic and mystery. 3m E of Lechlade. *Open: April-Sept Weds 11-1, 2-5, third Sat of the month 2-5. In addition first Sat in Jul and Aug 2-5. Tours for parties by arrangement Thurs and Fri; house open as garden. Entrance £6.00. Gardens only £2.00*

MILLETS FARM GARDEN CENTRE
KINGSTON ROAD, FRILFORD, NR ABINGDON OX13 5HB
TEL: 01865 391923 FAX: 01865 391567

Founded in 1987, **Millets Farm Garden Centre** shares its rural location with an excellent Farmshop, Pick-Your-Own and two Restaurants. The whole site has been sympathetically designed to complement surrounding Oxfordshire countryside. The Garden Centre has been a finalist in the Garden Centre of the Year Award, and prides itself on providing quality plants and products, value for money and unrivalled service. Set in the Vale of the White Horse, with rolling green countryside as a backdrop, the centre has an area devoted to farm animals and peacocks to visit and enjoy, helping to make a visit to Millets Farm a good day out for the whole family.

As with its sister centres - Willington near Bedford and Frosts at Woburn Sands - the garden centre guarantees all trees, shrubs and hardy garden plants sold for two years, and all foliage houseplants carry a 12-month guarantee. There is certainly a wealth of stock to choose from, with a fine range of healthy blooms, foliage plants, trees, shrubs, herbs, bedding and garden plants to fill your home, office, conservatory or garden with a myriad of different scents, colours and textures. Horticulturally trained staff are on hand to offer knowledgeable and courteous advice or information, and the Garden Centre's plant experts are here to help you in selecting the right plant for the correct location, whilst in the aquatic department staff are trained to give advice on water gardening and pond keeping.

The Garden Centre offers a professional design service. However, the landscaped grounds provide plenty of inspiration for those wishing to undertake a garden make-over themselves. Garden buildings, water features and landscape materials are displayed alongside imaginative planting schemes to provide a host of good ideas. A comprehensive range of cane, aluminium, cast iron and wooden garden furniture is available, together with a good selection of barbecues. There is a superb gift department, large displays of silk and dried flowers, interesting china and glassware, stationery and books.

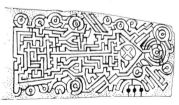

The Millets Farm Maize Maze, which achieved national and international press coverage when it first opened, is replanted annually to a different design and is open from August to October. *Open: opening hours are revised seasonally; please ring for details.*

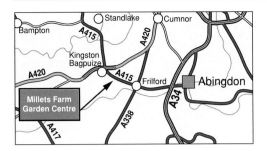

Directions:

From the Abingdon turning on the A34 take the A415 towards Witney. Millets Farm Garden Centre is on the left just after crossing the A338.

Aquatics	Dried & Artificial Flowers	Houseplants
Barbecues	Farm Shop	Information Desk
Books & Stationery	Fencing	Large Car Park
Childrens Play Area	Fruit Trees	Paving
Christmas & Seasonal Displays	Garden Construction	Pick Your Own
Clothing	Garden Design	Plant Guarantee
Conservatories	Garden Furniture	Plants
Credit Cards Accepted	Garden Machinery	Restaurant/Coffee Shop
Cut Flowers	Garden Products	Seeds & Bulbs
Disabled	Giftware	Trees
Display Gardens	Greenhouses & Sheds	

LOCAL GARDENS

Stanton Harcourt Manor, Stanton Harcourt, Witney 01865 880117

12 acres of grounds of the ruins of an impressive 14th- and 15th-century stone manor house with Chapel and Pope's Tower. Formal gardens, avenue of yews, herbaceous and rose borders, clematis, climbing roses, hydrangeas. Woodland area. Remains of moat and mediaeval stew ponds with water lilies, water-loving plants. Teas in mediaeval Great Kitchen. 9m W of Oxford, 5m SE of Witney off B4449. *Open: ring for details. Entrance: House and garden £4 (OAPs and children under 12 £2); garden only £2.50 (OAPs/children £1.50).*

Old Church House, 2 Priory Road, Wantage 01235 762785

Striking town garden running down to the Letcombe Brook. An exciting example of what can be achieved in under three years, it is set out as a series of rooms, with interspersed follies, water, mature trees. Sunken water garden, pergola garden, wild garden, Mediterranean garden. Tickets and teas at Vale & Downland Museum opposite. At junction of A417/A338. *Open: April-Oct Tues-Sat 10.30-4.30, Sun 2-5; private visits by arrangement. Entrance: £1 or donation to parish church next door (children free).*

Oxford Botanic Garden, Rose Lane, Oxford 01865 276920

Oldest botanic garden in Britain, founded in 1621, with 8,00 Magnificent Nicholas Stone gateway. One surviving yew; annuals and herbaceous plants, bog garden, roses, clematis, rock garden. National Collection of euphorbias. Opposite Magdalen College near bridge. *Open: April-Sept daily 9-5 (glasshouses 10-4.30), Oct-Mar daily 9-4.30 (glasshouses 10-4). Closed Easter Day and Xmas Day. Entrance: April-Aug £2 (children under 12 free); Sept-Mar by donation.*

BAYLEYS GARDEN CENTRE
BAYSTON HILL, SHREWSBURY, SHROPSHIRE SY3 0DA
TEL: 01743 874261 FAX: 01743 874208

Bayleys Garden Centre is situated on the edge of the medieval town of Shrewsbury in Shropshire. It is a county which has many outstanding gardens open to the public through the National Gardens Scheme, and every August the popular and prestigious Shrewsbury Flower Show draws thousands of visitors. Bayleys have won many awards for their displays at this show over the years. The centre combines a modern, attractive layout with traditional values of quality and service. Throughout the year you will find an extensive range of quality trees, roses, shrubs, alpines, conifers, heathers, herbaceous plants, fruit bushes and bedding plants.

During the first half of the year the Garden Centre has an extensive range of lawn products, tools, fertilisers, composts, bedding, seeds and hanging baskets. This is the busiest time of year in the garden. After the hard work is done, it's time to relax - and there's an excellent range of quality garden and cane furniture, barbecues and all accessories to help you do just that!

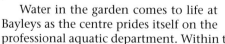

Water in the garden comes to life at Bayleys as the centre prides itself on the professional aquatic department. Within this area there is also a pet centre stocking small animals and birds - a great favourite with the children.

With the arrival of autumn the emphasis is again on planting and preparing the garden for winter and the following spring. The centre has a spectacular Christmas display of trees, garlands, lights, decorations and animated figures. The range of books, gifts and cards is extended for the Christmas season and people come from far and wide to do their Christmas shopping here.

Whatever the time of year the experienced and friendly staff are always available to give help and advice to customers. *Open: Mon-Thur and Sat 8.30-6, Fri 8.30-8, Sun 11-5.*

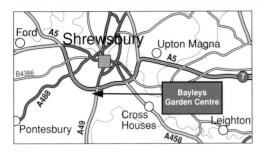

Directions

Bayleys Garden Centre lies adjacent to the Service area on the A5 Shrewsbury by-pass at the junction of the by-pass and the A49 to Church Stretton

Aquatics		Dried & Artificial Flowers		Information Desk
Barbecues		Fencing		Large Car Park
Books & Stationery		Fireworks		Paving
Childrens Play Area		Fruit Trees		Pet Products and/or Pets
Christmas & Seasonal Displays		Garden Furniture		Plant Guarantee
Clothing		Garden Products		Plants
Conservatories		Giftware		Restaurant/Coffee Shop
Credit Cards Accepted		Greenhouses & Sheds		Seeds & Bulbs
Disabled		Houseplants		Trees

LOCAL GARDENS

Hodnet Hall, Market Drayton 01630 685202

A 60-acre landscaped garden with great autumn colour provided by the magnificent acers, birches and sorbus. Grouped round a series of water gardens and lakes, with a great variety of flowers providing year-round colour: azaleas, magnolias and rhododendrons followed by fuchsias, gunneras, astilbes and water lilies. Also shrub roses, tree peonies and herbaceous borders. Teas and light lunches. 12m NE of Shrewsbury, at A53/A442 junction. *Open: April-Sept Tues-Sun and Bank Holiday Mon noon-5. Entrance: £3 (OAP £2.50, children £1.20).*

Attingham Park, Attingham, Shrewsbury 01743 709203

National Trust parkland set round grand neo-classical house. Landscaped by Leggett and Repton; spring daffodils, then azaleas and rhododendrons; autumn colour provided by the dogwoods and American thorns. Large trees and shrubs - grove of Lebanon cedars. Deer park, choice of walks. Naturalised narcissi along the river bank.18th-century orangery. Tea room. 4m SE of Shrewsbury off B4380. *Open: late Mar-Oct, Fri-Tues 1.30-5; Bank Holiday Mon 11-5. Parties by arrangement. Entrance: £1.80 (children 90p; house and grounds £4/£2).*

Acton Scott Historic Working Farm, Nr Church Stretton 01694 781306/7

Living history with heavy horse work, vintage machinery, rare breeds, butter making, hand milking and farm cottage. There are special events including craft demonstrations as well as facilities for children such as children's maze and picnic area. Shop and cafe on site but sorry no dogs. *Open: 30 Mar-31 Oct Tues, Sun & Bank Holidays 10-5. Adm: adults £3.50, Snr Citizens £3.00, Children £1.50 (under 5's free).*

PERCY THROWER'S GARDENING CENTRE
OTELEY ROAD, SHREWSBURY, SHROPSHIRE SY2 6QW
TEL: 01743 352311 FAX: 01743 351614 WEBSITE: www.percy.thrower.co.uk

Percy Thrower's Gardening Centre in the beautiful and historic town of Shrews-bury, home of the annual Shrewsbury Flower Show, is run by Percy Thrower's three daughters, who carry on the legacy of the most famous name in gardening. One of few family-run Centres, Margaret, Sue and Ann grow a high percentage of the plants they sell, making them supremely qualified to offer advice gained from practical experience of growing and caring for the plants they sell. They and their able, friendly staff, backed by in-depth knowledge of horticulture, are well-equipped to cater for both the keen experienced gardener and the enthusiastic amateur. Always promoting new specimens to an apprecia-tive public, recent years have seen them foster the popularity of surfinia petunias and Million Bells - and, of course, the Centre's speciality: award-winning fuchsias. Over the years they have championed many new and exciting varieties.

The Centre's Cedar Room is a licensed restaurant and cof-fee shop serving hot meals and tasty snacks. The home-made cakes, afternoon cream teas and Sunday roast are all firm fa-vourites. Other features include the Aquatic display, Mower House, Shed Centre and 'The Shropshire Poacher', a farm shop specialising in fresh foods, with over 40 cheeses, home-made pies and much more.

Throughout the year there are regular weekend demonstrations and weekly workshops, covering a range of topics including alpine gardens, planting indoor gardens, hanging baskets and flower arranging, with helpful advice on all aspects of gardening. There are also regular craft fairs and shows and exhibitions, such as the Cacti Show and Chrysanthemum Show. Group tours of the greenhouses can also be arranged. *Open: Mon-Sat 9-6 (5.30 in winter months), Sun 10.30-4.30; closed 25th/26th Dec, 1st Jan, Easter Sunday.*

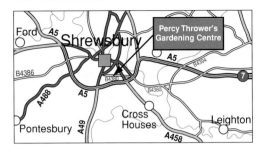

Directions:

Percy Thrower's Gardening Centre is situated on the B4380 just to the south of Shrewsbury. Follow the brown tourist signs from the A5.

Aquatics	Fencing	Houseplants
Barbecues	Floristry	Information Desk
Books & Stationery	Fruit Trees	Large Car Park
Christmas & Seasonal Displays	Garden Construction	Paving
Conservatories	Garden Design	Plant Guarantee
Credit Cards Accepted	Garden Furniture	Plants
Cut Flowers	Garden Machinery	Restaurant/Coffee Shop
Disabled	Garden Products	Seeds & Bulbs
Dried & Artificial Flowers	Giftware	Trees
Farm Shop	Greenhouses & Sheds	

LOCAL GARDENS

Wollerton Old Hall Garden, Wollerton, Nr Market Drayton 01630 685760

Delightful 20th century formal garden surrounding 16th century house (house is not open to the public). A profusion of imaginatively planted borders combine to create small separate gardens each with a different character. - Knot garden, lime allee, old roses and clematis collection. Lunches, teas and plants for sale. *Open: May to August Fri, Sun & Bank Hols 12-5*

The Shrewsbury Quest, 193 Abbey Foregate, Shrewsbury 01743 243324

Inspired by the Brother Cadfael novels, The Shrewsbury Quest has been created opposite Shrewsbury Abbey. It features a herb garden, considerately and meticulously laid out in the style of the Abbey of Fontevraud in France. Trellised walk with gallica roses and honeysuckles. Herbarium with dried herbs; demonstrations of the kinds of activities that Cadfael and his brethren might have undertaken. *Open: daily 10-5 (closed 25th Dec, 1st Jan). Entrance: garden and Quest £4.25 (OAPs/students £3.60, children £2.95, family £13).*

Powis Castle Gardens, Welshpool 01938 557018

National Trust garden originally laid out in 1720, founded on an even earlier design. World-famous hanging terraces, giant clipped yew hedges, lead urns and statuary, large wild garden, orangery, kitchen garden, fruit trees, flower garden, fine views. Tender plants and climbers in the shelter of hedges and walls. Tea rooms. 12m W of S off the A458. *Open: daily Apr - Nov except Mons & Tues. Open Tues in Jul and Aug and Bank Holiday Mondays throughout the season; Entrance: Garden only £5 (OAP's & children 5-17 £2.50) National Trust members free.*

CADBURY GARDEN CENTRE
SMALLWAY, CONGRESBURY, BRISTOL, SOMERSET BS49 5AA
TEL: 01934 876464 FAX: 01934 876485 EMAIL: info@cadburygc.co.uk

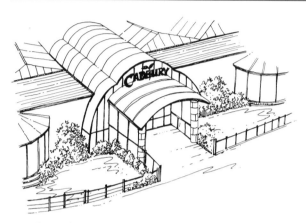

Cadbury Garden Centre was founded in 1982. Quality, choice and service are the bywords here, coupled with expertise in the various fields of gardening to help you create and maintain a healthy, happy garden. Over a million people visit this comprehensive garden centre every year. Medal winner at the presitigious Chelsea Flower Show and also voted Garden Centre of the Year for 1994 by the GCA, Cadbury offers a very wide range of products and services.

The selection here is truly outstanding. There are more than 5 acres of plant displays for you to browse through, with both common favourites and more unusual plants for the collector. The Plant Advice Centre is open every day to answer any of your gardening or plant questions. The Leisure Department offers an extensive range of quality garden furniture, barbecues, gazebos and more. Everything you need to enjoy yourself in the garden or conservatory is here

The extensive layout - both indoors and outdoors - also boasts dedicated areas for trees, conifers, shade-loving plants, herbaceous plants, fuchsias, geraniums and houseplants. Other areas focus on landscape design, water-gardening and patio products, aquatics and pets. Specialist departments include tools, watering and irrigation, floral art, gifts and amazing Christmas and seasonal displays. The centre's display gardens offer a wealth of ideas and inspiration. The Gardening Department can show you the easiest way to spend less

time toiling in the garden and more time enjoying it. The Orangery Coffee House serves a tempting variety of hot and cold snacks, meals and beverages. Demonstrations are hosted throughout the year, covering topics such as planting bulbs, preparing hanging baskets, and decorating ideas for Christmas. *Open: Mon to Sat 9-5.30, Sun 10.30-4.30. Late night Wed until 8 p.m. From mid Nov until Christmas late nights Wed, Thurs and Fri.*

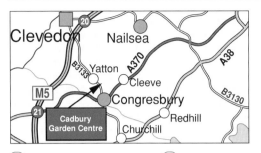

Directions:

Travelling southbound on the M5 take junction 20, B3133. From junction 21 off the M5 take the A370 towards Bristol and at the second set of traffic lights turn left. Cadbury Garden Centre can be found on the right.

(Aquatics icon) Aquatics	(Fireworks icon) Fireworks	(Houseplants icon) Houseplants
(Barbecues icon) Barbecues	(Floristry icon) Floristry	(Information icon) Information Desk
(Books icon) Books & Stationery	(Fruit Trees icon) Fruit Trees	(P icon) Large Car Park
(Christmas icon) Christmas & Seasonal Displays	(Garden Construction icon) Garden Construction	(Paving icon) Paving
(Clothing icon) Clothing	(Garden Design icon) Garden Design	(Pet Products icon) Pet Products and/or Pets
(Conservatories icon) Conservatories	(Garden Furniture icon) Garden Furniture	(Plant Guarantee icon) Plant Guarantee
(Credit Cards icon) Credit Cards Accepted	(Garden Machinery icon) Garden Machinery	(}) Plants
(Disabled icon) Disabled	(Garden Products icon) Garden Products	(Restaurant icon) Restaurant/Coffee Shop
(Display Gardens icon) Display Gardens	(Giftware icon) Giftware	(Seeds icon) Seeds & Bulbs
(Dried Flowers icon) Dried & Artificial Flowers	(Greenhouses icon) Greenhouses & Sheds	(Trees icon) Trees
(Fencing icon) Fencing		

LOCAL GARDENS

Clevedon Court, Tickenham Road, Clevedon 01275 872257

National Trust. Steeply terraced gardens of impressive 14th-century house. The south-facing terraces boast various species including the strawberry trees (Arbutus unedo), myrtles, a judas tree, fuchsias, palms, Canna iridiflora and magnolias. Bowling green; Gothick gazebo; 18th-century octagonal summerhouse. The upper terrace has an ornamental woodland as a backdrop, with holm oaks, ancient mulberry tree, London planes and ilex. 1½m e of Clevedon on the B3130. *Open: April-Sept Weds-Thurs, Sun and Bank Holiday Mon 2-5 (last admission 4.30). House open as garden. Entrance: house and garden £4 (children £2). Coaches by appointment.*

Milton Lodge, Wells 01749 672168

Mature Grade II listed terraced garden, which was replanted in the 1960s by the current owner. Cultivated down the side of a hill, it offers spectacular views of Wells Cathedral and the Vale of Avon. A wide variety of plants suitable for alkaline soil provide year-round interest and a succession of colours throughout the seasons. Fine trees, mixed borders, roses. Separate 7-acre arboretum. ½m N of Wells off the A39. From A39 take Old Bristol Road and entrance is first gate on left. *Open: Good Friday - End Oct, Sun-Fri (except Good Friday). Private visits welcome, please telephone for details. Entrance: £2 (children under 14 free).*

Sherbourne Garden, Litton 01761 241220

4½-acre landscaped garden of horticultural interest. Wide selection of herbaceous plants, shrubs and trees. Collections of 250 hardy ferns, 150 hollies, together with rose species, hemerocallis, hostas and grasses. All plants are well labelled. Also pinetum and ponds. Picnic area. 15m S of Bristol on the B3114. *Open: June-end Sept Sun-Mon 11-6; other times by private arrangement, please telephone for details. Entrance: £2.00 (children free).*

MONKTON ELM GARDEN AND PET CENTRE
MONKTON HEATHFIELD, TAUNTON, SOMERSET TA2 8QN
TEL: 01823 412381 FAX: 01823 412745

Founded in 1918, **Monkton Elm Garden and Pet Centre** has developed from a small nursery to a thriving concern renowned for providing a comprehensive selection of strong, healthy plants. The Centre has more than 10,000 varieties of outdoor plants on offer - bedding and indoor plants for a blaze of colour, striking shrubs, trees and conifers, alpine plants. Whatever you require for your garden, you are almost certain to find it here.

Finding the right tools is a vital part of creating the perfect garden, and Monkton Elm stocks a comprehensive range of garden tools and labour-saving products. The Centre prides itself on keeping abreast of the newest and most useful supplies for maintaining the garden in pristine condition. Greenhouses, sheds, paving and patio supplies help you add the finishing touches.

The Pet Centre is one of the largest in the South West, with an ever-changing selection of animals, birds and fish, as well as foods, accessories and expert advice for helping to look after them. The Aquatic Centre is well stocked with cold water and tropical fish, ponds, pumps and indoor and outdoor water features. The selection of house plants is superb, helping you to grace your home, office or conservatory. The horticulturally trained and qualified staff are always on hand for help, advice and information.  Other features of this superior Centre are the Decorative Effects department, Gorgeous Gift department - with a variety of books, cards and ceramics - and well-equipped children's play area.

The licenced Four Seasons restaurant serves morning coffee, lunches and afternoon tea, offering a range of traditional favourites and innovative dishes, which can be enjoyed on the attractive outdoor verandah when the weather is fine. *Open: Mon-Sat 9-5.30, Sun 10.30-4.30.*

Directions:

From junction 25 of the M5 take the A385 towards Taunton. At the first set of traffic lights turn right and Monkton Elm is found two miles on the left at the junction of the A38 and A361.

- Aquatics
- Barbecues
- Books & Stationery
- Camping Equipment
- Childrens Play Area
- Christmas & Seasonal Displays
- Clothing
- Conservatories
- Credit Cards Accepted
- Cut Flowers
- Disabled

- Dried & Artificial Flowers
- Fencing
- Fireworks
- Fruit Trees
- Garden Design
- Garden Furniture
- Garden Machinery
- Garden Products
- Giftware
- Greenhouses & Sheds

- Houseplants
- Information Desk
- Large Car Park
- Paving
- Pet Products and/or Pets
- Plant Guarantee
- Plants
- Restaurant/Coffee Shop
- Seeds & Bulbs
- Trees

LOCAL GARDENS

Cothay Manor, Greenham 01823 672283

Laid out by Reginald Cooper, a friend of Harold Nicolson of Sissinghurst and Lawrence Johnston of Hidcote in the 1920's this outstanding garden has been totally restored over the past few years. Original yew hedges, garden rooms: white garden, cottage garden, ox bow bog garden.One of the finest small medieval manors in the country. Plants propagated from the garden available to buy. 5m w of Wellington off the A38. *Open: May-Sept Weds-Thurs, Sun and Bank Holiday Mon 2-6, also on certain days for the NGS. House open for groups by arrangement. Entrance: £3 (children free).*

Hatch Court, Hatch Beauchamp 01823 480058

5-acre garden, with superb walled kitchen garden, roses, clematis, shrubs and young trees. 1995 Historic Garden Restoration Award. Very large walled kitchen and cutting garden, horse chestnut avenue. 30 acres of parkland and deer park; ancient cedars, impressive copper beech, Irish yews. Glorious views. All set round magnificent 1750 Palladian mansion. Teas. 5m SE of Taunton off the A358. *Open: 5th April-Sept daily 10-5.30. House open 10th June-9th Sept Thurs 2.30-5. Parties by appointment. Entrance: £2.50 (children 12-16 £1); house and garden £3.50.*

Hestercombe Gardens, Cheddon Fitzpaine 01823 413747

Over 3 centuries of gardening history in 50 acres of formal and landscape gardens. Famous Edwardian gardens designed by Sir Edwin Lutyens and planted by Gertrude Jekyll with terraces, pools and Orangery. Landscape garden designed by Coplestone Warre Bampfylde in the 1750s. 40 acres of woodland walks, lakes, Doric temple, mausoleum and rebuilt witch's hut. 4m NE of Taunton off the A361. *Open: all year daily 10-6 (last admission 5); parties by written appointment. Entrance: £3.50 (children 5-15 £1).*

BYRKLEY PARK CENTRE

RANGEMORE, BURTON UPON TRENT, STAFFORDSHIRE DE13 9RN
TEL: 01283 716467 FAX: 01283 716594 EMAIL: byrkleypark@dial.pipex.com

Set within a victorian walled garden deep in the beautiful Staffordshire country-side, **Byrkley Park Centre** once formed part of the old Bass family estate. The present owners bought the site in 1985, when it was a run-down nursery. It has been extensively developed to become one of the country's leading garden centres. This family-run business incorporates two other distinct garden centres. Each has its own character, yet all three are united in the high standards they strive to maintain. Offering top-quality gardening products, value for money and, above all, customer service, any shopping excursion to these centres will be a pleasant and inspiring experience.

During its lifetime Byrkley Park has been honoured with a host of awards, including Caring Garden Centre of the Year. Everything imaginable for the keen gardener and the potterer alike is here, including a stunning variety of superb plants and everything else for the perfect garden. Byrkley is so confident about the quality of their plants that all hardy varieties come with a special two-year guarantee.

The choice and variety continues through all ranges offered by this comprehensive garden centre, including specialist conservatory centres and water gardening and aquatic centres. The expert staff are happy to help with any gardening questions you may have. The award-winning tea-room and carvery serves a range of delicious snacks, meals and beverages. There's also a safe and attractive children's play area and farm yard animals. A visit to Byrkley will prove its motto, 'Everything for gardens and more'. Disabled and baby changing facilities, wheelchair loan and delivery service are all available. *Open: April to August Monday to Saturday 9-6 (late night on Friday until 9 p.m.), Sunday 10.30-4.30.; September to March Monday to Saturday 9-5 (late night on Friday until 9 p.m.), Sunday 10.30-4.30.*

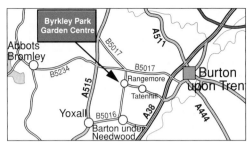

Directions:

Byrkley Park Garden Centre is situated at Rangemore, just 4 miles west of Burton-on-Trent. From the north, take the 2nd Burton exit off the A38 (from the south take the 1st exit) then head for Tatenhill and follow the signposts.

Aquatics	Display Gardens	Giftware
Barbecues	Dried & Artificial Flowers	Houseplants
Books & Stationery	Fencing	Information Desk
Childrens Play Area	Floristry	Large Car Park
Christmas & Seasonal Displays	Fruit Trees	Plant Guarantee
Clothing	Garden Construction	Plants
Conservatories	Garden Design	Restaurant/Coffee Shop
Credit Cards Accepted	Garden Furniture	Seeds & Bulbs
Cut Flowers	Garden Products	Trees
Disabled		

LOCAL GARDENS

Calke Abbey, Ticknall 01332 863822

National Trust. Extensive walled garden constructed late in the 18th century. Kitchen garden, Flower garden, Physic garden with Vinery. Restoration, which began in 1987, continues. Pleasure grounds around the walled garden. Orangery. Garden produce on sale. 10m S of Derby off the A514. *Open: end Mar-Oct Sat-Weds and Bank Holiday Mon 11-5. House open as garden but 12.45-4.45. Entrance: £2.30 (children £1.10); house and garden £5 (children £2.50).*

Melbourne Hall Gardens, Melbourne 01332 862502

A living record of a late 17th-/early 18th-century design in the style of Le Notre, laid out by London and Wise. Terraces down to a lake; grotto; lovely lead statuary including Van Nost's lead urn of The Four Seasons; fountains. Birdcage iron arbour dating from 1706, visible from the house along a long yew-hedged walk. 8m S of Derby off the B587. *Open: April-Sept Weds, Sat-Sun and Bank Holiday Mon 2-6. House open: please telephone for details. Entrance: £3 (OAPs £2, children £2).*

Kedleston Hall, Kedleston 01332 842191

Informal 18th-century garden with broad open lawn bounded by a ha-ha. More formal layout west of the Hall - ancient home to the Curzon family. Orangery, summerhouse. Rhododendrons, azaleas, lovely spring colour. Long Walk through woodlands. 4½m NW of Derby between the A6/A52. *Open: 17 Mar-31 Oct 11-6. 1 Nov - 19 Dec Sat & Suns 12-4. House (contains Lord Curzon's Indian Museum) open as garden but 12-4.30; Entrance: park (Thurs/Fri only) £2 per vehicle; park and garden £2.10 (children £1); hall, park and garden £4.90 (children £2.40).*

DOBBIES GARDENING WORLD
WATLING STREET, GAILEY, STAFFORDSHIRE ST19 5PP
TEL: 01902 791555 FAX: 01902 791120

Dobbies Garden Centres have been established for 130 years, with nine (soon to be ten) garden centres located throughout the UK. They are among the largest and most respected garden centres in Britain.

The range of products on offer undergoes continuous expansion, progressively growing as the centre goes from strength to strength in offering the greatest range of plants and garden features and accessories, including houseplants, fruit and ornamental trees, roses, shrubs, conifers, herbaceous plants, climbers, ground cover plants, heathers and alpines.

To complement this excellent range of plants, the centre stocks a comprehensive choice of gardening sundries and accessories, including ceramics and stoneware, containers in all sizes, floristry sundries, silk flowers, composts and fertilisers, and gardening tools.

Everything in this light and airy modern building is pristine and well laid out, with no clutter. Visitors could definitely spend half a day or more here, browsing, buying and being inspired with ideas for the home, garden, conservatory or office.

The speciality of this superior garden centre is its wonderful range of garden ornaments in a variety of shapes, sizes and materials, to add grace and charm to any garden. Pride of place goes to The Mezzanine Floor, a delightful and attractive feature here as it is in the Dobbies Centre at Lasswade.

Dobbies place an enormous emphasis on staff and training. The majority of staff are horticulturists, with the know-how and expertise to advise all customers on the best plants to choose for any situation and soil type, and on how to maintain and cultivate a beautiful and healthy garden. The 'Planter's' tearoom serves a variety of delicious hot and cold snacks and meals. *Open: Monday - Saturday 9:00 - 6:00, Sunday 11:00 - 5:00*

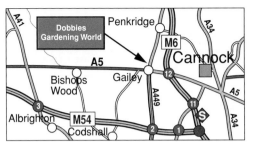

Directions:

From junction 12 on the M6 take the A5 towards Telford. Dobbies Garden Centre is at Gailey where the A5 crosses the A449.

Aquatics	Dried & Artificial Flowers	Greenhouses & Sheds
Barbecues	Farm Shop	Houseplants
Books & Stationery	Fencing	Information Desk
Camping Equipment	Fireworks	Large Car Park
Childrens Play Area	Floristry	Paving
Christmas & Seasonal Displays	Fruit Trees	Pet Products and/or Pets
Clothing	Garden Construction	Plant Guarantee
Conservatories	Garden Design	Plants
Credit Cards Accepted	Garden Furniture	Restaurant/Coffee Shop
Cut Flowers	Garden Machinery	Seeds & Bulbs
Disabled	Garden Products	Trees
Display Gardens	Giftware	

LOCAL GARDENS

Moseley Old Hall, Moseley Old Hall Lane, Fordhouses 01902 782808

National Trust small modern reconstruction of 17th-century garden with formal box parterre, knot garden, small herb garden. Old roses, herbaceous plants, wooden arbour. Fruit trees include medlars, a morello cherry and a mulberry. The Elizabethan house harboured Charles II after the Battle of Worcester. 4m N of Wolverhampton off the A460. *Open: 1.30-5.30 late Mar-May Sat-Sun; June and Sept-Oct Weds, Sat-Sun; July-Aug Tues-Weds and Sat-Sun; Nov-Dec Sun 1.30-4.30. House open. Entrance: house and garden £3.90 (children £1.95).*

Shugborough, Milford 01889 881388

Fine Victorian layout, terraces by Nesfield. Edwardian rose garden. Early example of a Chinoiserie and of English neoclassicism. Many buildings and monuments ascribed to James 'Athenian' Stuart. 6m E of Stafford on the A513. *Open: daily end Mar-end Sept 11-5; Oct Sun only. Open to pre-booked groups all year from 10.30 a.m. Entrance: parkland, gardens, picnic area, walks and trails £2 per vehicle; house, County Museum and Park Farm £8 (OAPs/students £6, children under five free); all-in-one ticket £4 (OAPs/students £3).*

Weston Park, Weston-under-Lizard, Shifnal 01952 850207

Capability Brown landscaped these gardens and parkland. Almost 1,000 acres of woodland with fine azaleas and rhododendrons. The formal gardens have been restored to their original 19th-century design. Rose garden, long wall, colourful Broderie Garden. Lovely pools. Rose walk to the deer park, long border. Temple of Diana, Orangery, Roman bridge. Events throughout the year. 7m W of junction 12 of the M6. *Open: April-Sept - Park and Gardens 11-7 last admission 5pm; House open 1 -5 last admission 4:30 pm. Entrance: £3.80 (OAPs £2.80, children £2.20); House, park and gardens £5.50 (OAPs £4.30, children £3.40).*

MARLOWS DIY & GARDEN CENTRE
HOLLOW ROAD, BURY ST EDMUNDS, SUFFOLK IP32 7AP
TEL: 01284 763155 FAX: 01284 703902

Marlows DIY & Garden Centre sells a comprehensive variety of everything you'll need to create and maintain a beautiful and thriving garden. Their range includes everything from mowers and trimmers, leaf collectors, mulch machines and a selection of power tools to garden furniture, pots, urns, ceramics and candles. In addition they sell more heavy-duty implements such as cement mixers, carpentry supplies, irrigation devices, garden lighting appliances and much more. In addition to this there is a fine selection of trees, shrubs and flowering plants, accompanied by expert advice from the friendly and efficient staff, specially trained at the Centre, which believes that from good training springs good service.

The business began over 65 years ago with just six men and a handcart. It was still the age of the horse, with Suffolks or Shires being used on both farmland and on the roads. By the late 1930s Marlows had established itself as one of the leading builder's merchants in the area, and business continued to grow. The specialised Garden Centre was added in 1983. Today it remains first and foremost a family business, offering the benefit of over six decades of experience to all customers. One speciality is the extensive range of birds for sale, part of the Centre's Pets Corner department. Here, in addition to guinea pigs, rabbits, hamsters and other small pets there is a superb range of lovebirds, canaries, cockatiels, budgerigars and finches. As will be expected from a premier DIY outlet, there is also the full complement of equipment, tools and supplies for plumbing, roofing, insulation and other home-improvement products, including a complete kitchen, shower and bath fitting and design service. *Open: Mon-Fri 8.30-8, Sat 8.30-6, Sun 10-4.30, Bank Holidays 8.30-8.*

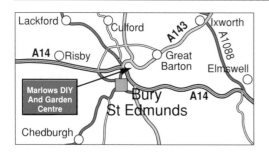

Directions:

Take the A143 out of Bury St Edmunds and follow signs to Eastern Industrial Estate. Marlows DIY and Garden Centre can be found on the Estate.

Barbecues	Fireworks	Houseplants
Books & Stationery	Floristry	Information Desk
Childrens Play Area	Fruit Trees	Large Car Park
Christmas & Seasonal Displays	Garden Construction	Paving
Clothing	Garden Design	Pet Products and/or Pets
Credit Cards Accepted	Garden Furniture	Plant Guarantee
Disabled	Garden Machinery	Plants
Dried & Artificial Flowers	Garden Products	Seeds & Bulbs
Fencing	Giftware	Trees

LOCAL GARDENS

Abbey Gardens, Bury St Edmunds 01284 757090

Gardens of the historic Abbey, beautifully maintained by St Edmundsbury Borough Council. Approached through one of the original gates, with parts of the historic abbey to the rear. Fine trees, huge beds of flowers. Rose garden planted by US servicemen stationed in Bury during the Second World War. Perennial borders and small heather planting. Light refreshments. Croquet and bowls greens. Particularly nice in spring and summer. *Open: daily til dusk. Entrance: free.*

Wyken Hall, Stanton 01359 250287/250240

Wonderfully coloured and scented garden, especially in high summer. 4-acre garden laid out as a series of rooms. Knot and herb gardens, yew hedge, wild garden, winter garden, nuttery, old-fashioned rose garden, hornbeam hedge, rose-laden pergola. Gazebo and copper beech maze, old orchard, herbaceous borders. Also woodland walk and dell, and vineyard. Kitchen and 'edible' garden. Restaurant, wine and teas. 9m NE of Bury along A143. *Open: April-1st Oct Thurs, Fris & Suns 10-6. Entrance: £2.00 (OAPs £1.50, children under 12 free).*

Ickworth House, Park & Gardens, Horringer 01284 735270

70 acre-gardens divided into north and south; south gardens restored to stylised Italian landscape, fitting unusual design of the House. Agapanthus, fatsias, geraniums, orangery. North gardens informally planted with wildflower lawns and woodland walk. Evergreens, Buxus collection, Victorian stumpery. New planting of cedars. 18th-century Albana Wood, laid out by Capability Brown, includes a circular walk. Restaurant, teas. 3m SE of Bury W of A143. *Open: House 20 Mar-31 Oct daily 10-5 except Mons & Thurs but open Good Friday & Bank Holiday Mondays 1-5, 1 Nov-31Mar daily 10-4 except Sat & Sun. Park open daily 7-7 except 25th December. Entrance: (house, garden and park) £5.20 (children £2.20); (park and garden) £2.20 (children 70p). Private group visits welcome.*

CHESSINGTON GARDEN CENTRE
LEATHERHEAD ROAD, CHESSINGTON, SURREY KT9 2NF
TEL: 01372 725638 FAX: 01372 740859

From humble beginnings as a shed where they cultivated roses and potatoes, Alex Martin and his family have developed and extended this wonderful garden centre over more than 30 years. **Chessington Garden Centre** now comprises a light and airy temperature-controlled indoor viewing area, and specialises in citruses and exotic plants, predominantly tropical plants from India, Polynesia, China, other parts of Asia and Central and South America. Cacti and a comprehensive variety of citrus plants - limes, lemons, oranges, grapefruit, clementines, Maltese sanguine and kumquat, to name just the most popular species - are featured here.

Every strain and type of plant, bush, flower and shrub includes details of how to keep and nurture it, including advice on where best to plant it out in your garden to give it the light, heat and conditions it needs to flourish. The uniformed staff are friendly, helpful and knowledgeable, offering advice on everything for the novice, enthusiast and professional gardener.

The Centre also boasts an impressive range of exterior garden items in ceramic and wood - everything from vast urns to tiny gnomes, including an unusual range of ceramic pots and vases in interesting glazes - as well as garden lighting, a section devoted to garden ponds and aquatics, and a big selection of greenhouses and fully furnished conservatories. The Centre's Landscape Department features fencing, buildings and paving, ornamental rocks, bricks and flagstones in a wonderful variety of shapes and colours. The dedicated garden furniture area has garden chairs and tables in wood and cast iron, gas-fired barbecues, gazebos and pergolas. The Centre's other attractions include the gift shop, which has a comprehensive range of gardening books. *Open: daily Jan 9-5; Feb-Dec Mon-Sat 9-6, Sun 10-4.*

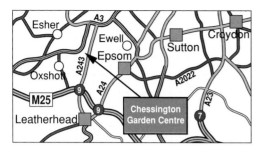

Directions

Follow the Chessington Ad ture Park signs from Junction of the M25 onto the A243 to wards Kingston. Chessington Garden Centre lies on the left just before Chessington World of Ad ventures and half-way between Junction 9 and the A3.

Aquatics	Fencing	Information Desk
Barbecues	Fruit Trees	Large Car Park
Books & Stationery	Garden Construction	Paving
Christmas & Seasonal Displays	Garden Design	Pet Products and/or Pets
Clothing	Garden Furniture	Plant Guarantee
Conservatories	Garden Machinery	Plants
Credit Cards Accepted	Garden Products	Restaurant/Coffee Shop
Disabled	Giftware	Seeds & Bulbs
Display Gardens	Greenhouses & Sheds	Trees
Dried & Artificial Flowers	Houseplants	

LOCAL GARDENS

9 Raymead Close, Fetcham 01372 373728

This 1/3-acre plantsman's garden has an unusual design, with narrow paths, secluded corners, ponds and a small sunken garden. Features include plantings designed to provide year-round colour, with trees, shrubs, perennials and annuals. Also an interesting selection of berries and winter bark. Teas available. A245 out of Cobham, through Stoke D'Arbonam and Fetcham, then second left after Raymead Way. *Open: telephone for details. Entrance: £1.50 (children £1).*

Painshill Landscape Garden, Portsmouth Road, Cobham 01932 868113/864674

Landscaped 160-acre park restored by the Painshill Park Trust. Centred around the winding 14-acre lake, it features a Chinese bridge leading to an island and grotto. The mausoleum features on Catherine the Great's Wedgwood 'Frog Service'. The garden's focal point is the elegant Gothick temple. The cedar of Lebanon is reputedly the largest in Europe. 1m W of Cobham on A245. *Open: April-Oct Tues-Sun and Bank Holiday Mon 10.30-6; Nov-March Tues-Thurs and Sat/Sun 11-4 (or dusk) last entry 4.30 (Summer), 3.00 (Winter). Closed 25th, 26th Dec. Entrance: £3.80 (concessions £3.30, children 5-16 £1.50).*

Knightsmead, Rickman Hill Road, Chipstead 01737 551694

Half-acre plantsman's garden, designed and maintained by the owners, with scented shrub roses and clematis, spring bulbs and woodland plants including trilliums, erythroniums and pure-colour bred hellebores, perennials for year-round interest, pond, raised alpine and peat beds, and hardy geraniums. Small craft exhibition onsite. 1m SW of Coulsdon off B2032. *Open: 14th April 10-4; 12th-13th June 2-5.30; 8th Sept 10-4; and by appointment. Entrance: £2 (children 50p).*

ST LODGE GARDEN CENTRE

HOLT POUND, FARNHAM, SURREY GU10 4LD
TEL: 01420 23275 FAX: 01420 22376

Forest Lodge Garden Centre is set in 6½ acres and boasts a full range of indoor and outdoor plants in all sizes, including a selection of specimen plants. A previous winner of the Garden Centre of the Year Award, as well as four Awards of Merit from the GCA for excellence, it supplies everything needed for the garden. More like a large garden which sells plants and gardening supplies than just another commercial garden centre, each area flows naturally into the next. Some areas are laid to grass with borders in typical domestic-garden style. Statues, stepping stones and water features enhance the 'user-friendly' feeling of these gardens.

Topiary plants are one speciality of this comprehensive garden centre. The Garden Style department nearby, concentrates on supplying an extensive range of large scale specimen outdoor plants, available both wholesale and retail. This selection includes trees, shrubs, conifers, herbaceous plants, climbers, topiary and feature plants, all in containers, ranging in height from 1m to 8m high - one of the widest selections in the UK.

The fine range of garden furniture on offer includes a good assortment of hardwoods, including Westminster Teak. Giftware such as candles, aromatics, Portmeirion crockery and ceramics, a unique selection of Jane Asher Victorian-style trinket boxes, and other popular and attractive items such as Strahl unbreakable outdoor 'glassware' in a range of stylish designs and colours, Dartington glass and crystal, books of every type and a full range of Stormafit outdoor clothing are all available here. The Squirrel's Pantry has an extensive menu. Its large windows open out onto an attractive patio area where pergolas, plants and statues are tastefully arranged. Free delivery service within a 20-mile radius. *Open: Monday to Saturday 8.30-5.30, Sunday 10.30-4.30, Bank Holidays 8.30-5.30.*

Directions:

From Farnham take the A31 towards Alton and at the A31/A325 roundabout take the A325 towards Bordon and Petersfield. Forest Lodge Garden Centre is on the right just after Birdworld. Follow the brown signs with the white cockatoo for Birdworld.

Aquatics	Fencing	Information Desk
Barbecues	Fireworks	Large Car Park
Books & Stationery	Floristry	Paving
Christmas & Seasonal Displays	Fruit Trees	Pet Products
Clothing	Garden Construction	Plant Guarantee
Credit Cards Accepted	Garden Furniture	Plants
Cut Flowers	Garden Machinery	Restaurant/Coffee Shop
Disabled	Garden Products	Seeds & Bulbs
Display Gardens	Giftware	Trees
Dried & Artificial Flowers	Houseplants	

LOCAL GARDENS

Birdworld, Holt Pound 01420 22140

Extensive gardens form the backdrop to this impressive bird sanctuary with childrens farm, aquarium and Puddleducks restaurant. Rose garden, ornamental grass border, white garden, pergola and climbing roses, heather bed, pond. Also summer bedding, wall baskets, hanging baskets. Colour and interest throughout the year. 3m S of Farnham on the A325. *Open: weekends Jan-Feb; daily mid-Feb-early Nov; weekends early Nov-Dec; 9.30-6 summer, 9.30-4.30 winter (last admission one hour before closing). Entrance: £7.50 (OAPs £5.95, children 3 plus £3.95, family £19.95).*

Bury Court, Bentley 01420 23202

New garden that has been laid out in co-operation with famous Dutch landscape designer Piet Oudolf. Unique example of continental 'naturalistic' style. Asymmetrical geometric beds with various grasses and vigorous perennials provide an extended season of interest. Superb mid- and late summer herbaceous borders. Plants for sale in nursery, adjacent. 5m SW of Farnham on the road signed Crondall. *Open: Thurs-Sat Mar 18-Oct 30, 10-6. Entrance: 50p.*

Gilbert White's House and Garden, The Wakes, Selborne 01420 511275

This is the house where White penned his Natural History of Selborne, published in the late 18th century. The gardens are in the process of being restored. Originals from White's time include the sundial and ha-ha. Beds and borders containing plants of his time, such as sweet Williams, pinks, hollyhocks, species foxgloves, martagon lilies, santolina and old rose species including Damasks and Gallicas. Tulip tree, herb garden, yew topiary, laburnum tunnel. Historic fruit varieties. 4m S of Alton on the B3006. *Open: daily 1 Jan-24 Dec 11-5; Evening openings for groups by appointment. House open as garden. Entrance: £4.00 (OAPs/students £3.50, children £1).*

GARSON FARM

WINTERDOWN ROAD, WEST END, ESHER, SURREY KT10 8LS
TEL: 01372 460181 FAX: 01372 460961 WEBSITE: http//www.garson-farm.co.uk

Situated by a picturesque village green, **Garson Farm** has been in the same family since 1871. Today it boasts an extensive Garden Centre, over 150 acres of Pick-your-own crops and an award-winning Farm Shop.

The gardening calendar begins with starter plants in February, progressing to larger versions until, by late spring, there is a vast expanse devoted to colourful bedding and other annuals. Garson Farm is also renowned for its splendid selection of planted hanging baskets and tubs which form a breathtaking display from April onwards. All year the outdoor planteria offers top quality perennials, shrubs and small trees as well as rock plants and herbs. Inside is a wide range of houseplants, as well as gardening products and equipment. Many unusual gift and household items can be found in the large gift department, also books and silk and dried flowers.

The Farm Shop is sited in a charming 140 year-old barn and specialises in traditionally produced British food It offers extensive ranges of cheeses and dairy produce, including sheep's and goats' products, free range eggs, meats and sausages, smoked fish from Scotland and numerous luxury brands of ice cream. Fresh fruit and vegetables form the largest section and many crops in season are harvested from the farm's own fields. There are also more uncommon brands of biscuits, confectionery, preserves, dressings, oils and vinegars, and home-made cakes. Fresh bread is available seven days per week.

Pick-your-own crops start in May with asparagus. Around 30 different fruit and vegetable crops can be harvested throughout the summer months and strawberries and raspberries can be picked until the first frosts in October. The PYO season ends with pumpkins around Halloween. *Open: Summer Mon-Sat 9-6, Sun 11-5; Winter Mon-Sat 9-5, Sun 11-5.*

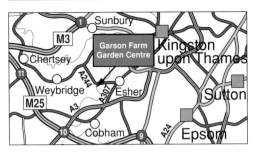

Directions:

Take the A244 from Esher towards Hersham. Turn left into West End Lane then right at the Prince of Wales public house.

Aquatics	Dried & Artificial Flowers	Houseplants
Barbecues	Farm Shop	Information Desk
Books & Stationery	Fencing	Large Car Park
Christmas & Seasonal Displays	Floristry	Pick Your Own
Clothing	Fruit Trees	Plant Guarantee
Conservatories	Garden Construction	Plants
Credit Cards Accepted	Garden Design	Restaurant/Coffee Shop
Cut Flowers	Garden Furniture	Seeds & Bulbs
Disabled	Garden Products	Trees
Display Gardens	Giftware	

LOCAL GARDENS

RHS Garden, Wisley, Woking 01483 224234

Primary garden of the RHS and hub of its scientific and education activities. 240 acres incorporating formal gardens, arboretum, rock garden, alpine and wild garden, model gardens, mixed borders, rose garden, orchard, fruit and vegetable garden, woodland garden, azaleas, lillies, hydrangeas, Mediterranean garden, glasshouses, canal, trial grounds. 7m NE of Guildford on A3. *Open to non-members all year (except Christmas Day) Mon-Sat 10-6 (Feb-Oct) 10-4.30 (Nov-Jan), Sun for members only. Entrance: by membership or £5 (children 6-16 £2).*

Dunsborough Park, Ripley, Woking 01483 225366

Restored gardens of distinguished Georgian house. Attractive herbaceous borders lead to extensive walled gardens redesigned as pleasure gardens by Penelope Hobhouse; unusual 70-ft gingko hedge (gingkos were grown to be sold but became established), water garden with bridge and belvedere, Victorian wooden glasshouses. Hidden garden enclosing an ancient mulberry tree. Teas. Antique Garden Ornament Centre. 6m NE of Guildford on A3/A247. *Open: by appointment. Entrance: £2.50 (children £1.25).*

Claremont Landscape Garden, Esher 01372 467806

50-acre National Trust garden (only part of the original estate), one of the earliest surviving English landscape gardens, begun before 1720 by Vanbrugh and Bridgeman, extended by Kent and Brown. Sensitive reconstruction of 18th-century English style. Favourite 19th-century retreat of Queen Victoria. Lake, grotto and turf amphitheatre, island with pavilion, superb views and avenues. Teas. 1m SE of Esher, on A307. *Open: Nov-Mar Tues-Sun 10-5 or sunset; Apr-Oct Mon-Fri 10-6, Sat/Sun/Bank Holiday Mon 10-7, open to 2.00 only on Jul 14 - Jul 18; closed 13th July, 25th Dec, 1st Jan. Entrance: £3 (children £1.50; family and group tickets available).*

SECRETTS GARDEN CENTRE

OLD PORTSMOUTH ROAD, MILFORD, GODALMING, SURREY GU8 5HL

TEL: 01483 426633 FAX: 01483 426855

Secretts Garden Centre is a family business that was founded in 1908. It has grown into a thriving garden centre, delicatessen, farm shop, flower shop, coffee shop and flower nursery - even a pick your own where you can gather delicious fresh fruit, vegetables and flowers. This award-winning garden centre is a plant-lover's paradise. Enjoy a peaceful stroll around the beautifully maintained land-scaped display gardens - a connoisseur's delight. The centre holds National Collections of Cornus florida and Kalmia latifolia.

Expert advice is always on hand, together with a comprehensive Information Centre for all your gardening questions. The Garden Design Service can also help with ideas, advice and inspiration. There is a wide selection of trees, conifers, shrubs, climbers and herbaceous peren-nials including herbs, cottage garden plants and many unusual varieties, to-gether with rockery and alpine plants. Houseplants and conservatory plants are the centre's speciality. They offer the wid-est selection in the South of England, from exotic plants to bowls, baskets, hanging arrangements and more. From baby starter plants to stunning seasonal displays, the range of bedding plants is also superb. Tubs, urns, hanging baskets - whatever you require, for any season, you'll find it here. From June to Septem-ber you can pick your own soft fruits and English country flowers.

The Rendezvous Coffee Shop serves teas, cakes, sandwiches, light meals and goodies of all descriptions, many of which are home-baked and home-made. Also on site there's a superb florist, fishmonger and farm shop offering a comprehen-sive selection of fruits and vegetables, many grown by Secretts at its Milford farm and cheeses from all over Europe, hand-made chocolates, fresh herbs and spices and much more. Nursery tours are available for groups of 10 or more by appoint-ment only. General enquiries 01483 426655. *Open: Monday to Saturday 9-5.30, Sunday 10.30-4.30, Bank Holidays 9-5.*

Directions:

Take the A3 out of Gui... wards Portsmouth and a... B3001 junction at Milford tu... and follow the signs towards Godalming. Secrett's Garden Centre is on the left.

Aquatics	Farm Shop	Houseplants
Barbecues	Fencing	Information Desk
Books & Stationery	Fresh Fish	Large Car Park
Childrens Play Area	Flower Shop	Pet Products
Christmas & Seasonal Displays	Fruit Trees	Pick Your Own
Conservatories	Garden Construction	Plant Guarantee
Credit Cards Accepted	Garden Design	Plants
Cut Flowers	Garden Furniture	Restaurant/Coffee Shop
Disabled	Garden Products	Seeds & Bulbs
Display Gardens	Giftware	Trees
Dried & Artificial Flowers		

LOCAL GARDENS

Loseley Park, Compton 01483 304440

Walled garden covering 2½ acres. Over 1,000 old fashioned rose bushes; herb garden illustrating the use of herbs for culinary medicinal dyeing and cosmetic purposes as well as flower garden; the newly planted fountain garden. Herbaceous borders, ancient wisteria, moat walk, terrace. 3m SW of Guildford off the B3000. *Open: Weds-Sat May-Sept, 11-5. House open same days as garden but June-Aug only, 2-5. Entrance: £2.50 (OAPs/disabled £2, children £1.50); house and garden £5.00 (OAPs/disabled £4, children £3).*

Winkworth Arboretum, Hascombe Road, Hascombe 01483 208477

95 acres on a hillside, planted with rare shrubs and trees. 60 plant families and 150 genera are grown here, providing year-round interest and variety: bluebells, then rhododendrons, azaleas and cherries, then autumn liquidambars, nyssas, acers and sorbus. National Collection of whitebeams. Spectacular views over the North Downs. Two lakes, wildfowl. Views over the water from the balcony of the newly renovated boathouse. 2m SE of Godalming off the B2130. *Open: daily all year, dawn-dusk; may be closed in bad weather, particularly high winds. Entrance: £2.50 (children 5-16 £1.25). Guided tours available. Coaches must pre-book.*

Chilworth Manor, Chilworth 01483 561414

17th-century house with 18th-century additions on the site of an 11th-century monastery. Monastic stewponds in the garden. Something to see all year round, particularly in spring and summer. The 18th-century walled garden was created by Sarah, Duchess of Marlborough. Herbaceous borders, flowering shrubs, spring flowers, lavender walk. The house is decorated with flowers by different Surrey flower clubs in turn. 3m SE of Guildford on the A248. *Open: 5 weekends a year - please telephone for details. Entrance: £2 (children free); house and garden £1.50.*

GARDEN CENTRE, HERSHAM

WOOD ROAD, HERSHAM, SURREY KT12 4AR
TEL: 01932 247579 FAX: 01932 254794

Founded in 1935, the Squire's group is a family business which comprises seven garden centres, a rose nursery and herbaceous and bedding plant nurseries. The company seeks to maintain high standards combining quality plants and gardening products with the best service to gardeners and a tradition of working with the local community.

The **Squire's Garden Centre at Hersham** is set round a quadrangle of Victorian farm buildings and is located within easy reach of Painshill Park Gardens, Esher and Cobham. The shop was damaged by fire in the autumn of 1998. However, an exciting building project is in progress with every effort being made to ensure that the rebuilt shop will be in keeping with, and maintain the character of, its predecessor. It is anticipated that the new shop and restaurant will be open in time for Christmas 1999. In the meantime a large temporary shop is in place so that a wide range of garden products, houseplants and gifts can still be offered.

The centre offers a fine selection of trees, shrubs, herbaceous bedding plants, terracotta pots and garden ornaments. It is particularly known for its specialisation in garden furniture including wood, resin, cast aluminium, tubular steel and the latest extruded aluminium furniture. The centre offers a very high standard of customer service and advice.

Special Customer Evenings are held each year offering a mixture of talks and demonstrations as well as the opportunity to wander around the Centre, browse and chat over a glass of wine. *Opening Times: Monday to Saturday 9.00 am - 6.00 pm; Sunday 10.30 am - 4.30 pm; Spring late-night opening Friday and Saturday to 7 pm. until end of June.*

Directions:

From Junction 10 of the M25 take the A3 towards London. At the first roundabout turn left and then immediately right into Seven Hills Road. At the next roundabout turn right and Squire's Garden Centre is on the right.

Barbecues	Fencing	Large Car Park
Books & Stationery	Fruit Trees	Paving
Christmas & Seasonal Displays	Garden Furniture	Plant Guarantee
Credit Cards Accepted	Garden Products	Plants
Disabled	Giftware	Seeds & Bulbs
Display Gardens	Houseplants	Trees
Dried & Artificial Flowers	Information Desk	

LOCAL GARDENS

Hampton Court Palace, East Molesey 0181 781 9500

Mixture of tastes and styles over 66 acres plus over 600 acres of informal deer park. Great Vine planted in 1768 (grapes for sale every September); world-famous maze. Fabulous bedding plants, knot garden, fountain garden, wilderness garden. Laburnum walk, rose garden, pond garden and largest herbaceous border in the south of England. Privy Garden with parterres, 17th-century plants. On A308 at junction of A309. *Open: Daily all year, dawn - dusk. Entrance: Park free; Maze £2.10 (children £1.30); Rose Gardens, Wilderness and East Front Gardens free; King William III Privy Garden, Sunken Garden and Great Vine £2 (children £1.30) - free to Palace ticket-holders.*

RHS Garden, Wisley, Woking 01483 224234

Primary garden of the RHS and hub of its scientific and education activities. 240 acres incorporating formal gardens, arboretum, rock garden, alpine and wild garden, model gardens, mixed borders, rose garden, orchard, fruit and vegetable garden, woodland garden, azaleas, lillies, hydrangeas, Mediterranean garden, glasshouses, canal, trial grounds. 7m NE of Guildford on A3. *Open to non-members Feb-Oct Mon-Sat 10-7 or dusk; Nov-Jan 10-4.30 (Sun for members only). Entrance: by membership or £5 (children 6-16 £2).*

Painshill Landscape Garden, Portsmouth Road, Cobham 01932 868113/864674

Landscaped 160-acre park restored by the Painshill Park Trust. Centred around the winding 14-acre lake, it features a Chinese bridge leading to an island and grotto. The mausoleum features on Catherine the Great's Wedgwood 'Frog Service'. The garden's focal point is the elegant Gothick temple. The cedar of Lebanon is reputedly the largest in Europe. 1m W of Cobham on A245. *Open: April-Oct Tues-Sun and Bank Holiday Mon 10.30-6; Nov-March Tues-Thurs and Sat/Sun 11-4 (or dusk). Closed 25th, 26th Dec. Entrance: £3.80 (concessions £3.30, children 5-16 £1.50).*

SQUIRE'S GARDEN CENTRE, WEST HORSLEY
EPSOM ROAD, WEST HORSLEY, LEATHERHEAD KT24 6AR
TEL: 01483 282911 FAX: 01483 281380

Founded in 1935, the Squire's group is a family business which comprises seven garden centres, a rose nursery and herbaceous and bedding plant nurseries. The company seeks to maintain high standards combining quality plants and gardening products with the best service to gardeners and a tradition of working with the local community. The **Squire's Garden Centre at West Horsley** situated close to the National Trust properties of Hatchlands and Polesden Lacey. It is an extensive garden centre which shares its site with Squire's herbaceous and bedding plant nurseries. This was the only Garden Centre in Surrey to receive a Garden Centre Association Award of Excellence for 1997/8. It offers a wide range of plants including trees, shrubs and the very freshest stock of herbaceous and bedding plants, many of which were grown at the nursery on site. Qualified staff are on hand to provide knowledgeable gardening advice. As well as gardening products and houseplants, the shop offers an exciting range of gifts and garden furniture. Visitors are welcome to view the specialist herbaceous bedding plants nurseries

The licensed Orchard Restaurant offers delicious lunches and snacks as well as tea and coffee and tempting cakes. There are also facilities for the disabled and a baby changing area. The centre has a large pet shop and aquatics centre featuring a magnificent range of tropical and cold water fish together with all the materials necessary for creating a water garden or indoor aquarium.

Special Customer Evenings are held each year offering a mixture of talks and demonstrations as well as the opportunity to wander around the Centre, browse and chat over a glass of wine. *Opening Times: Monday to Saturday 9.00 am - 6.00 pm; Sunday 10.30 am - 4.30 pm*

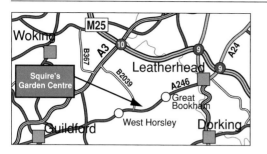

Directions:

Squire's Garden Centre at West Horsley lies on the northern side of the A246 between the villages of West Horsley and Great Bookham. It is midway between Leatherhead and Guildford.

⊛ Aquatics	⊞ Fencing	℗ Large Car Park
🍖 Barbecues	Ⓒ Fruit Trees	🐾 Pet Products and/or Pets
▊ Books & Stationery	⊟ Garden Furniture	🛡 Plant Guarantee
❄ Christmas & Seasonal Displays	⛢ Garden Products	🌱 Plants
▣ Credit Cards Accepted	⊞ Giftware	🍴 Restaurant/Coffee Shop
⚬ Disabled	◭ Houseplants	⦿ Seeds & Bulbs
🌷 Dried & Artificial Flowers	ⓘ Information Desk	🌴 Trees

LOCAL GARDENS

RHS Garden, Wisley, Woking 01483 224234

Primary garden of the RHS and hub of its scientific and education activities. 240 acres incorporating formal gardens, arboretum, rock garden, alpine and wild garden, model gardens, mixed borders, rose garden, orchard, fruit and vegetable garden, woodland garden, azaleas, lillies, hydrangeas, Mediterranean garden, glasshouses, canal, trial grounds. 7m NE of Guildford on A3. *Open to non-members Feb-Oct Mon-Sat 10-7 or dusk; Nov-Jan 10-4.30 (Sun for members only). Entrance: by membership or £5 (children 6-16 £2).*

Polesden Lacey, Great Bookham 01372 452048

National Trust formal gardens: winter garden, walled rose garden, iris garden, lavender garden, lawns. Wonderful views. Regency villa dating back to the early 17th century, re-modelled in the early 20th. King George VI and his Queen (now Elizabeth, the Queen Mother) spent part of their honeymoon here. 5m NW of Dorking off the A246. *Open: daily all year, 11-6 (or dusk). Last admission 5 pm. House open end Mar-Oct Weds-Sun 1.30-5.30; Bank Holiday Mon 11-5.30 (last admission half-hour before closing). Entrance: £3 (house and grounds £6). Family rate available for up to 2 adults and 3 children.*

Hatchlands Park, East Clandon 01483 222482

National Trust-owned garden and park designed by Repton in 1800. Three newly restored walks in the park. Small parterre, now restored, designed by Gertrude Jekyll in 1914 to flower in May and June. Wildflower meadow. N of the A246. *Open: 1st Apr-end Oct Tues-Wed, Thurs, Sun and Bank Holiday Mon 2-5.30 (also Fridays in August). Last admission 5 pm. Park walks and grounds April-Oct daily 11.30-6. Parties Tues and Weds only. House open but closes at 31st Oct. Entrance: park walks and grounds £1.80 (house and garden £4.20).*

SQUIRE'S GARDEN CENTRE, WOKING
LITTLEWICK ROAD, HORSELL, WOKING, SURREY GU21 4XR
TEL: 01276 858446 FAX: 01276 855664

Founded in 1935, the Squire's group is a family business which comprises seven garden centres, a rose nursery and herbaceous and bedding plant nurseries. The company seeks to maintain high standards combining quality plants and gardening products with the best service to gardeners and a tradition of working with the local community.

Extended in 1999, **Squire's Garden Centre at Woking** boasts a comfortable and compact shopping environment as well as a fine range of quality garden plants, houseplants, garden products, gifts and garden furniture. It is located close to the attractive village of Cobham and Horsell Common. Trained staff are on hand to give advice to novice and experienced gardeners alike. In addition the Centre displays a fine range of garden sheds.

The licenced Grapevine Cafe serves lunches, snacks and teas and there are disabled facilities on site.

Each year the garden centre hosts the St John's Floral Art Group Show - ask at the centre for details.

Special Customer Evenings are held each year offering a mixture of talks and demonstrations as well as the opportunity to wander around the Centre, browse and chat over a glass of wine. *Opening Times: Monday to Saturday 9.00 am - 6.00 pm; Sunday 10.30 am - 4.30 pm; Spring late-night opening Friday and Saturday to 7 pm. until end of June.*

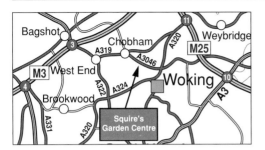

Directions:

From Junction 11 of the M25 take the road towards Woking. After a couple of miles turn right along the A245 towards Chobham and at the first roundabout turn left along Littlewick Road. Squire's Garden Centre is on the right hand side.

Barbecues	Fruit Trees	Large Car Park
Books & Stationery	Garden Furniture	Plant Guarantee
Christmas & Seasonal Displays	Garden Products	Plants
Credit Cards Accepted	Giftware	Restaurant/Coffee Shop
Disabled	Greenhouses & Sheds	Seeds & Bulbs
Dried & Artificial Flowers	Houseplants	Trees

LOCAL GARDENS

RHS Garden, Wisley, Woking (01483) 224234

Primary garden of the RHS and hub of its scientific and education activities. 240 acres incorporating formal gardens, arboretum, rock garden, alpine and wild garden, model gardens, mixed borders, rose garden, orchard, fruit and vegetable garden, woodland garden, azaleas, lillies, hydrangeas, Meditteranean garden, glasshouses, canal, trial grounds. 7m NE of Guildford on A3. *Open to non-members Feb-Oct Mon-Sat 10-7 or dusk; Nov-Jan 10-4.30 (Sun for members only). Entrance: by membership or £5 (children 6-16 £2).*

Great Fosters, Stroude Road, Egham (01784) 433822

Grade II listed garden of late 16th-century hunting lodge, now a hotel. The garden developed in 1918 and has recently been restored. Lengthy paved terrace, large semi-circular lawn, lime avenue. Four knot gardens with statuary, topiary, box edging, 16th-century sundial. Saxon moat, wisteria-covered Japanese bridge. Sunken rose garden, fountain and lily pool. Pergola underplanted with lavender. Orangery, iris and peony gardens. 1m S of Egham off junction 13 of the M25. *Open: All year daily, daylight hours. Entrance: free.*

Polesden Lacey, Great Bookham 01372 452048

National Trust formal gardens: winter garden, walled rose garden, iris garden, lavender garden, lawns. Wonderful views. Regency villa dating back to the early 17th century, re-modelled in the early 20th. King George VI and his Queen (now Elizabeth, the Queen Mother) spent part of their honeymoon here. 5m NW of Dorking off the A246. *Open: daily all year, 11-6 (or dusk). Last admission 5 pm. House open end Mar-Oct Weds-Sun 1.30-5.30; Bank Holiday Mon 11-5.30 (last admission half-hour before closing). Entrance: £3 (house and grounds £6). Family rate available for up to 2 adults and 3 children.*

THE MILLBROOK GARDEN COMPANY
ROTHERFIELD ROAD, JARVIS BROOK, CROWBOROUGH, EAST SUSSEX TN6 3RJ
TEL: 01892 663822 FAX: 01892 654176

Nestling in the hills between Crowborough and Rotherfield, **Millbrook Garden Centre** is of necessity set on an attractive series of terraces - the large carpark at the top leading to the various levels of products and merchandise, where the wealth of garden plants, tools and accessories can be viewed. The Centre stocks a superb grouping of trees, shrubs, container plants, bedding and houseplants, as well as a huge range of pots and garden decorations, making it a good deal simpler to create and maintain a healthy and attractive garden.

Highlights of this far-reaching Garden Centre include the Conservatory department, complete with a wide range of choices and expert advice from the able and friendly staff, and Millbrook Water Gardens, which offers a range of items to create the perfect pond, aquarium or other water feature. The Centre's Swimming Pool display is truly impressive. Millbrook Mowers is another speciality of this first-class Centre, providing an extensive selection of mowers, strimmers and more, to suit every garden's requirements.

The Centre also features a wide range of fencing, paving, walling and other products. With dedicated areas devoted to books, toys, gifts, clothing, glassware, ceramics, body products, cards, candles, and silk and dried flowers, this is a comprehensive site with a wealth of attractive and tasteful items for the discerning consumer. The small Acorns Restaurant/Coffee Shop area is partitioned off from the rest of the premises with trellis fencing. Hanging from this fencing are numerous pictures and prints, many by local artists, which add grace and charm to the restaurant and which can also be purchased. There's an attractive sister centre, also called Millbrook, at Gravesend in Kent (tel: 01474 331135). *Open: Summer Mon-Sat 9-5.30; Winter Mon-Sat 9-5; Suns (all year) 10.30-4.30*

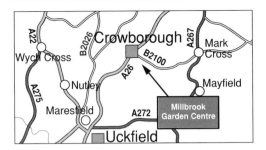

Directions:

From the centre of Crowborough take the B2100 towards Wadhurst. After going under the railway bridge at Jarvis Brook Millbrook Garden Centre is on the right.

Aquatics	Fencing	Houseplants
Barbecues	Floristry	Information Desk
Books & Stationery	Fruit Trees	Large Car Park
Christmas & Seasonal Displays	Garden Construction	Paving
Clothing	Garden Design	Plant Guarantee
Conservatories	Garden Furniture	Plants
Credit Cards Accepted	Garden Machinery	Restaurant/Coffee Shop
Disabled	Garden Products	Seeds & Bulbs
Display Gardens	Giftware	Trees
Dried & Artificial Flowers	Greenhouses & Sheds	

LOCAL GARDENS

Sissinghurst Castle Garden, Sissinghurst, Cranbrook 01580 712850

Created by Vita Sackville-West and her husband Sir Harold Nicolson, now managed by the National Trust. Herb garden, spring garden, rose garden; superb white garden, orange and yellow cottage garden, orchard. Influential for its design as a series of 'outdoor rooms'. Daily visitor numbers are restricted and timed tickets are used. 2m NE of Cranbrook off the A262. *Open: 1 Apr-15 Oct Tues-Fri 1-6.30 (last admission 6), Sat-Sun 10-5.30 (last admission 5). Parties of 11 or more by arrangement. Entrance: £6 (children £3).*

Sheffield Park Garden, Uckfield 01825 790231

Laid out by Capability Brown for the Earl of Sheffield in 1776, and modified in the 20th century, 120-acre NT landscape garden and arboretum. Rare trees, shrubs and fine waterlilies. Four lakes, waterfall and cascades; year-round beauty and interest. National Collection of Ghent azaleas. 5m NW of Uckfield off the A275. *Open: Jan-Feb weekends, Mar-23rd Dec Tues-Sun 10.30-6 (Nov-Mar 4 p.m. or dusk). Entrance: £4.20 (children £2.10/family ticket £10.50/ parties £3.20 per person).*

Moorlands, Friars Gate 01892 652474

4 acres of fine wetland garden developed over the past 70 years in lush valley in the Ashdown Forest. Many unusual shrubs and trees, water garden with pools and streams; azaleas, primulas, irises, rheums, lysichitons, rodgersias, rhododendrons. Liquidambar, larches and scarlet oak. Lovely terrace by the house. River walk. 2m N of Crowborough off the B2188. *Open: April-Oct Weds 11-5, Sun 23 May 2-6, Sun 18 Jul 2-6; always open on request please ring for details. Entrance: £2 (children free).*

OLD BARN NURSERIES LTD
DIAL POST (A24), HORSHAM, WEST SUSSEX RH13 8NR
TEL: 01403 710000 FAX: 01403 710010

Old Barn Nurseries Ltd is an award-winning centre which has been a thriving concern since 1992. Run by a horticulturist and house plant specialist, this excellent centre is situated conveniently on the A24, 12 miles north of Worthing. It is particularly well laid out, with each plant individually flagged with information on giving it the care and attention it needs to flourish. The stunning primrose display in spring is a feature of this extensive and comprehensive centre. Areas within areas highlight distinct garden features, plants and gift ideas. The range of plants for sale include fruiting banana and citrus trees, a large selection of rhododendrons and azaleas, shade-loving plants, acers and hardy ferns, and cacti, each given its own dedicated area.

The centre's speciality is its vast range of sculpture and ornaments for the garden, which includes stone and terracotta garden features, a selection of glazed ceramics - from small pots to huge 'Ali Baba' urns - and a truly amazing 5-foot-high Chinese decorated urn. There's a special display of the nursery's statuary, as well as areas devoted to waterfalls, fountains and other water features. Also on hand are a range of tailor-made hardwood conservatories, and ornamental and hedging features.

The nursery offers a plant information and advisory service, with knowledgeable and helpful staff on hand to advise on every aspect of creating and maintaining a healthy, attractive garden with year-round interest. The superb Old Barn restaurant/coffee shop is an impressive exposed beamed space with minstrels gallery, mock medieval candle chandelier and original high open-beamed roof. Long wooden (medieval-style) tables and large leaded windows add to the traditional ambience. Here visitors can stop for breakfast, hot and cold snacks and meals, and delicious cakes and puddings. *Open: Monday-Saturday 9:00 - 6:00, Sunday 10:30 - 4:30, Barn open daily 9:00 - 6:00*

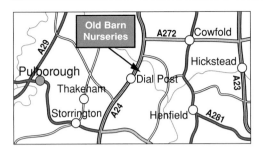

Directions:

Old Barn Nurseries lies on the A24 8 miles south of Horsham and 12 miles northof Worthing near the small village of Dial Post.

Aquatics

Barbecues

Books & Stationery

Christmas & Seasonal Displays

Clothing

Conservatories

Credit Cards Accepted

Cut Flowers

Disabled

Display Gardens

Dried & Artificial Flowers

Fencing

Floristry

Fruit Trees

Garden Construction

Garden Furniture

Garden Products

Giftware

Houseplants

Information Desk

Large Car Park

Paving

Pet Products

Plant Guarantee

Plants

Restaurant/Coffee Shop

Seeds & Bulbs

Trees

LOCAL GARDENS

St Mary's House, Bramber 01903 816205

Surrounding 15th-century Grade I timber-framed house, formal gardens with amusing topiary in animal and bird shapes. Large example of living fossil Gingko bilboa tree, magnolia grandiflora. Water features, pools and fountains, ancient ivy-clad 'Monk's Walk'. Adjacent 'Lost Gardens': recently rediscovered Victorian walled and pleasure gardens, rare circular orchard, 40-metre fruit wall, Boulton and Paul potting shed. Teas. 8m NE of Worthing off A283. *Open: April-Sept Thurs, Suns, Bank Holiday Mons 2-6 (last tour 5); groups at any other times by arrangement. Entrance: formal gardens £2 (chidlren 50p), lost garden £1.00 (children free), house and formal gardens £4.*

Little Thakeham, Merrywood Lane, Storrington 01903 744416

Edwin Lutyens house, now an hotel, surrounded by 4-acre garden. Long rose pergola walk, clematis, romneyas, flowering shrubs, herbaceous borders with peonies, thalictrums, geraniums, dicentras, columbines and catmints. Simple entrance court with squares of lawn, low pots filled withivy, ferns and hostas. Specimen trees, apple orchard, paved walks, spring daffodils. Paved parterre to the front of the house. Small water garden, bog garden. Teas. 10m SW of Horsham off A24. *Open: ring for details.*

Parham Gardens, nr Pulborough 01903 742021

In the heart of ancient deer park, gardens of Elizabethan house. 4 acres of walled garden with shrubs, herbaceous plants, rose garden, potager, orchard, charming miniature house. 7 acres of pleasure grounds with lake, views to the South Downs. Brick-and-turf maze, white-flowering cherry tree. Picnic area, teas. 4m SE of Pulborough on A283. *Open: April-Oct Wed, Thurs, Sun, Bank Holiday Mon noon-6 (last admission 5); parties by arrangement. Entrance: £3 (children 50p); house and garden £5 (OAPs £4, children £1).*

SNOWHILL PLANT AND GARDEN CENTRE
SNOWHILL ROAD, COPTHORNE, CRAWLEY, WEST SUSSEX RH10 3EY
TEL: 01342 712545 FAX: 01342 716477

Every corner of the **Snowhill Plant and Garden Centre** is filled with objects and plants to beautify not just the garden but the home as well. As well as a wonderful selection of flowering and foliage plants, shrubs and trees for all seasons, climates and soil types, this Centre boasts a full range of garden machinery, from basic hand mowers and strimmers to motorised driveable mowers. All products are well laid out and well presented. A Crutchfield's established Dahlia grower, this Centre boasts specialised seasonal trimmings including a most unusual fibre-optic Christmas tree - the ends of the pine needles themselves change colour continually. With fencing and paving sections, landscape material and garden buildings area, Snowhill offers a truly comprehensive selection of everything needed to create comfortable and attractive indoor and outdoor rooms.

Cane and wooden furniture are specialities of this distinguished Centre. Visitors will find a wealth of ideas on tasteful conservatory and outdoor furniture, and all the materials with which to create the perfect ambience in the garden. The staff are helpful, courteous and very knowledgeable, and offer specialist knowledge on self-assembled sheds, laying patios and much more, to complement the Centre's comprehensive selection of sheds, outhouses, summer pavilions and children's playhouses - many of these tastefully decorated and furnished. A full advisory and delivery service is also available.

The extensive and comprehensive book shop has books covering not just gardening matters but a wealth of other interesting titles. The restaurant/coffee shop is large and well appointed, with an excellent menu including dishes such as lamb steaks, haddock and king prawn bake, wild mushroom strudel and chicken and asparagus pie, and a selection of mouth-watering puddings. *Open: summer daily 9-6; winter daily 9-5.30, restaurant open: Mon-Fri 9.30-4.45, Sun 10-30-4.30.*

Directions:

From Junction 10 of the M23 take the A264 towards East Grinstead. Snowhill Plant and Garden Centre lies on the left opposite the Effingham Park Hotel

- 🍖 Barbecues
- 📕 Books & Stationery
- 🎄 Christmas & Seasonal Displays
- 👕 Clothing
- Conservatories
- ⬛ Credit Cards Accepted
- ♿ Disabled
- 🌼 Display Gardens
- 💐 Dried & Artificial Flowers

- 🏭 Fencing
- 🍒 Fruit Trees
- 🌺 Garden Design
- 🪑 Garden Furniture
- Garden Machinery
- 🪓 Garden Products
- 🎁 Giftware
- Greenhouses & Sheds
- Houseplants

- ⓘ Information Desk
- Ⓟ Large Car Park
- 🧱 Paving
- 🎍 Plant Guarantee
-) Plants
- 🍴 Restaurant/Coffee Shop
- Seeds & Bulbs
- 🌳 Trees

LOCAL GARDENS

Standen, East Grinstead 01342 323029

12-acre National Trust hillside garden. House and estate connected with William Morris. Succession of small English gardens, including 12 areas or features such as quarry garden, bamboo garden, rose garden, three summer houses. Wonderful views over the Medway and Ashdown Forest. Teas. 2m S of East Grinstead off the B2110/A22. *Open: late Mar-early Nov Weds-Sun, Bank Holiday Mon 12.30-6; early Nov-mid Dec Fri-Sun 1-4. Entrance: £3/£2 Nov-Dec (children £1.50/£1); house and garden £5 (children £2.50).*

Orchards, Wallage Lane, Rowfant, Crawley 01342 718280

Impressive woodland garden created by the late renowned horticulturalist Arthur Hellyer and his wife Gay, their daughter continues the replanting and restoration work. This 7-acre woodland garden boasts mature trees, orchards, bluebell wood, herbaceous and mixed borders, heather/conifer meadow, wild orchid meadow, and rhododendrons and camellias, for year-round interest. Owners nursery. 4m E of Crawley. Teas. *Entrance: £2 (children free).*

Wakehurst Place, Ardingly 01444 894067

Managed by the Royal Botanic Gardens, Kew, since 1965, with one of the finest collections of rare trees and flowering shrubs in an area of outstanding natural beauty. Hardy plants arranged geographically. National Collections of betulas, nothofagus, skimmias, hypericums. Heath garden, walled gardens, pinetum. Glade planted with species that grow at over 3,000 metres in the Himalyas. Steep wooded valley with scenic walks, lakes, large bog garden, attractive water course. Restaurant. 5m N of Haywards Heath on B2028. *Open: daily, all year, except 25th Dec, 1st Jan; Nov-Jan 10-4, Feb and Oct 10-5, March 10-6, April-Sept 10-7. Entrance: £5 (concs £3.50, children £2.50, under-5s free; family tickets available). Group bookings with discounts available by arrangement..*

COWELL'S GARDEN CENTRE
MAIN ROAD, WOOLSINGTON, NEWCASTLE UPON TYNE NE13 8BW
TEL: 0191 286 3403 FAX: 0191 271 2597

The Cowells started this garden centre from a small nursery and hobby as dahlia-growers back in 1978. Their son Martin, having trained at Pershore Agricultural College, joined the family business in 1996 to lend his help, support and practical knowledge. Customers benefit from the expertise of the centre's skilled and growing staff.

At **Cowell's Garden Centre**, plants are the number-one priority. The centre maintains impeccable standards for quality and service, and was voted the second best garden centre for 1998/9 by the Gardening Centre Association. This small but perfectly formed garden centre is a centre of excellence for hanging baskets. This has been acknowledged by the significant number of awards it has received - having been rewarded by the GCA no fewer than 12 times in the past few years. Owners Alan and Mavis Cowell are the resident experts on preparing and maintaining beautiful and healthy hanging baskets and are more than happy to give advice.

Whatever the season, a visit here is a real treat and an inspiration for all gardeners. In spring and early summer the accent is on patio and bedding plants, hanging baskets and containers. In autumn there is a similar choice of plants to bring colour and life to the garden. At Christmas there are attractive and magical seasonal displays.

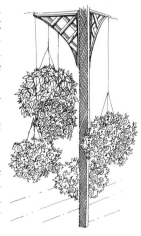

The centre's houseplant department offers year-round a superb choice of foliage and flowering plants. Planted arrangements are also available throughout the year to provide a spectacle of colour for home, office or conservatory.

To complement its excellent range of plants, the centre stocks a choice of gardening sundries and accessories, including stoneware, ceramics, composts and fertilisers, gardening tools, gifts and more. *Open: daily 9.00-6.00*

Directions:

From the A1/A696 junction take the B6918 towards Ponteland. Cowell's Garden Centre lies on the left just after the village of Woolsington.

Aquatics	Fencing	Information Desk
Barbecues	Fruit Trees	Large Car Park
Christmas & Seasonal Displays	Garden Construction	Plant Guarantee
Credit Cards Accepted	Garden Furniture	Plants
Disabled	Garden Products	Seeds & Bulbs
Display Gardens	Giftware	Trees
Dried & Artificial Flowers	Houseplants	

LOCAL GARDENS

Wallington, Cambo 01670 774283

National Trust fine house and grounds with lawns, terraces, flower beds. Superb walled garden. Fine species roses and shrubs, heathers and herbaceous plants. Edwardian conservatory with excellent fuchsias. 100-acre woodland and lakes, terraces and flower beds. 20m NW of Newcastle off the A696. *Open: grounds open daily all year during daylight hours. Walled garden daily April-Sept 10-7, Oct 10-6 (or dusk); Nov-Mar 10-4. House April-Sept Weds-Mon 1-5.30, Oct 1-4.30 (last admission 1 hour before closing). Entrance: £3.80 (children £1.90); house and grounds £5.20 (children £2.60).*

Kirkley Hall College, Ponteland 01661 860808

10 acres of grounds that include a three-acre walled Victorian garden. From propagation on, all stages of horticulture are displayed here and all plants are labelled. Bedding plants, climbers, borders. Beds are composed of a variety of colours, textures and shapes. On the Hall terraces there are many lovely containers. National Collection of beeches. Sunken garden, wildlife pond. 11m NW of Newcastle off the A696. *Open: April-Sept Mon-Fri 10-3. Entrance: free.*

Belsay Hall, Belsay 01661 881636

English Heritage 30-acre gardens with rare, exotic and mature specimens. Flower garden, winter-flowering heathers, magnolia terrace, winter garden with 28-metre Douglas fir. Fine rhododendrons. Grand croquet lawn. Neoclassical mansion has formal terraces leading to woods, a wild meadow and a quarry garden. One-and-a-half mile Crag Wood walk along a serpentine path, passing a lake and the hanging woodlandsopposite the Hall. 14m NW of Newcastle on the A696. *Open: daily April-Oct 10-6, Nov-Mar (except 24th-26th Dec) 10-4. Hall and Castle open. Evening tours in summer. Entrance: £3.60 (OAPs £2.70, children £1.80, reduced rate for groups of 11 or more).*

Dobbies Garden Centre, Ponteland
Street House Farm, Ponteland, Newcastle-upon-Tyne
Tel: 01661 820202 Fax: 01661 860010

Dobbies Garden Centres have been established for 130 years, with nine (soon to be ten) garden centres located throughout the UK. The range of products on offer undergoes continuous expansion, as the centre goes from strength to strength in offering a wide range of plants and garden features and accessories, including houseplants, fruit and ornamental trees, roses, shrubs, conifers, herbaceous plants and more.

This centre is also home to a landscaping franchise, swimming pool and jacuzzi franchise, and huge and well-stocked Acorn pet area. To complement all this, the centre stocks a comprehensive choice of gardening sundries and accessories, including ceramics and stoneware, containers of all sizes, floristry sundries, silk flowers, composts and fertilisers, and gardening tools. Outside in the rock gardens you see the plants in their proper setting.

Covering 17,000 square feet, this garden centre is housed in a superb converted farm building and retains a countryside atmosphere despite its proximity to Newcastle Airport. Small enough to have a cosy feel, it is light, airy and warm. The attractive old walled garden and other outdoor areas are covered by lovely wooden pergolas.

Dobbies place enormous emphasis on staff and training. The majority of staff are horticulturists, with the know-how and expertise to advise all customers on the best plants to choose for any situation and soil type, and on how to maintain and cultivate a beautiful and healthy garden. The restaurant/tearoom serves a variety of delicious hot and cold snacks and meals. It has large windows which look north towards the Borders region. Leave yourself enough time to stop and admire the views along the way! *Open: January to March and December, Monday to Saturday 9-5, Sunday 11-5; April to November, Monday to Saturday 9-6, Sunday 11-5.*

Directions:

From the A1/A696 junction take the A696 towards Ponteland. Just past the airport on the right lies Dobbies Garden Centre.

Aquatics		Dried & Artificial Flowers		Greenhouses & Sheds	
Barbecues		Farm Shop		Houseplants	
Books & Stationery		Fencing		Information Desk	
Camping Equipment		Fireworks		Large Car Park	
Childrens Play Area		Floristry		Paving	
Christmas & Seasonal Displays		Fruit Trees		Pet Products and/or Pets	
Clothing		Garden Construction		Plant Guarantee	
Conservatories		Garden Design		Plants	
Credit Cards Accepted		Garden Furniture		Restaurant/Coffee Shop	
Cut Flowers		Garden Machinery		Seeds & Bulbs	
Disabled		Garden Products		Trees	
Display Gardens		Giftware			

LOCAL GARDENS

Belsay Hall, Belsay 01661 881636

English Heritage 30-acre gardens with rare, exotic and mature specimens. Flower garden, winter-flowering heathers, magnolia terrace, winter garden with 28-metre Douglas fir. Fine rhododendrons. Grand croquet lawn. Neoclassical mansion has formal terraces leading to woods, a wild meadow and a quarry garden. One-and-a-half mile Crag Wood walk along a serpentine path, passing a lake and the hanging woodlandsopposite the Hall. 14m NW of Newcastle on the A696. *Open: daily April-Oct 10-6, Nov-Mar (except 24th-26th Dec) 10-4. Hall and Castle open. Evening tours in summer. Entrance: £3.80 (OAPs £2.80, children £1.90, reduced rate for groups of 11 or more).*

Wallington, Cambo 01670 774283

National Trust fine house and grounds with lawns, terraces, flower beds. Superb walled garden. Fine species roses and shrubs, heathers and herbaceous plants. Edwardian con-servatory with excellent fuchsias. 100-acre woodland and lakes, terraces and flower beds. 20m NW of Newcastle off the A696. *Open: grounds open daily all year during daylight hours. Walled garden daily April-Sept 10-7, Oct 10-6 (or dusk); Nov-Mar 10-4. House April-Sept Weds-Mon 1-5.30, Oct 1-4.30 (last admission 1 hour before closing). Entrance: £3.80 (children £1.90); house and grounds £5.20 (children £2.60).*

Meldon Park, Morpeth 01434 603351

About 8 acres of gardens and woodland. Walled kitchen garden, mature trees, shrub bor-ders, rhododendrons, herbaceous borders with a fine variety of irises and peonies, rose beds, box hedges. Woodland walks, orangery, wild meadow walks. Neoclassical house faces ha-ha and dene below. 7m W of Morpeth on the B6343. *Open: please telephone for details. House open. Entrance: £3 (OAPs £2, children 50p).*

PETER BARRATT'S GARDEN CENTRE
GOSFORTH PARK, NEWCASTLE UPON TYNE NE3 5EN
TEL: 0191 236 7111 FAX: 0191 236 5496

Peter Barratt's Garden Centre was established in 1982, growing from a bedding plants nursery on an attractive greenfield site into this large and comprehensive garden centre. Hellebores (the Easter rose) are the speciality of this extensive garden centre. The plantarea offers a wide range of these lovely plants, together with bulbs, bonsai, bedding and perennial plants, fruit and ornamental trees, shrubs, conifers, climbers, alpines and heathers. To complement this excellent range of plants, the centre stocks a comprehensive choice of gardening sundries and accessories, including containers in all sizes, stoneware, ceramics, floristry sundries, silk flowers, composts, gardening tools and implements, and fertilisers. Exterior displays feature a classic collection of frost-resistant pottery, including the Himalayan Collection, Thai sunrise, Vietnamese and Aegean ranges of ceramics.

Complete garden pool kits are sold here, together with fountains, fonts, cascades and statues that spout water in every way. There is also a significant range of pumps, ponds, fish, tanks, aquariums and sundries, with a large area of the centre devoted to these water features and aquatics. The trained staff are always available to advise on choosing plants for particular situations. Other attractions of this centre are the range of clothing, including Stormafit and Acorn fleeces and a selection of sweaters and outdoor wear. The small and well-stocked giftshop has ornaments, pictures and frames, wind chimes and a range of candles. There is also a well-stocked bookshop. The restaurant/  coffee shop, 'Peter's Eater', serves tempting hot and cold meals and snacks and there is a dedicated safe play area for children. To the rear there's a landscaped water feature with pergolas and plants. *Open: Monday to Saturday 9-5 (peak season 9-7), Sunday 10.30-4.30.*

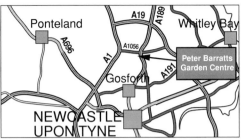

Directions:
From the A1/A1056 junction just north of Gosforth take the A1056 east towards Whitley Bay. At the third roundabout take the fifth road and Peter Barratts Garden Centre can be found on the left.

Aquatics	Dried & Artificial Flowers	Information Desk
Barbecues	Fencing	Large Car Park
Books & Stationery	Fireworks	Paving
Childrens Play Area	Floristry	Pet Products and/or Pets
Christmas & Seasonal Displays	Fruit Trees	Plant Guarantee
Clothing	Garden Furniture	Plants
Conservatories	Garden Products	Restaurant/Coffee Shop
Credit Cards Accepted	Giftware	Seeds & Bulbs
Disabled	Greenhouses & Sheds	Trees
Display Gardens	Houseplants	

LOCAL GARDENS

Jesmond Dene, Jesmond 0191 281 0973
The famous engineer Lord Armstrong presented these gardens and parkland to the city of Newcastle in 1883. Extensive walks through thickly wooded, steep-sided dene, taking in a ruined mill, waterfall and some excellent old buildings along the way. The upper park has a pond and children's play area. Pets' corner. 1m E of Newcastle city cenre along Jesmond Road. *Open: daily all year. Visitor Centre open at weekends. Entrance: free.*

Belsay Hall, Belsay 01661 881636
English Heritage 30-acre gardens with rare, exotic and mature specimens. Flower garden, winter-flowering heathers, magnolia terrace, winter garden with 28-metre Douglas fir. Fine rhododendrons. Grand croquet lawn. Neoclassical mansion has formal terraces leading to woods, a wild meadow and a quarry garden. One-and-a-half mile Crag Wood walk along a serpentine path, passing a lake and the hanging woodlandsopposite the Hall. 14m NW of Newcastle on the A696. *Open: daily April-Oct 10-6, Nov-Mar (except 24th-26th Dec) 10-4. Hall and Castle open. Occassional evening tours in summer. Entrance: £3.80 (OAPs £2.90, children £1.90, reduced rate for groups of 11 or more); wheelchair access to grounds and ground floor of building.*

Kirkley Hall College, Ponteland 01661 860808
10 acres of grounds that include a three-acre walled Victorian garden. From propagation on, all stages of amenity horticulture are displayed. Bedding plants, climbers, borders. Beds are composed of a variety of colours, textures and shapes. On the Hall terraces there are many lovely containers. National Collection of beeches. Sunken garden, wildlife pond. 11m NW of Newcastle off the A696. *Open: April-Sept Mon-Fri 10-3. Entrance: free.*

WHITACRE GARDEN CENTRE

TAMWORTH ROAD, NETHER WHITACRE, COLESHILL, BIRMINGHAM B46 2DN
TEL: 01675 481306 FAX: 01675 481762 EMAIL: whitacregc@dial.pipex.com

With a new name and look, **Whitacre Garden Centre** is a must for gardeners at all levels of expertise. Situated in the village of Nether Whitacre, with its newly designed plant areas this Centre has fast gained a reputation for quality and service. You'll find an extensive collection of plants, shrubs and seeds at this gardener's garden centre. This family-run business incorporates two other distinct garden centres. Each has its own character, yet all three are united in the high standards they strive to maintain.

Everything imaginable for the keen gardener and the potterer alike is here, including a stunning variety of superb plants and everything else for the perfect garden. Whitacre is so confident about the quality of their plants that all hardy varieties come with a special two-year guarantee. Local growers are used whenever possible, to offer you the widest range of the freshest plants. The expert staff are happy to help with any gardening questions you may have. In addition to the wide selection of trees, shrubs and plants for the garden, as well as a superb range of gardening tools and supplies, a special feature of this comprehensive garden centre is its wide range and variety of houseplants, to add grace, colour and style to any garden, home, office or conservatory.

Inside, you'll find gifts - from floating candles to fabulous cards, garden furniture, barbecues and much more. The choice and variety continues through all ranges offered by this comprehensive garden centre, including a specialist conservatory centre and World of Water, a must for all your water gardening and aquatic needs.

The Windmill Coffee Shop serves a range of tempting snacks, meals and beverages. A visit to Whitacre will prove its motto, 'Come and enjoy the difference'.
Open: Monday to Saturday 9-5.30, Sunday 10.30-4.30.

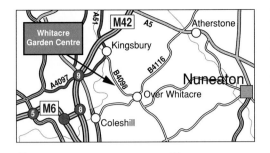

Directions:
From junction 9 of the M42 take the A4097 towards Kingsbury. Follow the tourist signs and turn right at the second roundabout on the B4098. Whitacre Garden Centre lies on the right just after the village of Nether Whitacre.

Aquatics	Fencing	Houseplants
Barbecues	Floristry	Information Desk
Books & Stationery	Fruit Trees	Large Car Park
Childrens Play Area	Garden Construction	Plant Guarantee
Christmas & Seasonal Displays	Garden Design	Plants
Conservatories	Garden Furniture	Restaurant/Coffee Shop
Credit Cards Accepted	Garden Products	Seeds & Bulbs
Disabled	Giftware	Trees
Dried & Artificial Flowers		

LOCAL GARDENS

Arbury Hall, Arbury 01203 382804
Wonderful 10-acre garden with a real feeling of tranquillity. Bulbs are followed by wisteria, rhododendrons and azaleas, then roses and autumn colours from shrubs and trees. Bluebell woods; lakes with wildfowl; formal rose garden. Old walled garden with arboretum; pollarded limes. 3½m SE of Nuneaton off the B4102. *Open: April-end Sept Sun and Bank Holiday Mon 2-6 (last admission 5). House open as garden but 2-5.30. Entrance: £3 (children £2); hall and gardens £4.50, children £2.50.*

Castle Bromwich Hall Garden Trust, Chester Road, Castle Bromwich 0121 749 4100
A shining example of the Formal English Garden style. Established in the 17th century, restoration began in 1985. 10 acres with a unique collection of historic shrubs, plants, culinary and medicinal herbs and vegetables. Summer house, greenhouse, orangery, orchard, kitchen garden, ponds, maze, wilderness. Guided tours. 4m E of Birmingham city centre off the M6/A38/A452. *Open: Easter-Sept daily 1.30-4.30, Sat-Sun and Bank Holiday Mon 2-6; April weekends only; Entrance: £2.50 (OAPs £1.50, children 50p).*

Botanical Gardens and Glasshouses, Westbourne Road, Edgbaston 0121 454 1860
15-acre garden of enormous interest and variety. Orangery, Tropical House, Cactus and Succulent House, waterfowl enclosure, cages with macaws and parrots. Raised alpine beds, sunken rose garden, rock garden with a range of primulas, astilbes, azaleas and alpine plants. Small display of carnivorous plants. Model domestic gardens with themes such as low-maintenance, children's garden, colour garden and plantsman's area. Lawn aviary. Adventure trail and children's playground. 2m from Birmingham city centre. *Open: daily all year 9 (10 on Sun)-7 (or dusk). Entrance: £4.20 (£4.50 on Sun in summer; OAPs/disabled/students/children £2.30, family £11, £12 on Suns and Bank Holiday Mons).*

WEBBS OF WYCHBOLD

WYCHBOLD, DROITWICH SPA, WORCESTERSHIRE WR9 0DG TEL: 01527 861777
FAX: 01527 861284 EMAIL: claire@webbsofwychbold.demon.co.uk

The origins of **Webbs of Wychbold** can be traced back to the mid-19th century, when Edward Webb, a successful agricultural seeds merchant, began trading from Wordsley near Stourbridge. In the 1970s his great-great-grandson Richard bought the present premises and took the development of Webbs further as both a garden centre and nursery. It now covers a 55-acre site, and is generally acknowledged as one of the leading horticultural centres in the country.

One special feature of this Centre is the charming thatched building, completed in 1937 as a reception area for visitors to Webbs Seed Trial Grounds. Today this atmospheric building provides a unique setting to display a magnificent range of silk flowers, plants and glassware. Completely redesigned over the last two years, the Award Winning Outdoor Plant Area caters for the green-fingered experienced gardener and keen novices alike, with display gardens throughout the Centre providing ideas and inspiration. From wonderful houseplants to books, cards and unusual gifts, garden furniture and the marvellous Christmas Wonderland, this Centre has it all.

The Nursery also plays its part in Webbs' success, growing over a million plants a year. It has been instrumental in introducing new plants to the garden, including Nemesia 'Confetti' and most recently Coreopsis 'Calypso'. Guided nursery tours can be arranged for groups of 10 or more (fee charged). This Centre has garnered many accolades, including 1998 Best GCA Garden Centre in the UK and 1998 GCA Winner for Best Outdoor Plant Area in the UK. The comfortable and attractive restaurant serves hearty and expertly prepared meals and snacks, as well as a selection of teas, coffees and soft drinks. Webbs produces a free mailing list to help you keep up with special events and the latest horticultural information. *Open: daily 9-6 except Suns 10.30-4.30. Extended opening Mon-Fri, Apr-Sep 9-8.*

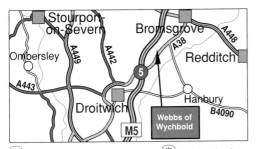

Directions:

From Junction 5 of the M5 take the A38 towards Bromsgrove. Webbs of Wychbold lies on the left.

Aquatics	Display Gardens	Houseplants
Barbecues	Dried & Artificial Flowers	Information Desk
Books & Stationery	Fencing	Large Car Park
Childrens Play Area	Floristry	Paving
Christmas & Seasonal Displays	Fruit Trees	Pet Products and/or Pets
Clothing	Garden Design	Plant Guarantee
Conservatories	Garden Furniture	Plants
Credit Cards Accepted	Garden Products	Restaurant/Coffee Shop
Cut Flowers	Giftware	Seeds & Bulbs
Disabled	Greenhouses & Sheds	Trees

LOCAL GARDENS

Avoncroft Museum of Historic Buildings, Stoke Heath (01527) 831886

Fascinating collection of buildings located on a beautiful open-air site. 600 years of history to experience; also rides, demonstrations, farm animals. Magnificent hall with medieval carved roof. Model railway rides most weekends. National telephone kiosk collection including working exchange. Horse-driven cider mill operating seasonally. Working windmill. Medieval merchant's house. Picnic area, tea room, craft gallery. 2 miles south of Bromsgrove off the A38. *Open: daily 10.30-5 (5.30 at weekends) July-Aug; Tues-Sun 10.30-4.30 (5 at weekends) April-June and Sept-Oct; Tues-Fri and Sat-Sun 10.30-4 Mar and Nov. Open Bank Holidays. Entrance: £4.50 (OAPs £3.60, children £2.25).*

Hanbury Hall, Droitwich 01527 821214

Outstanding William and Mary red-brick house, famed for its beautiful painted ceilings and staircase. Re-creation of an 18th century formal garden, as designed by George London. Sunken parterre, fruit orchard, wilderness. Orangery with citrus trees, Ice -house, pond and two bowling green pavilions. 4½m E of Droitwich (B4090). *Open: mid-Mar to mid-Oct Sun-Weds 2-6 (last admission 5.30 or dusk). National Trust members free. Garden only: £2.50; house and garden £4.40.*

Botanical Gardens and Glasshouses, Westbourne Road, Edgbaston 0121 454 1860

15-acre garden of enormous interest and variety. Orangery, Tropical House, Cactus and Succulent House, waterfowl enclosure, cages with macaws and parrots. Raised alpine beds, sunken rose garden, rock garden with a range of primulas, astilbes, azaleas and alpine plants, display of carnivorous plants. Model domestic gardens with themes such as low-maintenance, children's garden, colour garden and plantsman's area. Lawn Aviary. Adventure trail and children's playground. 2m from Birmingham city centre. *Open: daily all year 9 (10 on Sun)-7 (or dusk). Entrance: £4.20 (£4.50 on Sun in summer; OAPs/disabled/students/children £2.30, family £11, £12 on Suns and Bank Holiday Mons).*

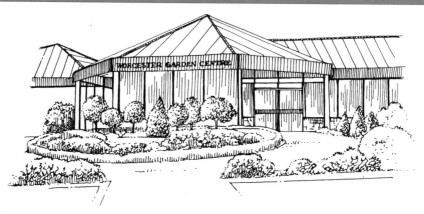

WORCESTER GARDEN CENTRE
DROITWICH ROAD, WORCESTER WR3 7SW
TEL: 01905 451231 FAX: 01905 755371 EMAIL: worcestergc@dial.pipex.com

The modern design of **Worcester Garden Centre** reflects a commitment to giving today's gardeners exactly what they want. The centre is built around an extensive selection of high-quality products that allow you to create the garden of your dreams. This family-run business incorporates two other distinct garden centres. Each has its own character, yet all three are united in the high standards they strive to maintain. Offering top-quality gardening products, value for money and, above all, customer service, any shopping excursion to these centres will be a pleasant and inspiring experience.

Everything imaginable for the keen gardener and the potterer alike is here, including a stunning variety of superb plants and everything else for the perfect garden. Worcester is so confident about the quality of their plants that all hardy varieties come with a special two-year guarantee. The choice and variety continues through all ranges offered by this comprehensive garden centre. There is plenty to browse around - and if you don't know exactly what you need, or if you have a problem to solve, the experienced gardeners on hand can help. They will advise you on the best plants and products for your garden, and offer helpful hints and tips.

In addition to the wide selection of trees, shrubs and plants for the garden, as well as a superb range of gardening tools and supplies, a special feature of this comprehensive garden centre is its wide range of pot plants, to add grace, colour and style to any garden, home, office or conservatory. The Black Pear Cafe serves a tempting range of meals, snacks and beverages. A visit to Worcester Garden Centre will prove its motto, 'The Worcester source of gardening know-how'. *Open: Monday to Saturday 9-6 (late night on Thursday until 9 p.m.), Sunday 10-4.*

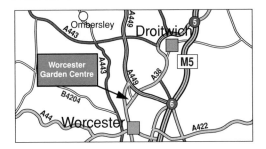

Directions:

From junction 6 of the M5 take the A449 towards Kidderminster. After 2 miles, at the first roundabout, take the first exit signed to Claines. Follow this road to the T junction, about 1 mile, and turn right on the A38 towards Worcester. Worcester Garden Centre is on the right.

Aquatics	Fencing	Houseplants
Barbecues	Floristry	Information Desk
Books & Stationery	Fruit Trees	Large Car Park
Childrens Play Area	Garden Construction	Paving
Christmas & Seasonal Displays	Garden Design	Plant Guarantee
Conservatories	Garden Furniture	Plants
Credit Cards Accepted	Garden Products	Restaurant/Coffee Shop
Disabled	Giftware	Seeds & Bulbs
Display Gardens	Sheds	Trees
Dried & Artificial Flowers		

LOCAL GARDENS

Eastgrove Cottage Garden Nursery, Sankyns Green, Shrawley, Little Witley 01299 896389

Unique and delightful country cottage flower garden, nearly 30 years in the making, which has attracted worldwide interest for its inspired and ever-changing planting. Profusion of colour, carefully planted and beautifully maintained. Variegated foliage and strongly-coloured shrubs lend a backdrop for a variety of herbaceous plants. Secret Garden with strong mauves, pinks, silver and burgundy. Arboretum. Range of unusual plants for sale, propagated at the nursery. 8m NW of Worcester on the road between Shrawley on the B4196 and Great Witley on the A443. *Open: April-July Thurs-Mon 2-5; Sept-early Oct Thurs-Sat 2-5. Entrance: £2 (children free).*

Witley Court, Worcester Road, Great Witley 01299 896636

English Heritage. Witley Court is an early Jacobean manor house which was renovated in the 1800s in Italianate style, with porticoes by John Nash. Now a ruin but none the less impressive, the gardens - William Nash's 'Monster Work' - feature enormous fountains of stone. The woodland walks are being restored. Evening guided tours by appointment. 10m NW of Worcester on the A433. *Open: daily April-Oct 10-6 (dusk in Oct); Nov-Mar Weds-Sun 10-4. Closed 25th-26th Dec. Entrance: £3.50 (OAPs £2.60, children £1.80), 15% group discounts for parties of 11 or more.*

Stone House Cottage Gardens, Stone, Kidderminster 01562 699902

This garden has been created since 1974. Follies and towers breal up the area and are covered with unusual climbers and shrubs. Yew hedges divide the garden. Raised beds. Unusual herbaceous plants, shrubs abd climbers are all labelled. Picnics allowed for a modest fee. *Open Mar-Sep wed - Sat 10-5.30. Oct - Mar by appointment. Entrance charged - ring for details.*

ARMITAGE'S MOWER WORLD & GARDEN CENTRE

BIRCHENCLIFFE HILL ROAD, BIRCHENCLIFFE, HUDDERSFIELD, WEST YORKSHIRE HD3 3NJ
TEL: 01484 536010 FAX: 01484 519554 WEBSITE: www.armitages-gc.co.uk

In 1842, 26 years before the first lawnmower was invented, William Armitage opened his small but well-stocked corn and seed merchants shop in the heart of Huddersfield. Over the years the business has expanded, and moved to these more extensive premises in the mid-1980s. Still family run, making it one of the oldest family-run businesses in the area, **Armitage's Garden Centres** now comprise two sites: this centre and Armitage's Pennine Garden Centre.

The centre's range of garden plants is one of the largest and most comprehensive in the region. Experts are always on hand to help you choose the right plant for the best results. All hardy outdoor plants are guaranteed for two years.

The centre also stocks a wide range of tubs, planters, troughs and pots from around the world, as well as statues and water features, to enhance the natural beauty of any garden.

As its name suggests, this centre specialises in garden machinery. The centre has over 200 different machines to choose from, and provides a complete garden machine service, from helping you to select the best machine to regular servicing and repair. Mower World has over 7,000 machinery spare parts and a team of advisors who can supply you with all you need to keep your machine in tip-top condition.

The garden furniture range is selected to offer the utmost comfort with durability, quality and value for money. This comprehensive centre also boasts a Pet Department and a Gift Department. The Coffee Shop onsite serves sandwiches and hot and cold snacks every day. *Open: Every day - please phone for seasonal variations.*

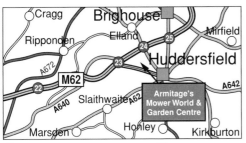

Directions:

From Junction 24 of the M62 take the Huddersfield road and turn right into Birchencliffe Hill Road. Armitage's Mower World and Garden Centre is on the right.

Aquatics	Fireworks	Houseplants
Barbecues	Floristry	Information Desk
Books & Stationery	Fruit Trees	Large Car Park
Christmas & Seasonal Displays	Garden Design	Paving
Clothing	Garden Furniture	Plant Guarantee
Credit Cards Accepted	Garden Machinery	Plants
Cut Flowers	Garden Products	Restaurant/Coffee Shop
Disabled	Giftware	Seeds & Bulbs
Dried & Artificial Flowers	Greenhouses & Sheds	Trees
Fencing		

LOCAL GARDENS

Harewood House, Harewood, Leeds 0113 288 6331

80 acres of gardens within the 1,000-acre parkland designed by Capability Brown. Victorian formal garden with box edging; statues, parterres and Italianate fountains, woodland walks, rock garden, majestic lake and cascade; bog garden, collections of rhododendrons. Formal terraces restored by original Sir Charles Barry specifications. Art gallery and bird garden. 7m N of Leeds off the A61. *Open: Mar-Oct daily 10-6 (or dusk); Nov-mid Dec weekends 10-6 (or dusk). House open 11-4.30. Entrance: Terrace Gallery, Bird Garden and grounds £6.95 (OAPs £6.25, children £4.75).*

Golden Acre Park, Otley Road, Leeds

Botanic garden and impressive public park. Pleasant rolling hills lead down to lake. Rock garden and alpine house, rhododendrons, fine collection of sempervivums, heathers. Extensive tree collection, most specimens are labelled. Demonstration plots where instruction is offered to amateur gardeners. This park also has a demonstration garden for Fleuroselect flowers. NW of Leeds off the A660. *Open: all year, daily during daylight hours. Entrance: free.*

East Riddlesden Hall, Bradford Road, Keighley 01535 607075

National Trust property with garden and traditional 17th-century Yorkshire manor house. After nearly two centuries of neglect, the house was restored in the mid-1980s. The great barn is deemed to be one of the best of its kind in northern England. The grounds boast a small but well- tended garden and a monastic fish pond. 1m NE of Keighley off the A650. *Open: April-June and Sept-Oct Sat-Weds noon-5; July-Aug Sat-Thurs noon-5. Last admission 4.30; groups must pre-book. House open. Entrance: £3.30 (children £1.80).*

ARMITAGE'S PENNINE GARDEN CENTRE
HUDDERSFIELD ROAD, SHELLEY, HUDDERSFIELD, WEST YORKSHIRE HD8 8LG
TEL: 01484 607748 FAX: 01484 519554

For over 155 years **Armitage's** has been the name synonymous with all things horticultural in the Huddersfield area. Still family run, Armitage's Garden Centres now comprise two sites: this centre and Armitage's Mower World and Garden Centre. The company never shies away from trying a new product or system. From state-of-the-art gardening technology to the basic border spade, the centre is at the forefront of innovative gardening products to help you create the perfect garden.

The centre's range of garden plants is one of the largest and most comprehensive in the region. Experts are always on hand to help you choose the right plant for the best results. All hardy outdoor plants are guaranteed for two years. If you are looking for a particular plant or have a difficult garden to work with, Armitage's can help you obtain plants of all shapes and sizes, as they buy in plants from all over the country and even from abroad.

The centre also stocks a wide range of tubs, planters, troughs and pots from around the world, as well as statues and water features, to enhance the natural beauty of any garden. The garden furniture range is selected to offer the utmost comfort with durability, quality and value for money. This comprehensive centre also boasts a Pet Department.

The Gift Department has a large selection of pot plants and planted bowls, to grace any home, office or conservatory with a splash of colour or lovely foliage. The Coffee Shop onsite serves sandwiches and hot and cold snacks every day. *Open: Every day - phone for seasonal variations.*

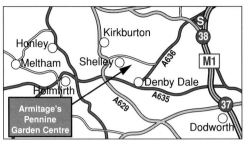

Directions:

From Holmfirth take the A635 towards Barnsley. At the Junction of the A636 turn left. After 1 mile turn left towards Shelley and Armitage's Garden Centre can be found on the left hand side just before the village.

Aquatics	Fireworks	Information Desk
Barbecues	Floristry	Large Car Park
Books & Stationery	Fruit Trees	Paving
Christmas & Seasonal Displays	Garden Design	Pet Products and/or Pets
Clothing	Garden Furniture	Plant Guarantee
Credit Cards Accepted	Garden Machinery	Plants
Cut Flowers	Garden Products	Restaurant/Coffee Shop
Disabled	Giftware	Seeds & Bulbs
Dried & Artificial Flowers	Greenhouses & Sheds	Trees
Fencing	Houseplants	

LOCAL GARDENS

Temple Newsam, Leeds 0113 264 5535

Leeds City Council garden incorporating part of a Capability Brown landscape. Large walled rose garden with some of England's finest herbaceous borders, Italian paved garden, bog garden, Jacobean-style parterre. Pleached lime walks, rhododendron and azalea walks. Greenhouses with cacti, climbing pelargoniums, ivies. National Collections of asters, phlox, delphiniums. 3m E of Leeds off the A63/A6120. *Open: Daily all year 9-dusk. National Collections open daily 11-3 (11-2 at weekends). House open Tues-Sun 10.30-6.15. Entrance: free (charge for house).*

Wentworth Castle Gardens, Lowe Lane, Stainborough 01226 731269

Considered one of the most exciting gardens in Yorkshire. Laid out mainly by William Wentworth in the mid- to late 18th century, the landscape has been designated Grade I by English Heritage. Camellias. Serpentine lake, Gothick folly of Stainborough Castle, monuments to Lady Mary Montagu and Queen Anne. One of the finest collections of rhododendrons in northern England, including National Collection for species rhododendrons, and also for species magnolias. 3m SW of Barnsley off the M1 junction 37. *Open: May Bank Holiday weekend 10-5, also guided tours in May and June - telephone for details. Entrance: £2 (OAPs £1, children under 16 free).*

Fir Croft, Froggatt Road, Calver 0114 257 8444

Plantsman's garden owned by botanist and botanical photographer, begun from scratch in 1985. Water garden and nursery, rockeries, tufa and scree beds. Extensive alpine garden. Massive collection of over 2,000 varieties of conifers, alpines, including 500 saxifrages, 600 sempervivums, 350 primulas. Plants for sale from nursery. 4m N of Bakewell off the A625/B6001. *Open: selected weekends in April, May and June 2-5 pm. Entrance: by donation.*

WHITELEY'S GARDEN CENTRE
WHITEGATE, LEEDS ROAD, MIRFIELD, WEST YORKSHIRE WF14 0DQ
TEL: 01924 495944 FAX: 01924 480465 EMAIL: max@whiteleys.demon.co.uk

Whiteley's Garden Centre is a family business that developed from a rose-growing concern the 1950s and 1960s, developing into a garden centre in the 1970s. One speciality of this excellent garden centre remains roses. Whiteley's specialise in high-quality unusual plants at Yorkshire prices - a combination that ensures outstanding value for money. As such they are proud to stock hardy plants from all the best of British growers - all with a two-year guarantee - and unusual alpines and bedding plants. They are stockists of products such as David Austin specialist roses, Blooms of Bressingham specimen conifers, shrubs and alpines, Anglia Alpines, Bridgemere wholesale nurseries, and Anglo Aquarium pond and marginal plants.

Winner of the GCA Plant Centre of the Year National Award 1995 & 1997, Garden Centre of Excellence National Award 1998, and Christmas Centre of the Year Regional Award 1995 and 1997, this centre boasts a 2-acre area with raised beds and a large outdoor covered area. This includes an aquatics department and retail space of 10,000 square feet, carpeted throughout. The staff number 40 strong, in a mixture of qualified horticulturists and keen amateur gardeners and florists, all of whom are available to answer questions and give good advice.

This jewel in the GCA crown has a spacious gift area with ideas and inspiration for a massive range of presents for friends, family - and yourself! In November and December the centre turns into a spectacular Christmas display, with of course Christmas trees in abundance, and floristry demonstrations. Throughout the year the centre hosts talks and demonstrations on such topics as bedding plants, pond construction, hanging baskets, barbecues and more. *Open: spring/ summer and December Monday to Saturday 9-9, Sunday 11-5; winter Monday to Saturday 9-5.30, Sunday 11-5.*

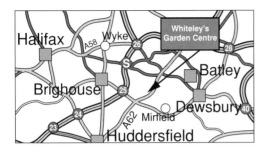

Directions:

From Junction 25 of the M62 follow signs to Huddersfield. Turn left onto the A62 and then 1st left into Far Common Road. Whiteley's Garden Centre is on the left.

Aquatics	Dried & Artificial Flowers	Houseplants
Barbecues	Fencing	Information Desk
Books & Stationery	Fireworks	Large Car Park
Christmas & Seasonal Displays	Floristry	Plant Guarantee
Conservatories	Fruit Trees	Plants
Credit Cards Accepted	Garden Furniture	Seeds & Bulbs
Disabled	Garden Products	Trees
Display Gardens	Giftware	

LOCAL GARDENS

Golden Acre Park, Otley Road, Leeds 0113 246 3504

Once a privately-owned pleasure park, now a botanic garden and impressive public park. Pleasant rolling hills lead down to lake. Rock garden and alpine house, rhododendrons, fine collection of sempervivums, heather. Extensive tree collection, most specimens are labelled. Demonstration plots where instruction is offered to amateur gardeners. This park also has a demonstration garden for Fleuroselect flowers. NW of Leeds off the A660. *Open: all year, daily during daylight hours. Entrance: free.*

Roundhay Park (Tropical World Canal Garden), Princes Avenue, Leeds 0113 266 1850

Extensively cultivated canal gardens once the kitchen and ornamental gardens of the Nicholson family. Parkland; canal gardens with formal bedding. Botanical gardens, rose gardens, exotic houses with the largest collection apart from those at Kew. Butterfly house, reptile house (tropical world), exotic birds, insect house, nocturnal house with bush babies, monkeys and other animals. Cafe and shop. A wonderful day out for all the family. 2m from city centre off the A58. *Open daily all year (except 25th Dec) 10-dusk. Entrance: £1 (children 8-16 50p).*

Oakwell Hall Country Park, Birstall 01924 326240

Beautiful 16th-century manor house with delightful period gardens, including large formal garden, cottage garden and herb garden with medicinal and fragrant herbs. Espaliered and fan-trained fruit trees, including eight 17th-century varieties. Also wildlife garden including a pond and wildflower meadow. Arboretum, 100-acre country park. Cafe and shop. Nature trails and picnic areas, equestrian arena and adventure playground. 10m SW of Leeds off the A652. *Open: Mon-Fri 11-5, Sat-Sun noon-5. Groups by arrangement. Entrance: hall and gardens £1.20 Mar-Oct (children 50p); free Nov-Feb.*

CLYDE VALLEY GARDEN CENTRE
LANARK ROAD, GARRION BRIDGE, LARKHALL ML9 2UB
TEL: 01698 888880 FAX: 01698 888860

Established in 1995, **Clyde Valley Garden Centre** is a family-run business located on the banks of the River Clyde midway between Glasgow and Edinburgh. It has quickly gained a reputation as one of the finest garden centres in the area. It offers a huge variety for the discerning gardener in a unique and welcoming shopping environment. The centre has quality hardy shrubs, fruit trees, heathers, rhododendrons, alpines, herbaceous plants, herbs and seasonal bedding plants from the best nurseries in the UK, Holland, Italy and throughout Europe, as well as many imports from the Far East, making for an exciting and unusual range of products. The fabulous range of houseplants changes with the seasons, and there are floral crafts and silk and dried flowers available, which can be arranged to your specifications. There is also a superb selection of garden and conservatory furniture, barbecues and accessories.

The centre boasts gifts to suit every occasion. In the comprehensive food hall you can choose from a wide variety of savouries, sauces, jams, shortbread and home-made sweets. Here you can also purchase Crabtree & Evelyn products or choose from among the other ranges of cosmetic goods. Toys, books, glassware, pottery, crockery and marble garden ornaments are also on offer, together with a vast array of unique basketware gifts in a varied range of shapes, sizes and designs, and ceramics imported from all corners of the world.

The unique feature of this centre is its decorative and very attractive licensed Top Deck Cafe Bistro. This overlooks the garden centre and the surrounding picturesque countryside. The bistro serves an impressive range of delicious home-made food, including fresly baked cakes and scones baked on the premises in the bistro's own bakery. *Open: summer daily 8.30-8; winter daily 9-5.*

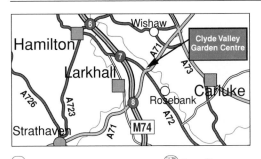

Directions:

From junction 7 of the M74 take the A72 towards Lanark and at the junction with the A71 turn left. Clyde Valley Garden Centre is on the junction.

Aquatics	Farm Shop	Greenhouses & Sheds
Barbecues	Fencing	Houseplants
Books & Stationery	Floristry	Information Desk
Christmas & Seasonal Displays	Fruit Trees	Large Car Park
Clothing	Garden Construction	Plant Guarantee
Credit Cards Accepted	Garden Design	Plants
Cut Flowers	Garden Furniture	Restaurant/Coffee Shop
Disabled	Garden Products	Seeds & Bulbs
Display Gardens	Giftware	Trees
Dried & Artificial Flowers		

LOCAL GARDENS

Broughton Place, Broughton, Biggar 01899 830234

Lovely 2-acre garden almost 900 feet above sea level. 18th-century beech avenue, wandering paths, National Collections of tropaeolums and thalictrums. Borders with interesting and rare plants. The walled garden is accessed through the magnificent turreted mansion designed earlier this century by Sir Basil Spence, now an art gallery. N of Broughton off the A701. *Open: end Mar-mid-Oct Thurs-Tues 10.30-6. Entrance: by donation to collection box.*

Culzean Castle Country Park, Maybole 01655 760269

National Trust for Scotland-managed castle and grounds, visited by over 200,000 people a year. 30 acres of gardens (including massive walled garden) and 563 acres of country park with woodland and cliff-top paths. Many prime architectural features throughout the grounds. Glasshouse dating from 1818, restored to its original status as an orangery. Fountain, lovely viaduct, restored pagoda. Originally a medieval fortified house, the castle was extensively reworked in the late 18th century by Robert Adam. 12m S of Ayr on A719. *Open: Country park and gardens April-Oct daily 10.30-5.30. Castle open. Entrance: £3.50 (children £2.50); additional charge for castle.*

Pollok House, Pollokshaws Road, Glasgow 0141 616 6410

National Trust for Scotland-managed house and gardens. Beautifully planted and maintained 19th-century woodland and parkland; charming formal terrace of box parterres. Wonderful show of spring bluebells. Stone gazebos with ogee roofs. House contains Stirling Maxwell collection of European art; Burrell Collection of decorative and fine arts also in the grounds. 3½m S of city centre. *Open: all year (except 25th Dec and 1st Jan) Mon-Sat 10-5, Sun 11-5. House and gallery open. Entrance: free 1 Nov - 1 Apr, charge at other times - call for admission charges.*

DOBBIES GARDEN WORLD
MELVILLE NURSERY, LASSWADE, MIDLOTHIAN EH18 1AZ
TEL: 0131 663 1941 FAX: 0131 654 2548

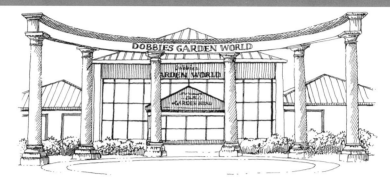

Dobbies Garden Centres have been established for 130 years. This centre is the flagship and headquarters for nine (soon to be ten) garden centres located throughout the UK. Dobbies in Lasswade is the oldest and most respected garden centre in Scotland. The range of products on offer undergoes continuous expansion, as the centre goes from strength to strength in offering the greatest range of plants and garden features and accessories.

Dobbies can almost be considered part of the leisure industry, such is the range of plants and products for home and garden on offer. To complement the excellent range of plants, the centre stocks a comprehensive choice of water features, gardening sundries and accessories, ceramics and stoneware, and containers in all sizes.

Covering 45,000 square feet, from the stunning entrance with its columns and fountain customers enter the light, airy and modern main building. Visitors could definitely spend half a day or more here, browsing, buying and being inspired with ideas for the home, garden, conservatory or office. Pride of place goes to The Mezzanine Floor, a delightful and attractive feature here as it is in the Dobbies Centres at Gailey and Dundee.

A large number of staff are horticulturists, with the expertise to advise customers on the best plants to choose for any situation, and on how to maintain and cultivate a beautiful and healthy garden. Also on site is the fascinating Butterfly World. The Birds of Prey centre offers a glimpse into the habits of these majestic creatures. The extensive and modern open-plan restaurant seats 120 and serves a variety of delicious hot and cold snacks and meals. Other features of this superb garden centre are the three children's play areas. *Open: Monday to Saturday 9-6, Sunday 10-6.*

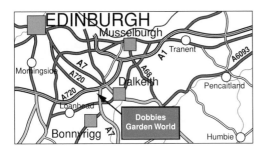

Directions:

Dobbies Garden World is on the west side of the A7 at the A7/A720 junction just north of Dalkeith.

Aquatics	Dried & Artificial Flowers	Greenhouses & Sheds
Barbecues	Fencing	Houseplants
Books & Stationery	Fireworks	Information Desk
Childrens Play Area	Floristry	Large Car Park
Christmas & Seasonal Displays	Fruit Trees	Paving
Clothing	Garden Construction	Pet Products and/or Pets
Conservatories	Garden Design	Plant Guarantee
Credit Cards Accepted	Garden Furniture	Plants
Cut Flowers	Garden Machinery	Restaurant/Coffee Shop
Disabled	Garden Products	Seeds & Bulbs
Display Gardens	Giftware	Trees

LOCAL GARDENS

Inveresk Lodge and Village Gardens, Musselburgh 0131 665 1855

Modern and semi-formal gardens, with views of Pentland Hills, of 17th-century house; wide range of exotic plants, climbers, flower beds, shrub roses and recently restored conservatory. The village is a pristine collection of late 17th- and early 18th-century gardens. 6m E of Edinburgh off the A6124. *Open: Mon-Fri all year 10-4.30, Sat-Sun 2-5 (closed Sat Oct-Mar). Entrance: Lodge £1 (honesty box); other gardens £1.50 each.*

Royal Botanic Garden Edinburgh, Inverleith Row 0131 552 7171

72 acres on a hillside with wonderful panoramic views of the city. Established in the 1600s, this is one of the finest botanic gardens in the world. Superb rock garden; rhododendrons, lilies, marsh orchids, saxifrages and campanulas. Peat garden, woodland garden, striking herbaceous border. Arboretum. Pringle Chinese Collection. Glasshouse Experience has Britain's tallest palm house, passion flowers, cycads. Interactive hands-on exhibitions in the Exhibition Hall. 1m N of city centre. *Open: daily all year (except 25th Dec, 1st Jan) from 9.30. Garden tours daily April-Sept at 11 and 2. Entrance: free (voluntary contributions invited).*

Stevenson House, Haddington 01620 823217

Ornamental pleasure garden with main lawn, stunning flower beds. Rockery, many very fine trees. Nearly two-acre old walled kitchen garden, designed in the 1700s to feed the household of 20 or 30 strong. The old herbaceous border has been revived. 18m E of Edinburgh. *Open: daily May-Oct 2-5. House open different times, with guided tours; please telephone for details. Entrance: £1 (children free - those under 12 must be accompanied); house and garden £2.50.*

CAERPHILLY GARDEN CENTRE
PENRHOS, NANT GARW, NR CARDIFF CF4 7UN
TEL: 01222 861511 FAX: 01222 862518

Caerphilly Garden Centre grew from the owners' own back garden. So many people came knocking on their door to buy, they decided to go into business. The site now covers 3½ acres, and the owners have 20 years' experience in gardening to offer their customers. They are ably assisted by a 30-strong staff of trained horticulturists. Billed as 'the perfect place for the perfect garden', this Centre makes a special feature of its selection of shrub and species roses, with a range found at few other garden centres.

Water features and fountains are also in evidence here. A lovely old watermill greets visitors at the entrance, and the reception area is housed in a charming chalet-style garden house. There are attractive fully furnished conservatories on display, and dedicated areas for cacti, patios, fountains and ornaments, pets and aquatics, and furnishings for the home. The dried flower display is particularly impressive.

Noted for its advanced customer care, the Centre has a garden consultancy and design department. The friendly and knowledgeable staff offer demonstrations of various gardening techniques, and host, among other special events, a monthly Bonsai clinic (first Sunday of every month from 1-4 p.m.). Christmas is the important annual festival at this Centre, with fantastic displays and festive food and drink on site in celebrations that are renowned far and wide.

This comprehensive Centre also sells sea shells, carpets and occasional rugs, Chinese pots and ceramics, windchimes, glassware, cards, home fragrances, aromatics and candles, and dolls' houses and furnishings. In addition there's an interesting range of traditional and modern garden accessories. Always looking to the future, plans are in place for a Millennium Garden on site. *Open: Mon-Sat 9-6; Sun 10.30-4.30.*

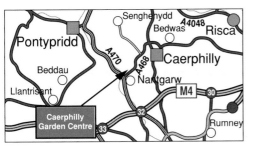

Directions:

From junction 32 of the M4 take the A470 towards Pontypridd. At the junction with the A468 turn right and Caerphilly Garden Centre can be found on the left at the top of the hill.

Aquatics	Fencing	Houseplants
Barbecues	Fireworks	Information Desk
Books & Stationery	Floristry	Large Car Park
Christmas & Seasonal Displays	Fruit Trees	Paving
Clothing	Garden Construction	Pet Products and/or Pets
Conservatories	Garden Design	Plant Guarantee
Credit Cards Accepted	Garden Furniture	Plants
Disabled	Garden Products	Restaurant/Coffee Shop
Display Gardens	Giftware	Seeds & Bulbs
Dried & Artificial Flowers	Greenhouses & Sheds	Trees

LOCAL GARDENS

Cefn Onn Park , Cardiff

Not the usual city park, this features large swathes of informally planted rhododendrons and azaleas, with lovely perfumes and colours wafting up to the tops of the tall trees, which are best viewed from the opposite bank. Magnolias, camellias. From Cardiff take A469; first right, then left opposite Lisvane Street - or at junction 32 of M4 turn S off the A470, first left to T-junction, then right, left at church, left at T-junction, pass over M4, first right, then left opposite Lisvane Street. *Open: daylight hours daily all year. Entrance: free.*

Clyne Gardens, Blackpill, Swansea 01792 401737

50 acres of well-kept Swansea City Council-managed gardens. Woodland garden with varied range of azaleas and rhododendrons, young magnolias. Grouping of large-leaved rhododendrons which are at their best in April, National Collections of rhododendron 'Falconera', 'Triflora' and pieris and enkianthus. Magnolia campbellii, bog grden, lake and waterfall with Japanese bridge. From Swansea, take the A4067 Mumbles Road, then turn right at Woodman Roast Inn. *Open: daily all year. Ring for information on garden tours. Entrance: free.*

Dyffryn Gardens, St Nicholas, Cardiff 01222 593328

Owned by Vale of Glamorgan Council, this is one of Wales' largest landscaped gardens. Edwardian garden based on a Thomas Mawson design. A series of garden rooms recently and continually being restored with Heritage Lottery funding. 4m SW of Cardiff off the A48. *Open daily all year, 10-dusk. Entrance: £3 (OAPs/children £2), family ticket £6.50.*

HOLLAND ARMS GARDEN CENTRE
GAERWEN (ON THE A5), ISLE OF ANGLESEY, NORTH WALES LL60 6LA
TEL: 01248 421655 FAX: 01248 421896

Holland Arms Garden Centre has been a family-run business since 1953, developing from a small nursery to the comprehensive centre you find here today. Small-scale but big in facilities and features, it stocks a range of shrubs, roses, climbers, hedging, border plants, herbs, alpines, heathers and trees, including fruit trees.

You will find houseplants of all types here, plus a wide choice of silk and dried flowers. To complement the selection of plants, there are garden ornaments, tools, patio pots, stoneware, bird tables and other garden accessories. The marvellous aquatics department featuring Lotus water garden equipment and sundries, from ponds and fountains to underwater lighting, filters, pumps, hoses and more. Orchids are the speciality here - the centre has a spectacular range of these beautiful and delicate blooms in all colours and shapes. It also stocks bonsai plants, cacti and terrariums. The centre also boasts a range of Swan Hattersley furniture, designed and manufactured in Shropshire where skilled woodworkers craft high quality timber using traditional methods to produce a range of beautiful hardwood garden tables, benches, chairs and more.

The Gardener's Cafe has a relaxing and pleasant atmosphere, and serves a good range of home-cooked breakfasts, meals, salads, snacks, cakes and drinks. In the Welsh Pantry you can purchase quality preserves made with liqueurs, produced locally, plus a range of other food and gift items such as chocolates, candles, books, pot pourri, incense and burners. Throughout the year the centre hosts special events, including seasonal displays, summer barbecues, and demonstrations by resident experts on topics such as hanging baskets or growing your own bedding. *Open: Mon to Sat 9-5.30, Sun 11-5, Bank Holidays 10-5.*

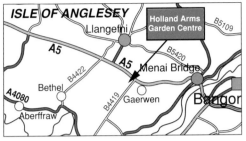

Directions:
From the A5 bridge over the Menai Straits take the A5 towards Holyhead. Holland Arms Garden Centre is on the left just past the village of Gaerwen.

- Aquatics
- Barbecues
- Books & Stationery
- Christmas & Seasonal Displays
- Credit Cards Accepted
- Cut Flowers
- Disabled
- Dried & Artificial Flowers
- Fireworks
- Fruit Trees
- Garden Furniture
- Garden Products
- Giftware
- Greenhouses & Sheds
- Houseplants
- Information Desk
- Large Car Park
- Pet Products and/or Pets
- Plant Guarantee
- Plants
- Restaurant/Coffee Shop
- Seeds & Bulbs
- Trees

LOCAL GARDENS

Penrhyn Castle, Bangor 01248 353084
National Trust. Large (48-acre) gardens with fine shrubs and specimen trees, wild garden, marvellous views. Spectacular bog garden, giant tree fern, gunnera, Australian bottle-brush plant. 1m E of Bangor on the A5122. *Open: end Mar-Jun and Sept-Oct Weds-Mon 11-5.30, July-Aug Weds-Mon 10-5.30. Castle open as for garden, but noon-5 (11-5 July/Aug). Entrance: £3 (children £1.50); castle and garden £5 (children £2.50).*

Plas Newydd, Llanfairpwll 01248 714795
Plas Newydd, the traditional home of the Marquess of Anglesey, is situated on the banks of the Menai Strait, This elegant eighteenth century house, built by James Wyatt, commands magnificent views of the beautiful mountains of Snowdonia. Plas Newydd houses an exhibition devoted to the work of Rex Whistler, and his largest painting commissioned by the 6th Marquess of Anglesey in the 1930's can be seen in the dining room. The military museum at Plas Newydd contains many fascinating relics of the first Marquess of Anglesey, who commanded the cavalry at the battle of Waterloo of 1815. In the gardens, exotic and mature woodlands provide tranquil walks. There is a fine spring garden, summer terrace, and later massed hydrangeas. A woodland walk gives access to a marine walk along the Menai Strait. Connoisseur and garden tours by prior arrangement. 2m SW of Menai Bridge off the A5. *Open: 27 Mar-31 Oct Sat-Weds 11-5.30 (last admission 5). Rhododendron garden open April-early June only. House/military museum open as for gardens, but noon-5. Entrance: £2.20 (children £1.10). House and gardens £4.20 (children £2.10). Guided tours by arrangement.*

Bodnant Garden, Tal-y-Cafn, Colwyn Bay 01492 650460
National Trust. 80 acres of one of Britain's finest gardens. Magnificent rhododendrons, camellias, magnolias in spring followed by herbaceous borders, roses and water lilies in summer. Good autumn colours. Lily terrace, stepped pergola, laburnum arch, dell garden, Pin Mill and canal terrace. 45-metre high Sequoia sempervirens, the tallest redwood in the country. 8m S of Llandudno off the A470. *Open: daily mid-Mar-Oct 10-5 (last admission 4.30). Entrance: £4.60 (children £2.30).*

TABLE OF FLOWER SHOWS AND EXHIBITIONS

	Location	Start Date	Duration
APRIL 1999			
Harrogate Spring Show	Harrogate	April 27, 1999	4 days
MAY 1999			
Milton Keynes Garden Show	Walton Hall, Milton Keynes	May 1, 1999	3 days
Amateur Gardening Spring Show	NAC Stoneleigh Park	May 1, 1999	2 days
Spring Gardening Show	Malvern, Worcestershire	May 7, 1999	3 days
Chelsea Flower Show Press Day	Chelsea London	May 24, 1999	1 day
Chelsea Flower Show	Chelsea London	May 25, 1999	4 days
Wrest Park Garden Show	Silsoe, Bedfordshire	May 29, 1999	3 days
JUNE 1999			
Scotland's National Gardening Show	Strathclyde Country Park	June 4, 1999	3 days
Woburn Abbey Garden Show	Woburn	June 5, 1999	2 days
Gardeners World Live	NEC Birmingham	June 16, 1999	5 days
Three Counties Agricultural Show	Malvern, Worcestershire	June 18, 1999	3 days
Royal Highland Show	Edinburgh	June 25, 1999	4 days
JULY 1999			
Royal Show - Stoneleigh	Warwickshire	July 5, 1999	4 days
Hampton Court Flower Show	Hampton Court, London	July 6, 1999	6 days
RHS Flower Show at Tatton Park	Manchester	July 22, 1999	4 days
Kildare Show	Kildare	July 22, 1999	2 days
Fruit Focus	Writtle College	July 28, 1999	1 day
AUGUST 1999			
Shrewsbury Flower Show	Shrewsbury	August 13, 1999	2 days
Southport Flower Show	Southport	August 19, 1999	3 days
Wisley Flower Show	RHS Wisley	August 24, 1999	2 days
Ayr Flower Show	Ayr	August 26, 1999	3 days
SEPTEMBER 1999			
National Amateur Gardening Exhibition	TBA	September 3, 1999	3 days
Dundee Flower Show	Dundee	September 3, 1999	3 days
Four Oaks	Cheshire	September 7, 1999	2 days
RHS Great Autumn Show	London	September 14, 1999	2 days
Veg Focus	TBA	September 15, 1999	1 day
Harrogate Autumn Show	Harrogate	September 17, 1999	1 day
Malvern Autumn Show	TCAS Showground, Malvern	September 25, 1999	2 days

	Location	Start Date	Duration
DECEMBER 1999			
RHS Christmas Show	London	December 14, 1999	1 day
APRIL 2000			
Dundee Spring Show	Dundee	April 1, 2000	2 days
MAY 2000			
Malvern Spring Show	TAC Showground, Malvern	May 5, 2000	3 days
Chelsea Flower Show	Chelsea, London	May 23, 2000	4 days
JUNE 2000			
Scotland's National Gardening Show	Strathclyde Country Park	June 2, 2000	3 days
Three Counties Agricultural Show	Malvern, Worcestershire	June 13, 2000	3 days
Royal Highland Show	Edinburgh	June 22, 2000	4 days
Wisley Flower Show	RHS Gardens, Wisley	June 26, 2000	2 days
JULY 2000			
The Royal Agricultural Show	Stoneleigh	July 3, 2000	4 days
Hampton Court Flower Show	Hampton Court, London	July 4, 2000	6 days
RHS Flower Show at Tatton Park	Manchester	July 20, 2000	4 days
AUGUST 2000			
Shrewsbury Flower Show	Shrewsbury	August 11, 2000	2 days
Southport Flower Show	Southport	August 11, 2000	2 days
Ayr Flower Show	Ayr	August 24, 2000	3 days
SEPTEMBER 2000			
Dundee Flower Show	Dundee	September 1, 2000	3 days
RHS Great Autumn Show	London	September 12, 2000	2 days
Harrogate Autumn Show	Harrogate	September 15, 2000	3 days
Malvern Autumn Show	TCAS Showground, Malvern	September 23, 2000	2 days
DECEMBER 2000			
RHS Christmas Show	London	December 12, 2000	2 days

INDEX OF GARDEN CENTRES

INDEX OF GARDENS

TABLE OF PRODUCTS & SERVICES

This table of products & services will enable readers to identify quickly which garden centres offer a specific product or service. It will also enable readers to check what products and services are offered by a specific garden centre.

The index is presented in tabular form and the products and services are listed alphabetically along the top whilst the garden centres are listed alphabetically within each county, down the side of each page.

Simply locate the product or service you are looking for and use the table to cross-reference to the garden centre of your choice. Alternatively, select the garden centre and cross-reference to the product or service of your choice. All garden centres offering that specific product or service are blocked out in dark green.

The products and services are categorised as follows:-

Aquatics		Garden Construction	
Barbecues		Garden Design	
Books & Stationery		Garden Furniture	
Camping Equipment		Garden Machinery	
Childrens Play Area		Garden Products	
Christmas & Seasonal Displays		Giftware	
Clothing		Golf	
Conservatories		Greenhouses & Sheds	
Credit Cards Accepted		Houseplants	
Cut Flowers		Information Desk	
Disabled		Large Car Park	
Display Gardens		Paving	
Dried & Artificial Flowers		Pet Products and/or Pets	
Farm Shop		Pick Your Own	
Fencing		Plant Guarantee	
Fireworks		Plants	
Fishing		Restaurant/Coffee Shop	
Floristry		Seeds & Bulbs	
Fruit Trees		Trees	

Column headings (left to right):

Aquatics · Barbecues · Books & Stationery · Camping Equipment · Childrens Play Area · Christmas & Seasonal Displays · Clothing · Conservatories · Credit Cards Accepted · Cut Flowers · Disabled · Display Gardens · Dried & Artificial Flowers · Farm Shop · Fencing · Fireworks · Fishing or Fresh Fish · Floristry · Fruit Trees

Bedfordshire

| Willington Garden Centre, Nr Bedford |

Berkshire

| Squire's Garden Centre, Windsor |

Buckinghamshire

| Booker Garden Centre, Nr Marlow |
| Frosts Garden Centre, Milton Keynes |

Cambridgeshire

| Brampton Garden Centre, Huntingdon |

Cheshire (including the Wirral)

| Barton Grange Garden Centre, Woodford |
| Bents Garden Centre, Nr Leigh |
| Brookside Garden Centre, Poynton |
| Burleydam Garden Centre, South Wirral |
| Gordale Garden Centre, South Wirral |
| Grosvenor Garden Centre, Chester |
| High Legh Garden Centre, Knutsford |

Cleveland

| Peter Barratt's Garden Centre, Stockton-on-Tees |

Cornwall

| Trelawney Garden Leisure, Wadebridge |

Cumbria

| Webbs Garden Centre, Kendal |

Derbyshire

| Chatsworth Garden Centre, Matlock |
| Ferndale Nursery & Garden Centre, Dronfield |
| Grangecraft Garden Centre, Mickleover |

Devon

| Endsleigh Garden Centre, Ivybridge |
| Otter Nurseries Garden Centre, Ottery St Mary |
| Otter Nurseries Garden Centre, Nr Plymouth |

Dorset

| Stewarts Country Garden Centre, Nr Wimborne |
| Stewarts Garden-Lands, Christchurch |

Garden Construction	Garden Design	Garden Furniture	Garden Machinery	Garden Products	Giftware	Golf	Greenhouses & Sheds	Houseplants	Information Desk	Large Car Park	Paving	Pet Products or Pets	Pick Your Own	Plant Guarantee	Plants	Restaurant or Coffee Shop	Seeds & Bulbs	Trees	

Bedfordshire
Willington Garden Centre, Nr Bedford

Berkshire
Squire's Garden Centre, Windsor

Buckinghamshire
Booker Garden Centre, Nr Marlow
Frosts Garden Centre, Milton Keynes

Cambridgeshire
Brampton Garden Centre, Huntingdon

Cheshire (including the Wirral)
Barton Grange Garden Centre, Woodford
Bents Garden Centre, Nr Leigh
Brookside Garden Centre, Poynton
Burleydam Garden Centre, South Wirral
Gordale Garden Centre, South Wirral
Grosvenor Garden Centre, Chester
High Legh Garden Centre, Knutsford

Cleveland
Peter Barratt's Garden Centre, Stockton-on-Tees

Cornwall
Trelawney Garden Leisure, Wadebridge

Cumbria
Webbs Garden Centre, Kendal

Derbyshire
Chatsworth Garden Centre, Matlock
Ferndale Nursery & Garden Centre, Dronfield
Grangecraft Garden Centre, Mickleover

Devon
Endsleigh Garden Centre, Ivybridge
Otter Nurseries Garden Centre, Ottery St Mary
Otter Nurseries Garden Centre, Nr Plymouth

Dorset
Stewarts Country Garden Centre, Nr Wimborne
Stewarts Garden-Lands, Christchurch

Columns: Aquatics · Barbecues · Books & Stationery · Camping Equipment · Childrens Play Area · Christmas & Seasonal Displays · Clothing · Conservatories · Credit Cards Accepted · Cut Flowers · Disabled · Display Gardens · Dried & Artificial Flowers · Farm Shop · Fencing · Fireworks · Fishing or Fresh Fish · Floristry · Fruit Trees

Essex

Altons Garden Centre, Wickford	
Frinton Road Nurseries, Kirby Cross	
Thurrock Garden Centre, South Ockenden	

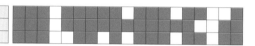

Hampshire

Brambridge Park Garden Centre, Eastleigh	
Redfields Garden Centre, Fleet	

Hertfordshire

Aylett Nurseries, St Albans	
The Van Hage Garden Company, Stevenage	
The Van Hage Garden Company, Chenies	
The Van Hage Garden Company, Great Amwell	
Woods of Berkhamsted, Berkhamsted	

Kent

Bybrook Barn Garden Centre, Ashford	
Cooling's Nurseries Ltd, Knockholt	
The Millbrook Garden Company, Gravesend	
Polhill Garden Centre, Badgers Mount	
Ruxley Manor Garden Centre, Sidcup	

Lancashire (including Merseyside and Greater Manchester)

All-in-One Garden Centre, Middleton	
Barton Grange Garden Centre, Bolton	
Barton Grange Garden Centre, Preston	
Daisy Nook Garden Centre, Failsworth	
Gateacre Garden Centre, Gateacre	
Lady Green Nurseries & Garden Centre, Formby	
Sefton Meadows Garden & Home Centre, Maghull	
Worsley Hall Garden Centre, Worsley	

Leicestershire

Woodlands Nurseries, Stapleton	

Lincolnshire

Baytree Nurseries & Garden Centre, Spalding	
Crowders Garden Centre, Horncastle	
Pennells Garden Centre, Lincoln	

The columns are labelled left to right:
1. Garden Construction
2. Garden Design
3. Garden Furniture
4. Garden Machinery
5. Garden Products
6. Giftware
7. Golf
8. Greenhouses & Sheds
9. Houseplants
10. Information Desk
11. Large Car Park
12. Paving
13. Pet Products or Pets
14. Pick Your Own
15. Plant Guarantee
16. Plants
17. Restaurant or Coffee Shop
18. Seeds & Bulbs
19. Trees

Essex

1	2	3	4	5	6	7	8	9	10	11	12	13	14	15	16	17	18	19	
■		■	■	■	■		■	■		■	■			■	■		■	■	Altons Garden Centre, Wickford
■	■	■	■	■	■		■	■		■	■			■	■		■	■	Frinton Road Nurseries, Kirby Cross
	■	■	■	■	■		■	■		■	■			■	■		■	■	Thurrock Garden Centre, South Ockenden

Hampshire

1	2	3	4	5	6	7	8	9	10	11	12	13	14	15	16	17	18	19	
■		■	■	■	■		■	■		■	■			■	■		■	■	Brambridge Park Garden Centre, Eastleigh
■		■	■	■	■		■	■		■	■			■	■		■	■	Redfields Garden Centre, Fleet

Hertfordshire

1	2	3	4	5	6	7	8	9	10	11	12	13	14	15	16	17	18	19	
	■	■	■	■	■		■	■		■	■			■	■		■	■	Aylett Nurseries, St Albans
■	■	■		■	■		■	■		■	■			■	■	■	■	■	The Van Hage Garden Company, Stevenage
■	■	■		■	■		■	■		■	■			■	■		■	■	The Van Hage Garden Company, Chenies
■	■	■		■	■		■	■		■	■	■		■	■	■	■	■	The Van Hage Garden Company, Great Amwell
	■	■	■	■	■		■	■		■	■			■	■		■	■	Woods of Berkhamsted, Berkhamsted

Kent

1	2	3	4	5	6	7	8	9	10	11	12	13	14	15	16	17	18	19	
	■	■	■	■	■		■	■		■	■			■	■	■	■	■	Bybrook Barn Garden Centre, Ashford
■	■	■		■	■		■	■		■	■			■	■		■	■	Cooling's Nurseries Ltd, Knockholt
	■	■	■	■	■		■	■		■	■			■	■		■	■	The Millbrook Garden Company, Gravesend
■	■	■		■	■		■	■		■	■			■	■	■	■	■	Polhill Garden Centre, Badgers Mount
	■	■	■	■	■		■	■		■	■			■	■	■	■	■	Ruxley Manor Garden Centre, Sidcup

Lancashire (including Merseyside and Greater Manchester)

1	2	3	4	5	6	7	8	9	10	11	12	13	14	15	16	17	18	19	
	■	■	■	■	■		■	■		■	■			■	■		■	■	All-in-One Garden Centre, Middleton
■	■	■		■	■		■	■		■	■			■	■		■	■	Barton Grange Garden Centre, Bolton
■	■	■		■	■		■	■		■	■			■	■	■	■	■	Barton Grange Garden Centre, Preston
	■	■	■	■	■		■	■		■	■			■	■		■	■	Daisy Nook Garden Centre, Failsworth
	■	■	■	■	■		■	■		■	■	■		■	■		■	■	Gateacre Garden Centre, Gateacre
	■	■	■	■	■		■	■		■	■			■	■		■	■	Lady Green Nurseries & Garden Centre, Formby
■	■	■		■	■		■	■		■	■			■	■		■	■	Sefton Meadows Garden & Home Centre, Maghull
	■	■	■	■	■		■	■		■	■			■	■		■	■	Worsley Hall Garden Centre, Worsley

Leicestershire

1	2	3	4	5	6	7	8	9	10	11	12	13	14	15	16	17	18	19	
	■	■		■	■		■	■		■	■			■	■		■	■	Woodlands Nurseries, Stapleton

Lincolnshire

1	2	3	4	5	6	7	8	9	10	11	12	13	14	15	16	17	18	19	
	■	■	■	■	■		■	■		■	■			■	■	■	■	■	Baytree Nurseries & Garden Centre, Spalding
	■	■	■	■	■		■	■		■	■			■	■	■	■	■	Crowders Garden Centre, Horncastle
	■	■	■	■	■		■	■		■	■			■	■	■	■	■	Pennells Garden Centre, Lincoln

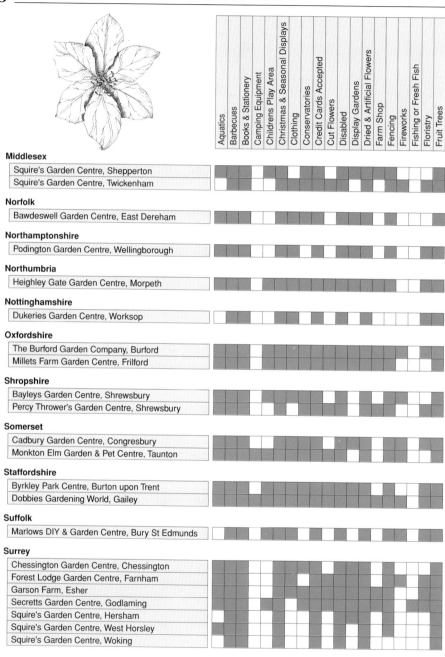

Middlesex
Squire's Garden Centre, Shepperton
Squire's Garden Centre, Twickenham

Norfolk
Bawdeswell Garden Centre, East Dereham

Northamptonshire
Podington Garden Centre, Wellingborough

Northumbria
Heighley Gate Garden Centre, Morpeth

Nottinghamshire
Dukeries Garden Centre, Worksop

Oxfordshire
The Burford Garden Company, Burford
Millets Farm Garden Centre, Frilford

Shropshire
Bayleys Garden Centre, Shrewsbury
Percy Thrower's Garden Centre, Shrewsbury

Somerset
Cadbury Garden Centre, Congresbury
Monkton Elm Garden & Pet Centre, Taunton

Staffordshire
Byrkley Park Centre, Burton upon Trent
Dobbies Gardening World, Gailey

Suffolk
Marlows DIY & Garden Centre, Bury St Edmunds

Surrey
Chessington Garden Centre, Chessington
Forest Lodge Garden Centre, Farnham
Garson Farm, Esher
Secretts Garden Centre, Godalming
Squire's Garden Centre, Hersham
Squire's Garden Centre, West Horsley
Squire's Garden Centre, Woking

	Garden Construction	Garden Design	Garden Furniture	Garden Machinery	Garden Products	Giftware	Golf	Greenhouses & Sheds	Houseplants	Information Desk	Large Car Park	Paving	Pet Products or Pets	Pick Your Own	Plant Guarantee	Plants	Restaurant or Coffee Shop	Seeds & Bulbs	Trees
Middlesex																			
Squire's Garden Centre, Shepperton		●	●	●	●			●	●	●	●	●	●			●	●	●	●
Squire's Garden Centre, Twickenham		●	●	●	●			●	●	●	●	●	●			●	●	●	●
Norfolk																			
Bawdeswell Garden Centre, East Dereham	●	●	●		●	●		●	●	●	●	●	●			●	●	●	●
Northamptonshire																			
Podington Garden Centre, Wellingborough	●	●	●	●	●			●	●	●	●	●	●			●	●	●	●
Northumbria																			
Heighley Gate Garden Centre, Morpeth		●	●	●	●			●	●	●	●	●	●			●	●	●	●
Nottinghamshire																			
Dukeries Garden Centre, Worksop		●		●	●			●	●	●						●	●	●	●
Oxfordshire																			
The Burford Garden Company, Burford	●	●	●	●	●	●		●	●	●	●	●			●	●	●	●	●
Millets Farm Garden Centre, Frilford	●	●	●	●	●	●		●	●	●	●	●		●		●	●	●	●
Shropshire																			
Bayleys Garden Centre, Shrewsbury		●		●	●			●	●	●	●	●				●	●	●	●
Percy Thrower's Garden Centre, Shrewsbury	●	●	●	●	●	●		●	●	●	●	●				●	●	●	●
Somerset																			
Cadbury Garden Centre, Congresbury	●	●	●	●	●	●		●	●	●	●	●				●	●	●	●
Monkton Elm Garden & Pet Centre, Taunton	●	●	●	●	●	●		●	●	●	●	●	●			●	●	●	●
Staffordshire																			
Byrkley Park Centre, Burton upon Trent	●	●	●		●	●		●	●	●	●	●				●	●	●	●
Dobbies Gardening World, Gailey	●	●	●	●	●	●		●	●	●	●	●				●	●	●	●
Suffolk																			
Marlows DIY & Garden Centre, Bury St Edmunds	●	●	●	●	●	●			●	●	●	●			●	●	●		●
Surrey																			
Chessington Garden Centre, Chessington		●	●		●	●		●	●	●	●	●	●			●	●	●	●
Forest Lodge Garden Centre, Farnham		●	●		●	●		●	●	●	●	●				●	●	●	●
Garson Farm, Esher		●	●		●	●		●	●	●	●	●		●		●	●	●	●
Secretts Garden Centre, Godlaming		●	●		●	●		●	●	●	●	●		●		●	●	●	●
Squire's Garden Centre, Hersham		●	●		●	●		●	●	●	●	●	●			●	●	●	●
Squire's Garden Centre, West Horsley		●	●		●	●		●	●	●		●	●			●	●	●	●
Squire's Garden Centre, Woking		●	●		●	●		●	●	●	●	●				●	●	●	●

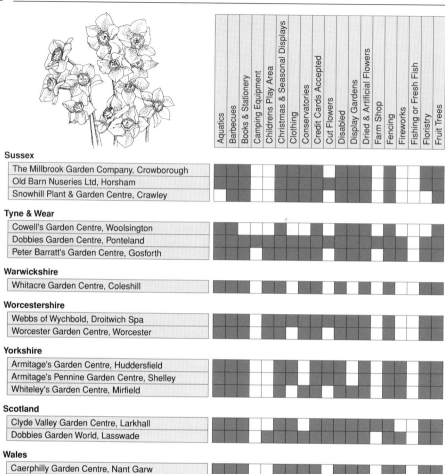

Column headings (left to right): Aquatics · Barbecues · Books & Stationery · Camping Equipment · Childrens Play Area · Christmas & Seasonal Displays · Clothing · Conservatories · Credit Cards Accepted · Cut Flowers · Disabled · Display Gardens · Dried & Artificial Flowers · Farm Shop · Fencing · Fireworks · Fishing or Fresh Fish · Floristry · Fruit Trees

Sussex

- The Millbrook Garden Company, Crowborough
- Old Barn Nuseries Ltd, Horsham
- Snowhill Plant & Garden Centre, Crawley

Tyne & Wear

- Cowell's Garden Centre, Woolsington
- Dobbies Garden Centre, Ponteland
- Peter Barratt's Garden Centre, Gosforth

Warwickshire

- Whitacre Garden Centre, Coleshill

Worcestershire

- Webbs of Wychbold, Droitwich Spa
- Worcester Garden Centre, Worcester

Yorkshire

- Armitage's Garden Centre, Huddersfield
- Armitage's Pennine Garden Centre, Shelley
- Whiteley's Garden Centre, Mirfield

Scotland

- Clyde Valley Garden Centre, Larkhall
- Dobbies Garden World, Lasswade

Wales

- Caerphilly Garden Centre, Nant Garw
- Holland Arms Garden Centre, Isle of Anglesey

Garden Construction	Garden Design	Garden Furniture	Garden Machinery	Garden Products	Giftware	Golf	Greenhouses & Sheds	Houseplants	Information Desk	Large Car Park	Paving	Pet Products or Pets	Pick Your Own	Plant Guarantee	Plants	Restaurant or Coffee Shop	Seeds & Bulbs	Trees	
																			Sussex
■	□	■	■	■			□	■					□		■				The Millbrook Garden Company, Crowborough
□	■	■	■	■			□	■					□		■				Old Barn Nuseries Ltd, Horsham
■	■	■	■	■			■	■					□		■				Snowhill Plant & Garden Centre, Crawley
																			Tyne & Wear
■	□	■	□	■			□	■							■	□			Cowell's Garden Centre, Woolsington
■	■	■	□	■			□	■							■	□			Dobbies Garden Centre, Ponteland
□	■	■	□	■			■	■							■	■			Peter Barratt's Garden Centre, Gosforth
																			Warwickshire
■	■	■	□	■			□	■					□		■				Whitacre Garden Centre, Coleshill
																			Worcestershire
■	□	■	■	■			□	■					□		■				Webbs of Wychbold, Droitwich Spa
■	■	■	■	■			□	■					□		■				Worcester Garden Centre, Worcester
																			Yorkshire
■	□	■	■	■			□	■					□		■				Armitage's Garden Centre, Huddersfield
□	■	■	■	■			□	■					□		■				Armitage's Pennine Garden Centre, Shelley
■	■	■	■	■			□	■					□		■				Whiteley's Garden Centre, Mirfield
																			Scotland
■	□	■	□	■			■	■					□		■				Clyde Valley Garden Centre, Larkhall
■	■	■	□	■			□	■					□		■				Dobbies Garden World, Lasswade
																			Wales
■	□	■	■	■			□	■					□		■				Caerphilly Garden Centre, Nant Garw
■	■	■	■	■			□	■					□		■				Holland Arms Garden Centre, Isle of Anglesey

MAP SECTION

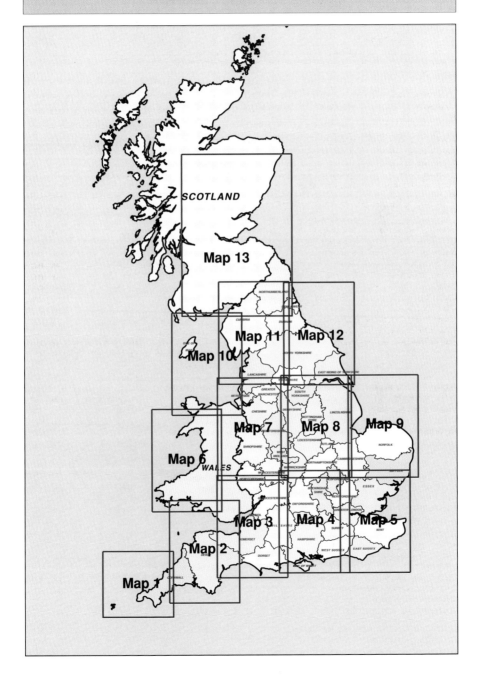

HOW TO USE THE MAP SECTION

- Each garden centre location is marked on the appropriate map. In order to find the entry in the guide, locate the area you are interested in and the approximate position of each garden centre is marked with a yellow box. The number in the box relates to the page number on which the entry can be found.

- At the start of this section (page 242) there is a full alphabetic list of all the Garden Centres included in this guide. The details for each of the Garden Centres gives the map number and grid reference of each centre together with the page number of the guide entry. The map refrence can be used to identify the approximate location of the Garden Centre. Detailed location maps are included with each directory entry.

Map 1

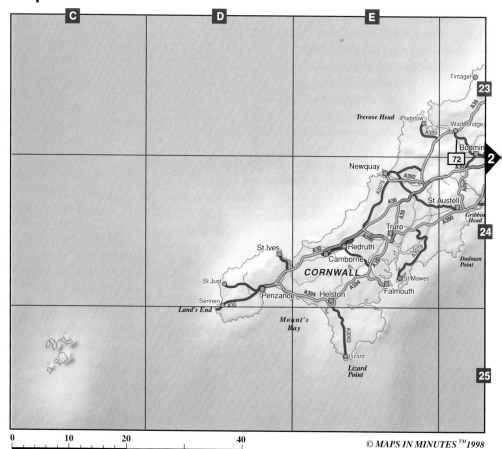

© MAPS IN MINUTES ™1998

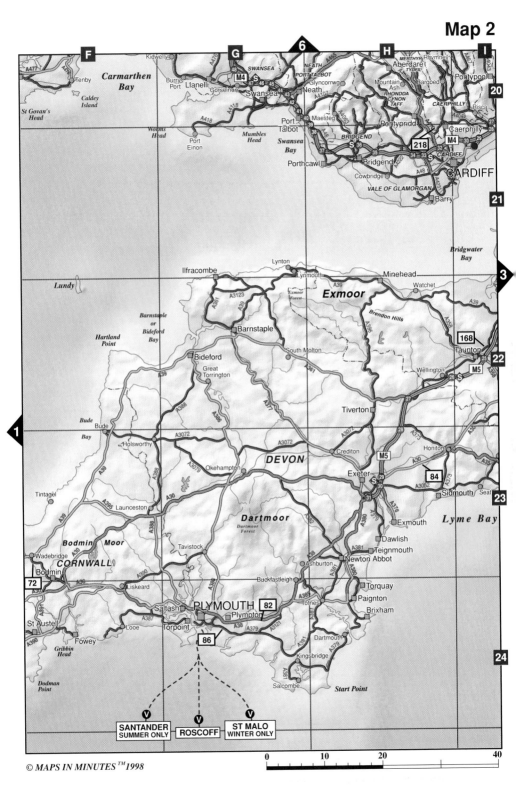

Map 3

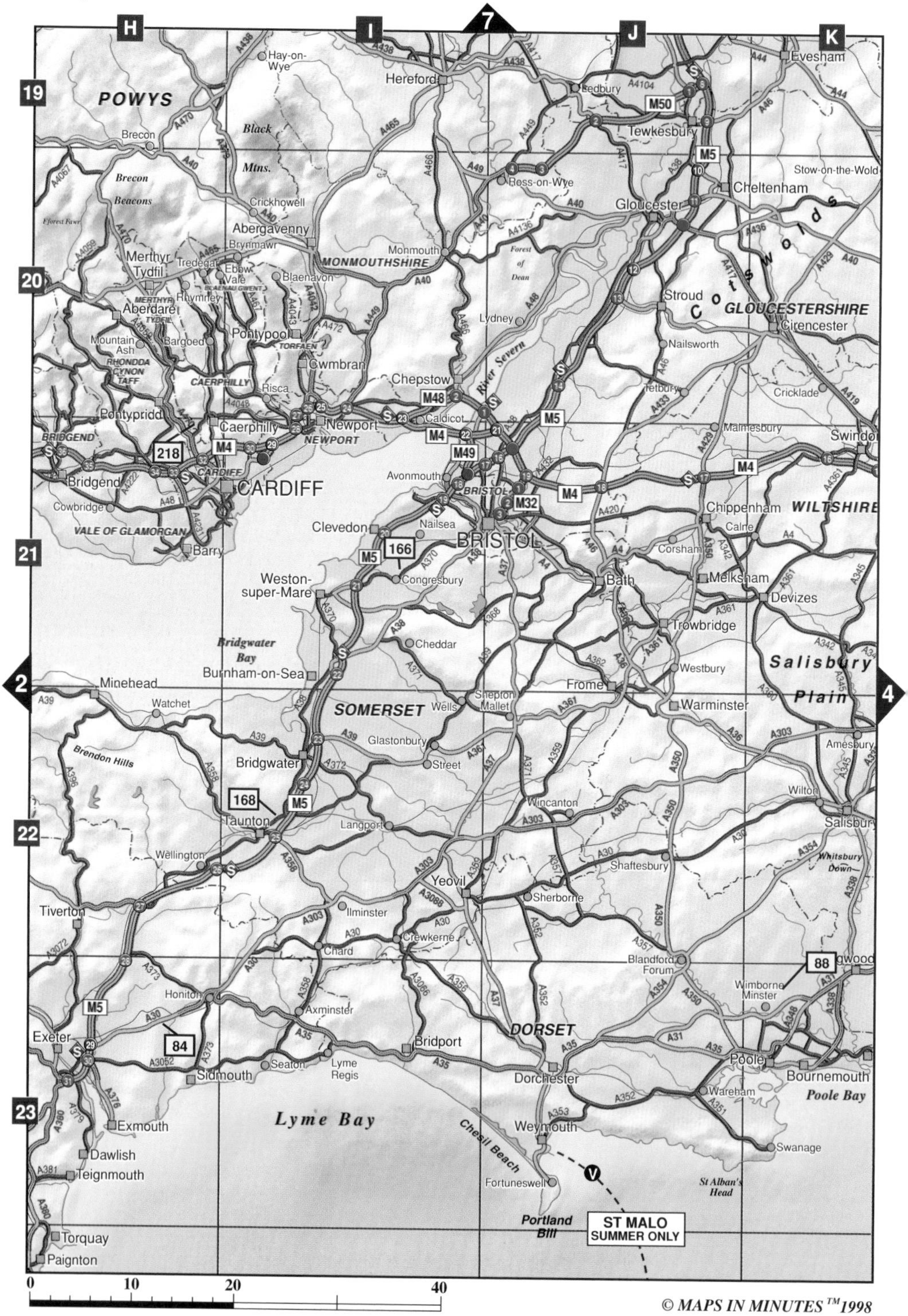

19

POWYS

Hay-on-Wye
Hereford
Ledbury
A4104
M50
Evesham
Tewkesbury
M5
10
Stow-on-the-Wold
Cheltenham

Brecon
Black
Mtns.
Brecon
Beacons
Fforest Fawr
Crickhowell
Ross-on-Wye
A40
Gloucester
12
Stroud
Cotswolds
GLOUCESTERSHIRE
Cirencester

Merthyr Tydfil
Abergavenny
Brynmawr
Mynydd
Monmouth
MONMOUTHSHIRE
Forest
of
Dean
Nailsworth
Cricklade

20

Aberdare
Tredegar
Ebbw Vale
Blaenavon
MERTHYR TYDFIL
Rhymney
BLAENAU GWENT
Pontypool
TORFAEN
Cwmbran
Lydney
Severn
Tetbury
Malmesbury
Swindon

Mountain Ash
Bargoed
CAERPHILLY
Risca
Chepstow
M48
Caldicot
M49
M5
A429

Pontypridd
Caerphilly
CARDIFF
Newport
NEWPORT
M4
Avonmouth
M5
BRISTOL
M32
Chippenham
WILTSHIRE
Calne
A4

BRIDGEND
218
M4
Bridgend
Cowbridge
VALE OF GLAMORGAN
Barry
Clevedon
Nailsea
BRISTOL
M5
166
Congresbury
Bath
Corsham
Melksham
Devizes

21

Weston-super-Mare
Cheddar
Wells
Shepton Mallet
Frome
Westbury
Trowbridge
Warminster
Salisbury Plain

2 · 4

Minehead
Watchet
Burnham-on-Sea
Bridgwater Bay
SOMERSET
Glastonbury
Street
Amesbury
Wilton

Brendon Hills
Bridgwater
168
M5
Langport
Wincanton
Shaftesbury
Salisbury
Whitbury Down

22

Taunton
Wellington
Ilminster
Yeovil
Sherborne
Blandford Forum
88
Wimborne Minster

Tiverton
Chard
Crewkerne
DORSET
Poole
Bournemouth
Poole Bay

M5
Honiton
84
Axminster
Bridport
Dorchester
Wareham
Swanage

23

Exeter
Sidmouth
Seaton
Lyme Regis
Lyme Bay
Weymouth
Chesil Beach
St Alban's Head

Exmouth
Dawlish
Teignmouth
Fortuneswell
Portland Bill
ST MALO
SUMMER ONLY

Torquay
Paignton

0 · 10 · 20 · 40

© MAPS IN MINUTES™ 1998

Map 4

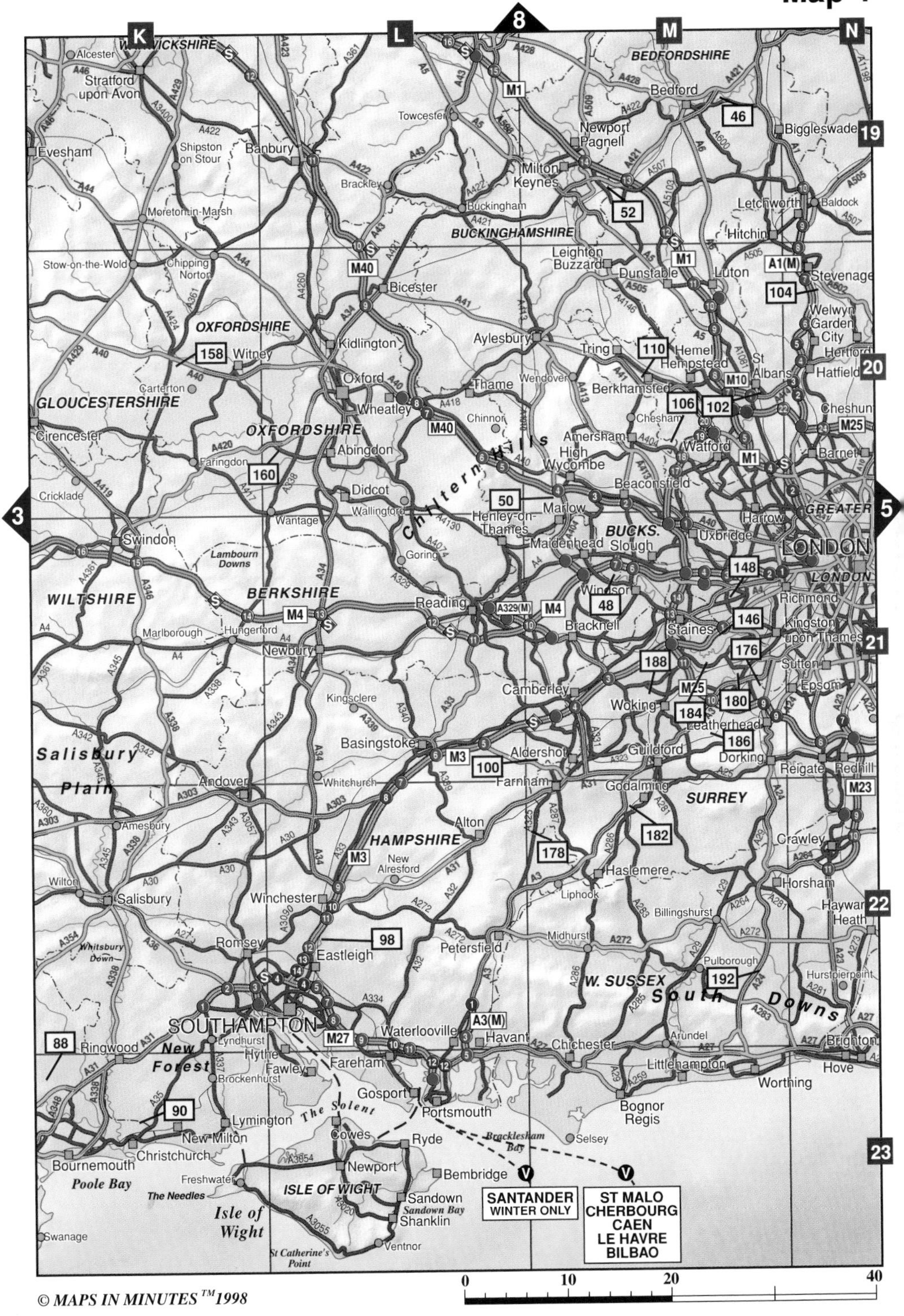
K
L
8
M
N
3
5
19
20
21
22
23
WARWICKSHIRE
BEDFORDSHIRE
Alcester
Stratford upon Avon
Evesham
Shipston on Stour
Banbury
Towcester
Bedford
46
Biggleswade
Newport Pagnell
Milton Keynes
Brackley
Buckingham
52
Letchworth
Baldock
Hitchin
BUCKINGHAMSHIRE
Moreton-in-Marsh
Stow-on-the-Wold
Chipping Norton
M40
Bicester
Leighton Buzzard
Dunstable
M1
Luton
A1(M)
Stevenage
104
Welwyn Garden City
Hertford
Hatfield
OXFORDSHIRE
Kidlington
Aylesbury
Tring
110
Hemel Hempstead
St Albans
158
Witney
Oxford
Thame
Wendover
Berkhamsted
M10
Carterton
GLOUCESTERSHIRE
Wheatley
Chinnor
106
102
Cheshunt
M25
Cirencester
OXFORDSHIRE
Chesham
Amersham
Watford
Abingdon
High Wycombe
Barnet
Faringdon
160
Chiltern Hills
Beaconsfield
Cricklade
Didcot
Wallingford
50
Henley-on-Thames
Marlow
GREATER
Wantage
BUCKS.
Harrow
Swindon
Maidenhead
Slough
Uxbridge
LONDON
Lambourn Downs
Goring
148
WILTSHIRE
BERKSHIRE
Windsor
Richmond
Reading
A329(M)
M4
48
Marlborough
Hungerford
Bracknell
Staines
146
Kingston upon Thames
Newbury
176
188
Sutton
Epsom
Camberley
Woking
184
180
Kingsclere
Leatherhead
Salisbury Plain
Basingstoke
M3
186
Aldershot
Guildford
Dorking
Reigate
Redhill
100
Andover
Whitchurch
Farnham
Godalming
SURREY
M23
Amesbury
Alton
182
HAMPSHIRE
Crawley
178
New Alresford
Haslemere
Wilton
Salisbury
Liphook
Horsham
Winchester
Billingshurst
Haywards Heath
Whitsbury Down
98
Romsey
Eastleigh
Petersfield
Midhurst
Pulborough
Hurstpierpoint
192
W. SUSSEX
South Downs
SOUTHAMPTON
A3(M)
Havant
Chichester
Arundel
Brighton
88
Ringwood
Lyndhurst
New Forest
Hythe
M27
Waterlooville
Fawley
Fareham
Littlehampton
Hove
Brockenhurst
Worthing
Gosport
Portsmouth
Bognor Regis
90
Lymington
The Solent
New Milton
Cowes
Ryde
Bracklesham Bay
Selsey
Christchurch
Bournemouth
Newport
Bembridge
Poole Bay
Freshwater
The Needles
ISLE OF WIGHT
Sandown
Sandown Bay
Shanklin
Isle of Wight
Swanage
Ventnor
St Catherine's Point
SANTANDER
WINTER ONLY
ST MALO
CHERBOURG
CAEN
LE HAVRE
BILBAO
0
10
20
40

Map 5

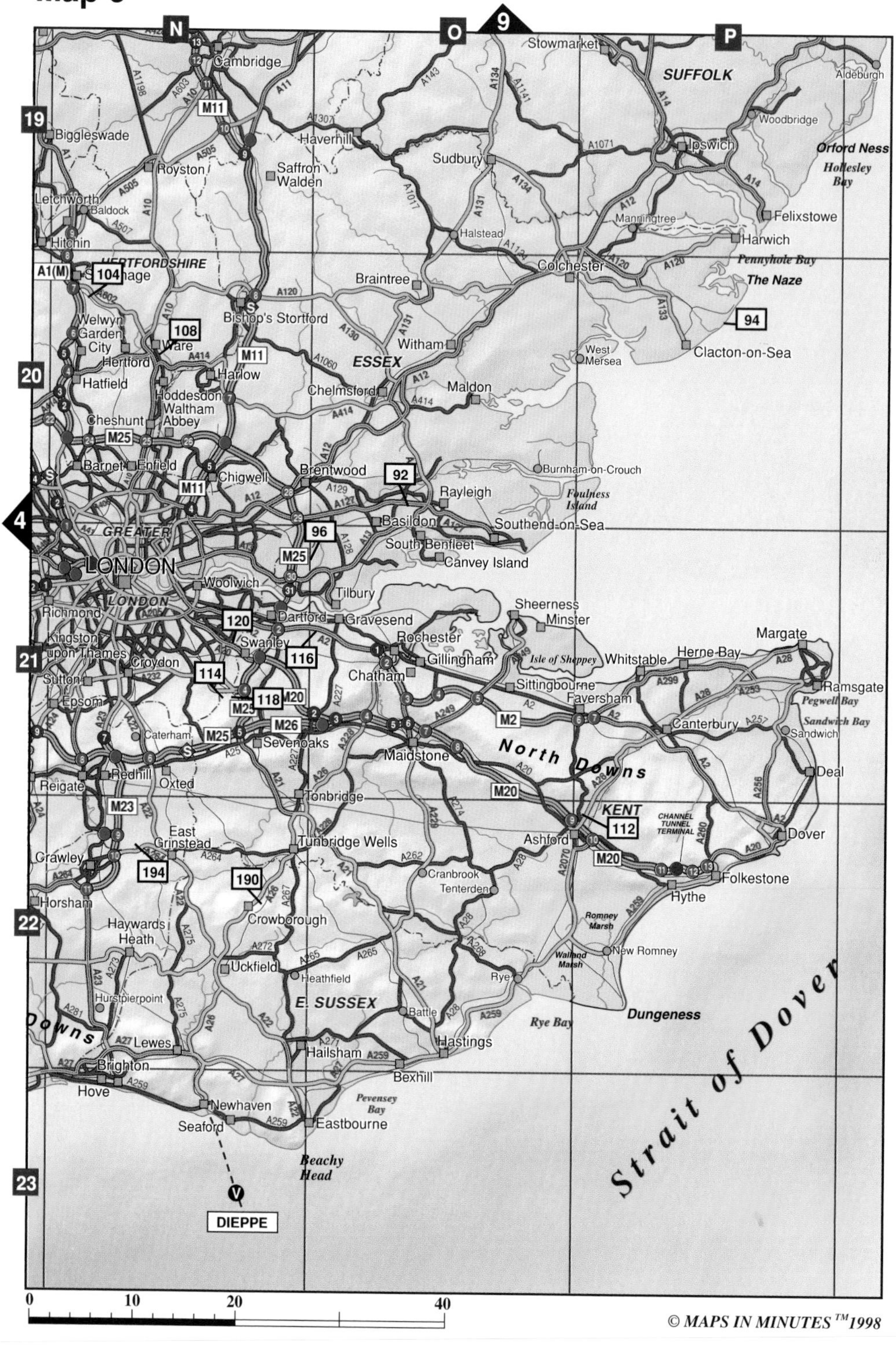

Stowmarket

SUFFOLK

Aldeburgh

Cambridge

Woodbridge

19

Biggleswade

Haverhill

A1071

Ipswich

Orford Ness

Hollesley Bay

Royston

Sudbury

Saffron Walden

A14

Felixstowe

Letchworth

Baldock

Hitchin

Halstead

Manningtree

Harwich

Pennyhole Bay

HERTFORDSHIRE

A1(M)

104 Stevenage

Braintree

Colchester

The Naze

94

Welwyn Garden City

108

Bishop's Stortford

Witham

West Mersea

Clacton-on-Sea

20

Hertford

Ware

M11

ESSEX

Hatfield

Harlow

Chelmsford

Maldon

Hoddesdon

Waltham Abbey

Cheshunt

M25

Barnet Enfield

Chigwell

Brentwood

92

Burnham-on-Crouch

M11

Rayleigh

Foulness Island

96

Basildon

Southend-on-Sea

GREATER

M25

South Benfleet

Canvey Island

4

LONDON

Woolwich

Tilbury

Sheerness

Minster

Richmond

120

Dartford

Gravesend

Margate

Kingston upon Thames

Swanley

Rochester

Isle of Sheppey

Whitstable

Herne Bay

21

Croydon

114

116

Gillingham

Sittingbourne

Faversham

Ramsgate

Pegwell Bay

Sutton

Epsom

118 M20

Chatham

M2

Canterbury

Sandwich Bay

Sandwich

Caterham

M25

M26

Sevenoaks

Maidstone

North Downs

Deal

Reigate

Redhill

Oxted

Tonbridge

M20

KENT

Crawley

M23

East Grinstead

Tunbridge Wells

Ashford

112

Dover

194

190

Cranbrook

Tenterden

M20

Folkestone

Horsham

22

Haywards Heath

Crowborough

Romney Marsh

Hythe

Uckfield

Heathfield

Rye

Walland Marsh

New Romney

Hurstpierpoint

E. SUSSEX

Battle

Rye Bay

Dungeness

Downs

Lewes

Hastings

Strait of Dover

Brighton

Hailsham

Bexhill

Hove

Newhaven

Pevensey Bay

Seaford

Eastbourne

23

Beachy Head

V

DIEPPE

0   10   20   40

© MAPS IN MINUTES ™1998

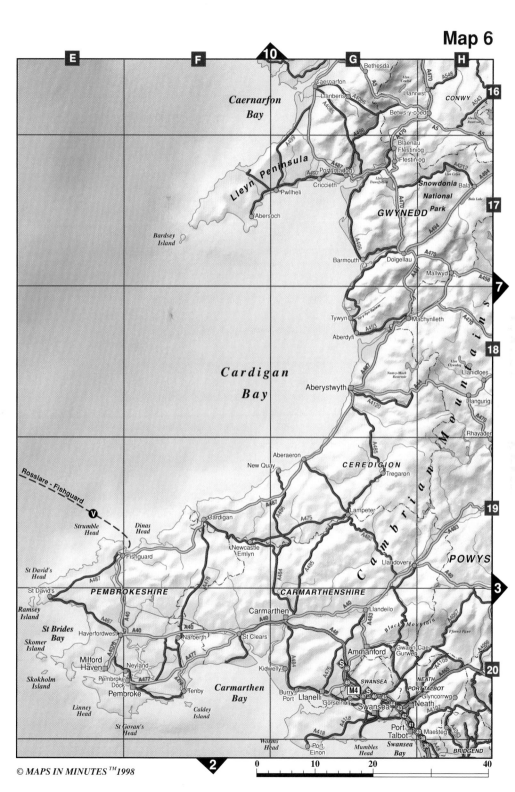

Map 6

Map 7

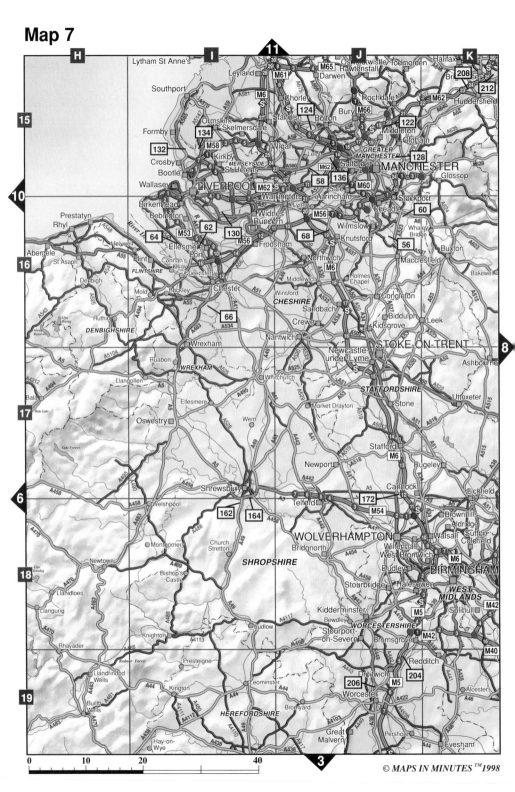

© MAPS IN MINUTES ™ 1998

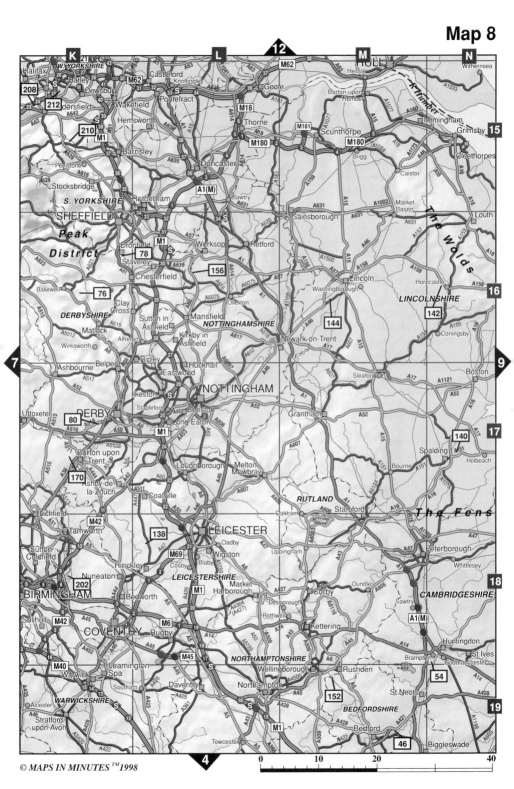

Map 8

© MAPS IN MINUTES ™ 1998

Map 9

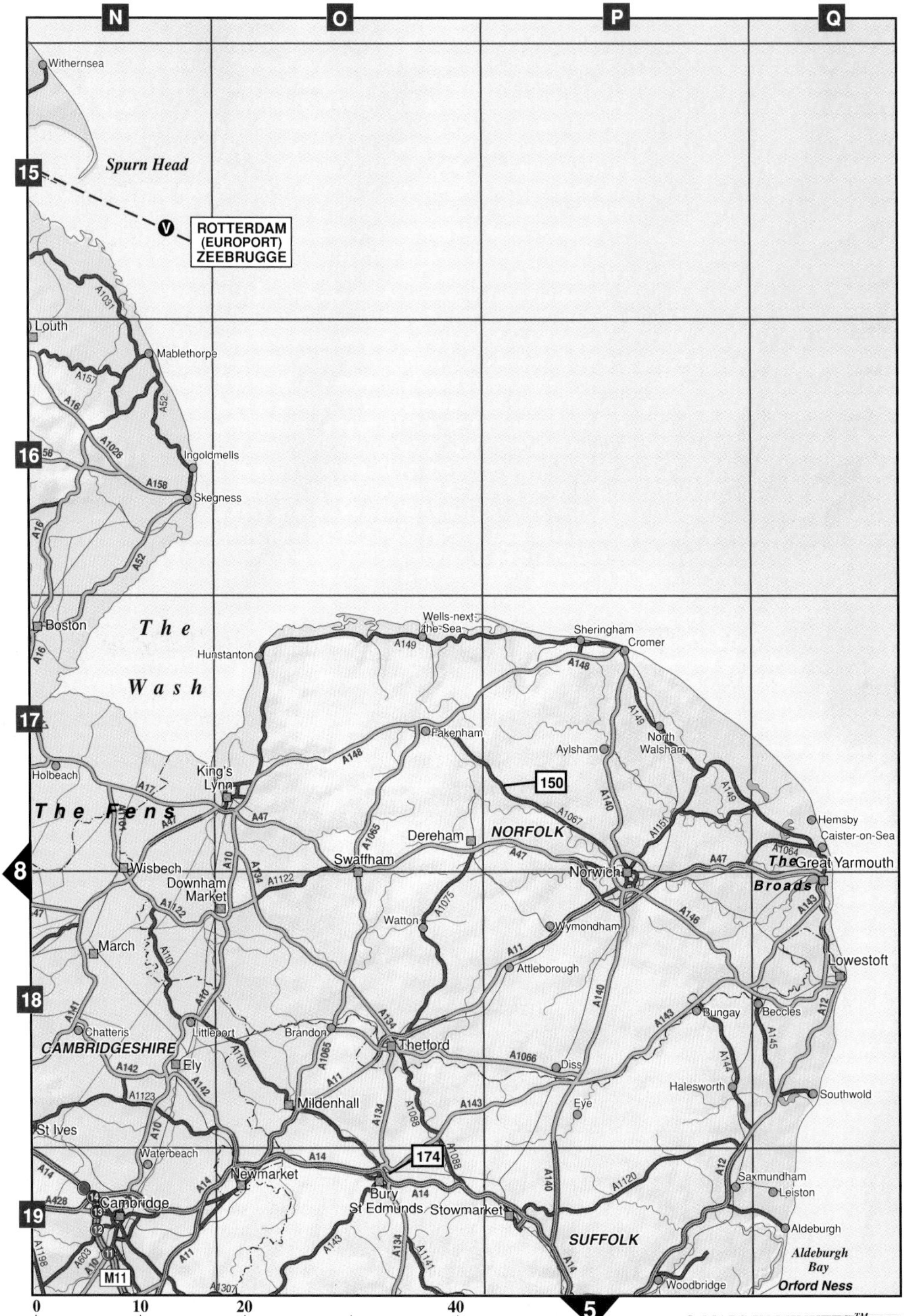

Withernsea

Spurn Head

V | ROTTERDAM (EUROPORT) ZEEBRUGGE

15

Louth

Mablethorpe

A157

A16

A52

16 | 58

A1028

Ingoldmells

A158

Skegness

A16

A52

Boston

The

Wells-next-the-Sea

Sheringham

Cromer

A149

Wash

Hunstanton

A148

17

Fakenham

Aylsham

North Walsham

A149

Holbeach

A17

King's Lynn

A148

150

A140

Hemsby

Caister-on-Sea

The Fens

A47

A1065

Dereham

NORFOLK

A1067

A1151

A149

8

Wisbech

A10

Downham Market

A47

Swaffham

A47

Norwich

A1064

TheGreat Yarmouth

A1122

A47

A1075

Watton

Wymondham

A146

Broads

A151

March

A1122

A11

Attleborough

A140

Lowestoft

18

A141

Littleport

Chatteris

Brandon

A134

Thetford

A1066

Diss

Bungay

A143

Beccles

A145

CAMBRIDGESHIRE

Ely

A142

A142

A11

A1065

Mildenhall

A134

A1066

A143

Eye

Halesworth

A144

Southwold

St Ives

A10

Waterbeach

A14

174

A140

A1120

Saxmundham

A12

Leiston

19

A428

Cambridge

A14

Newmarket

A14

Bury St Edmunds

A14

Stowmarket

SUFFOLK

Aldeburgh

Aldeburgh Bay

M11

A11

A143

A134

A1141

A14

Woodbridge

Orford Ness

0 10 20 40

5

© *MAPS IN MINUTES* ™ *1998*

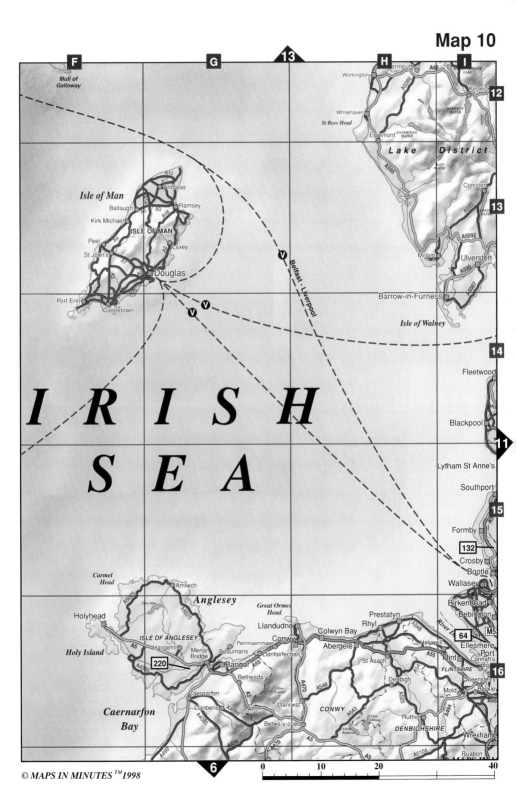

Map 10

F   G   **13**   H   I

12

Mull of
Galloway

Workington

A66   A596   BASSENTHWAITE
LAKE

Keswick

Whitehaven
St Bees Head

Egremont   ENNERDALE
WATER   DERWENT
WATER

Lake   District

A55

WAST
WATER

A10

Isle of Man   A11

Andreas

Coniston   A593

13

Ballaugh   A3   Ramsey

Kirk Michael   A18

A5   CONISTON
WATER

ISLE OF MAN

A5092

Peel   A4

St John's   Laxey

A7   Millom   Ulverston

A590

A2   A1   **Douglas**

V   A587

Port Erin   Castletown

Barrow-in-Furness

Isle of Walney

V   Belfast - Liverpool

V

14

Fleetwood

I R I S H

Blackpool

S E A

11

Lytham St Anne's

Southport

15

Formby

132

Crosby

Bootle

Wallasey

Carmel
Head   Amlwch

Anglesey   *Great Ormes
Head*

Birkenhead

Bebington

River Dee

M53

A5025   Llyn Alaw   A5025

Holyhead

Prestatyn

Rhyl   A548

ISLE OF ANGLESEY

Llandudno

Colwyn Bay

Holywell   64

A55   Ellesmere
Port

Holy Island   A5   Llangefni   Penmaenmawr   Conwy   Abergele   A548   A55   Flint   Connah's
Quay

220   Menai
Bridge   Beaumaris   Llanfairfechan   St Asaph   **FLINTSHIRE**   16

A4080   Bangor   A55   Denbigh   Mold   A494   Buckley

Holy Island   Bethesda   A5   Queensferry

Caernarfon   A470   A548   A525   Ruthin   A483

*Caernarfon
Bay*   Llanberis   A4086   Llanrwst   *CONWY*   Llyn Brenig   **DENBIGHSHIRE**   Wrexham

Betws-y-coed   Alwen Reservoir   A5104   Ruabon

A4085   A4086   A470   A5   A5   A525

© *MAPS IN MINUTES* ™ 1998

6

0   10   20   40

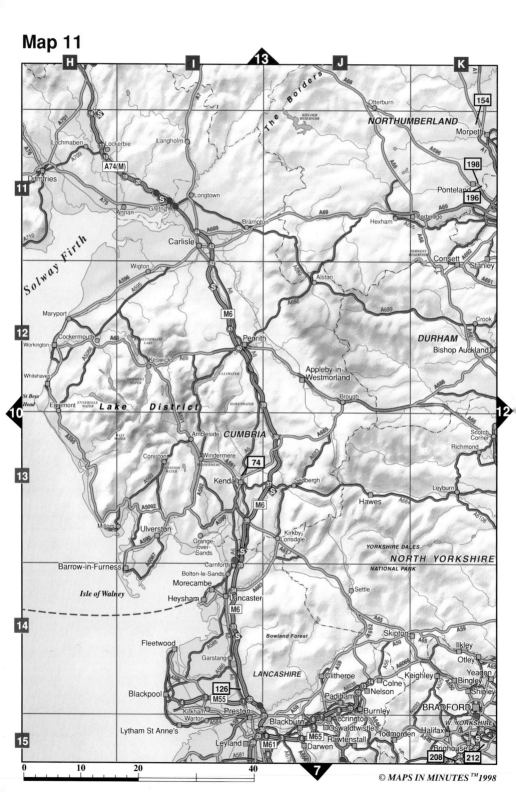

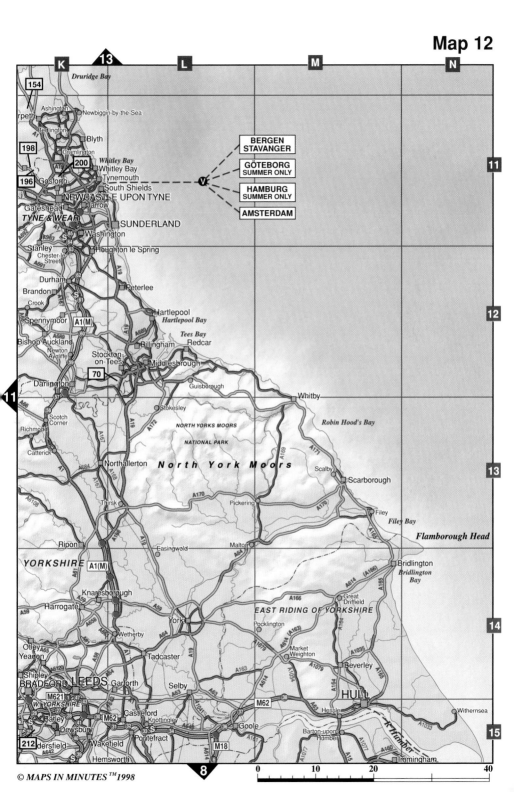

Map 12

BERGEN
STAVANGER

GÖTEBORG
SUMMER ONLY

HAMBURG
SUMMER ONLY

AMSTERDAM

© MAPS IN MINUTES ™ 1998

0   10   20   40

Map 13

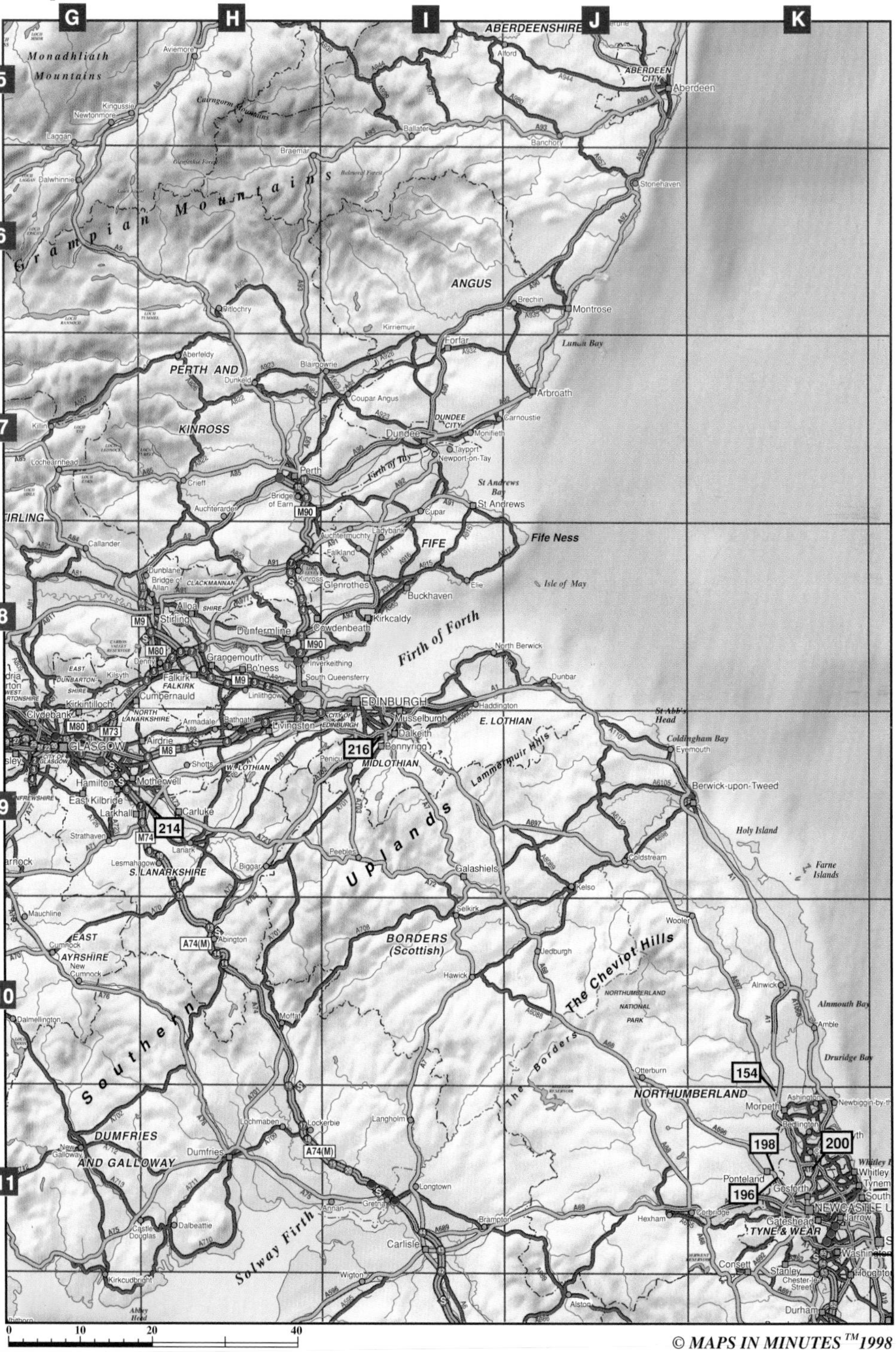

G H I ABERDEENSHIRE J K

5

Monadhliath Mountains Aviemore Alford ABERDEEN CITY Aberdeen

Kingussie Newtonmore Ballater Banchory

Laggan Braemar Stonehaven

6

Balmoral Forest

ANGUS Brechin Montrose

Kirriemuir Forfar Lunan Bay

Aberfeldy Blairgowrie

PERTH AND Dunkeld Coupar Angus Arbroath

KINROSS Dundee DUNDEE CITY Carnoustie

7 Kinloch Crieff Perth Dundee Monifieth

Lochearnhead Auchterarder Bridge of Earn Tayport Newport-on-Tay Firth of Tay

STIRLING Callander M90 Cupar St Andrews Bay St Andrews

Auchtermuchty Ladybank

Dunblane Falkland FIFE Fife Ness

Bridge of Allan CLACKMANNAN Kinross Glenrothes Elie Isle of May

8 Alloa SHIRE Buckhaven

M9 Stirling Kirkcaldy

Dunfermline Cowdenbeath Firth of Forth

M90 North Berwick

M80 Grangemouth Inverkeithing

EAST DUNBARTON Kilsyth FALKIRK Bo'ness South Queensferry Dunbar

WEST Cumbernauld M9 Linlithgow EDINBURGH Haddington

Clydebank NORTH LANARKSHIRE Armadale Bathgate Musselburgh St Abb's Head

M80 M73 GLASGOW Airdrie Livingston EDINBURGH Dalkeith E. LOTHIAN Coldingham Bay

M8 Shotts 216 Bonnyrigg Eyemouth

Hamilton W. LOTHIAN Penicuik MIDLOTHIAN Lammermuir Hills Berwick-upon-Tweed

9 East Kilbride Motherwell

RENFREWSHIRE Larkhall 214 Holy Island

M74 Lanark Peebles Coldstream Farne Islands

Strathaven Galashiels Kelso

S. LANARKSHIRE Biggar Selkirk

U p l a n d s

Mauchline Abington BORDERS (Scottish) Wooler

EAST Cumnock A74(M) Jedburgh NORTHUMBERLAND NATIONAL PARK Alnwick

AYRSHIRE New Cumnock Hawick Alnmouth Bay

10 Dalmellington Moffat Amble

S o u t h e r n Druridge Bay

Otterburn 154 NORTHUMBERLAND Morpeth

Lochmaben Lockerbie Langholm Ashington Newbiggin-by-the

DUMFRIES Dumfries Ponteland 198 200

New Galloway AND GALLOWAY A74(M) Whitley Bay Whitley Tynemouth

11 Longtown 196 Gateshead NEWCASTLE South Shields

Annan Gretna Hexham TYNE & WEAR Jarrow

Castle Douglas Dalbeattie Brampton Consett Washington

Carlisle Stanley Chester-le-Street

Kirkcudbright Wigton Houghton

Solway Firth Alston Durham

0 10 20 40

© MAPS IN MINUTES ™ 1998